Dedication

For my Dad Bill Coghlan,

Gerry Farnan,

Jumbo Elliott

and

Fanahan McSweeney.

I think of you everyday.

"Who can forget the look on Eamonn's face as he cruised past the Russian with less than 200 metres to go to the finish of the 1983 World Championships in Helsinki? It still stands out as one of the great sporting moments in my lifetime. Eamonn's success and dedication to his sport has helped others, particularly those involved in individual sport, to believe that they, too, can achieve success on the world stage."
Padraig Harrington, winner of the 2007 and 2008 Open Championship.

"A legend in world athletics. His unsurpassed achievements running indoors in America were heroic. Eamonn has an insatiable appetite for challenge, culminating in him breaking the once magical Four Minute Mile in 1994 at the age of forty-one. His contribution to Irish athletics is immense and reading his book is a must for all his admirers throughout the world."
Dr Ronnie Delany, Olympic Gold Medal winner at 1,500 metres, 1956 Melbourne Games.

"A great friend, a great guy, a great athlete. Growing up together in Drimnagh was a fantastic experience and the grounding we got there in life and sport has stood us both well in our respective careers. His contribution to athletics, to sport and to Irish society through his work at Our Lady's Hospital, is a measure of the man. He was always too bloody quick for me though."
Brian Kerr, former Irish soccer manager.

"Eamonn is one of the greatest Irish sportsmen of this or any other generation. He is a credit to his country and a phenomenal ambassador for the sport of athletics. Unquestionably the greatest indoor miler in the history of athletics. If ever the government gets around to erecting a statue for an athletics legend, surely Eamonn Coghlan must be the subject."
John O'Shea, Chief Executive and founder of GOAL.

"We all have an image of Eamonn Coghlan's seemingly effortless win in the World Championships 5,000 metres in 1983 – but it was achieved through enormous hard work and dedication. As a nation, we should be a very proud of his achievements."
John Giles, former Leeds United and Irish soccer International.

"Eamonn Coghlan was one of the all time greats of world middle distance running. It has been a privilege to have known him and to have raced against him. Eamonn embodies the legacy of great Irish middle distance running through his many successes."
Ray Flynn Irish Record for the Mile and 1,500 metres.

Eamonn wearing gold following his win in the 1983 World Championship 5,000 metre race in Helsinki, during which the country came to a virtual standstill.

Foreword
By Bertie Ahern T.D.

Many people reading this book might be envious of Eamonn for the obvious things. He was a world champion. He was a superstar international runner, and he was an Irish celebrity in the days when every other celebrity we knew about came from another country. This was years before Riverdance and U2 and Colin Farrell and Westlife made their way.

But I'm envious of Eamonn for another reason and that's because when he was a young lad and I wasn't too much older he had the best seats in Croker. His Da used to install and operate the sound systems in all the great venues from Shamrock Rovers in Glenmalure Park, to Santry Stadium, to the RDS and to, as he puts it himself "the pride of them all, Croke Park."

So on the days when all the other young Northsiders like myself could barely peek inside the gates, young Eamonn was standing in front of a pillar – supposedly helping out his Da – right in the middle of the Ard Chomhairle – the VIP seating area.

For a GAA fan it's hard to believe that watching some of the great games of the Seventies didn't convince Eamonn to drop the running; but it was in his blood and nothing was going to draw him away from it. My own brother Maurice was coaching athletics at the time, and I remember him saying how great this young fella from the Cooley Road in Drimnagh was.

I suppose younger people nowadays can't really understand just how great Eamonn's achievements on the track were, and how his success on the world stage lit up the country with excitement at a time when – to be honest – there wasn't too much to be excited about. I remember him coming home to Dublin in 1983 with his World Championship gold medal, and if Ireland had have won the World Cup, we couldn't have been happier.

But none of this came without a struggle. Even when he got that great scholarship to Villanova he had to battle his homesickness and came close to giving up at one point. I think it was the great support of his family and his mates and his coaches at home that got him back and got him moving onto the most successful

period of his life, for himself and for his family and also for his country.

When emigration was a sad reality for thousands of our people, Eamonn Coghlan was a great source of pride for Irish people everywhere but, in particular, in America. He was one of the biggest names in US sports and one of the most popular. He won the world renowned Wanamaker Mile an incredible seven times and there was always a big Irish contingent present to cheer the Chairman of the Boards home.

Eamonn's career is one of huge achievement. He has given Irish sports fans some of our most cherished memories. Who can forget his shattering the world record for the indoor mile, his World Championship victory in Helsinki and that brilliant day in Belfield when Eamonn, Marcus O'Sullivan, Ray Flynn and Frank O'Mara broke the world record for the 4 x 1 mile relay?

For me, Eamonn's greatest achievement was becoming the first athlete ever over forty to run a sub-four minute mile. This was a truly inspirational achievement and highlights not just Eamonn's great natural ability but also his unrivalled sense of dedication and commitment

Eamonn Coghlan is a great athlete. He is also a great gentleman, a role model and a great ambassador for Ireland. He deserves great credit for his fantastic work in building up athletics in this country, and he has inspired and encouraged many young people to be active in sport. The great human side of Eamonn also came out in his work for Our Lady's Children's Hospital and other charitable causes.

As a fellow Dubliner, I'm proud of Eamonn and the role he played in giving this country of ours great pride and confidence in what we could and did achieve. His book tells us how he did it.

He's a modest man but nothing can take from the fact that to achieve at the world level what Eamonn did took more than talent and determination – it took more than a few strokes of genius too.

Introduction
By Eamonn Coghlan
Chairman of the Boards
Master of the Mile

Some people nowadays write their biographies when it seems they're barely out of their teens. I often marvel at the fact that someone can fill a big fat book about themselves, when they've hardly even grown up!

I'm at the other end. I hope by now that I've grown up but I also hope that at last I know myself and what has made me the person I am and how I can shape, for the best, the person I would still like to become. Maybe in ten years time I'll say that I wrote this book too early.

Running was my life, still is in many ways. It took over my life when I was a kid, shaped it, directed it, filled it and – alongside my family – made it complete.

Writing this book took many years. I waited until long after I had stopped most of my competitive running before I began to map out that journey that my life has been to date. Maybe I couldn't or wouldn't accept that a phase – admittedly a very long phase – was ending and that it was time to examine that life and lay it out for people to see and to understand.

But as I got into it, and particularly as I started systematically to piece together that life, I realised that I wasn't just telling other people about me, I was also telling me about me. I was forced to look back and,

Continued on next page

when I did that looking back, I noticed things that maybe I had glimpsed before, but had failed at the time to understand.

This excavation of life began to uncover patterns or behaviour and mood that I realised weren't just the natural highs and lows of a fiercely competitive athlete. The highs were probably within the normal limits but the lows were definitely too low – even at the moments when a sense of failure gripped hold.

I realise now that the lows were due to depression, that my occasional disturbing withdrawal from life and loved ones were symptoms of something that had a name and, more than that, something which I now realise is capable of being dealt with. And that's now what I'm doing. At last.

It took the writing of this book, and the soul-searching that went with it, to find this out. Am I sad that I didn't make this discovery earlier? In ways – yes – obviously. But then sometimes the things that make a person succeed – even beyond their wildest dreams – aren't always the good things that people take for granted – like talent and positive attitudes and healthy living. Everyone has their dark side as well and maybe – even though we might not wish to acknowledge it – it's that dark side that also informs our choices and behaviour and also helps create our successful selves.

A lot goes into the making of a successful sportsman or woman. Yes it helps to have talent and good coaching and the occasional lucky break. But mainly it's what goes on in our head and not in your feet or your hands. When I nearly quit my early scholarship at Villanova it had nothing to do with what I was doing on the track, it had everything to do with what was going on in my head.

Later, when success was literally calling me up to the world championship tape, it was what my head was telling me as much as what my legs were capable of, that got me over that career defining line.

I hope that people who read this book, athletes, would be athletes, or just people with an interest in sport, will get more from it than just the detailing of one man's life in sport.

I hope that, just like me, it helps them to learn more about themselves.

In full flight ahead of Filbert Bayi during the Maple Leaf Games, Toronto, in the late Seventies.

Introduction
By George Kimball

We had just emerged from the restaurant in Temple Bar that August evening half a dozen years ago. It was my last night in Ireland at the conclusion of my usual summertime visit, and in honour of the occasion I'd met up with Eamonn and Yvonne Coghlan and their three sons for a farewell dinner.

We'd arrived in separate vehicles, so when it came time to leave, Michael and John, the two younger boys, piled into the car with Eamonn and Yvonne, while Eamonn Jr. opted to drive back with me. The two of us had crossed Dame Street and were just opening the door to my car outside Dublin Castle when the tableau flashed before us.

Two youths who appeared to be about 16-years-of-age came flying up the cobble-stoned road. They were sprinting so hard they seemed to be straining at the bit, and one of them clutched what looked like a small handbag. They were followed in short order by what appeared in the gathering darkness to be a middle-aged man in hot pursuit. It was barely light enough to see that the older fellow giving chase looked to be wearing a dark green jumper. It took a second for the penny to drop.

"Wasn't your dad wearing a green sweater?" I asked young Eamonn.

"Uh, I think he was," he replied.

With that we leapt into the car and headed off after them.

In the years since I've often wondered what the two young purse-snatchers must have been thinking at this moment. For all I know they might been practising their brazen trade with impunity for years, secure in the knowledge that even if someone were foolish enough to give chase, they had youth on their side and that they could surely outrun them.

Now, as they occasionally chanced a worried glance back over their shoulders, they must have been echoing the sentiments of Butch Cassidy and the Sundance Kid with the Bolivian posse in hot pursuit "Who is this guy, anyway?"

How could these kids have known that they had elected to commit a robbery right in front of what may have been the only 48 year-old man in Ireland who could outrun

them? And that, moreover, they had chosen as their escape route a system of back-alleys every bit as familiar to their pursuer as it was to themselves?

As the chase went on, these two juvenile delinquents were at least clever enough to split up, and Eamonn, forced to make a split-second decision, made the wrong one.

By the time he ran down his quarry and cornered him in a cul-de-sac a block or two further on, he realised that the fellow's mate had gotten away with the purse.

All of this came to light as the several parties simultaneously converged on the spot – Eamonn Coghlan with the cowering and, by now, gasping, mugger, young Eamonn and I in my rented Scenic, two Gardaí in a squad car along with the victims of the theft, and Yvonne and the boys in their car.

While we can only speculate about what might have been going through the minds of the young robbers in the course of this merry chase, it is somewhat less difficult to imagine what was going through Coghlan's.

"I didn't even think of it until those last few steps when I ran him into the alley," Eamonn admitted later. "But then it suddenly dawned on me: What am I going to do when I do catch him? What if he's got a knife? Or a gun?"

The lady whose purse had been stolen turned out to be an elderly American tourist. Eamonn apologised to the lady for having collared the wrong mugger. She assured him that after the initial fright, she was none the worse for it. And while she and her husband thanked Coghlan profusely for his intervention, it was obvious that they had no idea who he was.

The Gardaí, on the other hand, could not help but be amused by the entire turn of events. They took statements from all concerned and then led their prisoner away in the squad car. The poor fellow was probably still asking himself "How did I ever let that old man catch me?"

He couldn't have known it, of course, but for at least a quarter of a century, faster men than he had been wondering the same thing.

A life measured by time: how

WORLD RECORDS

Indoor Mile

3:52.6, San Diego, February 16, 1979

3:50.6, San Diego, February 20, 1981

3:49.78, East Rutherford, NJ, February 28, 1983

2,000 Metres

4:54.07, Inglewood, Calif., February 21, 1987

Distance Medley Relay

9:28.2, Philadelphia, April 25, 1975 (Ken Schappert, Greg Eckman, Tom Gregan, Coghlan)

4-Mile Relay

15:49.08, Belfield, August 17, 1985 (Coghlan, Marcus O'Sullivan, Frank O'Mara, Ray Flynn)

WORLD CHAMPIONSHIPS

First, 5,000 metres, Helsinki, 1983

OTHER NOTABLE CHAMPIONSHIPS

First, 5,000 metres, World Cup, Rome, 1981

First, 1,500 metres, European Indoor Championships, Vienna, 1979

First, 1,500 metres, US AAU, Los Angeles, 1976

First, US Indoor Championships, Three Mile, 1980, 1981,1985

First, US Indoor Championships, One Mile, 1977, 1979, 1983,1987

First, British AAA's, 5,000 metres, 1979,1981

First, British AAA's, 1,500 Metres, 1977

EAMONN COGHLAN'S COLLEGIATE CAREER AT VILLANOVA

NCAA (National Collegiate Athletic Association Championships)
1974 NCAA Indoors Sixth, 880-yard run
1975 NCAA Indoors First, One Mile Run
1975 NCAA Outdoors First, One Mile Run
1976 NCAA Indoors First, One Mile Run
1976 NCAA Outdoors First, 1,500 metres

Championship of America (Penn Relays) winning relay teams
1973 First, 4-Mile Relay (Coghlan, Brian McElroy, Ken Schappert, John Hartnett)

1974 First, Distance Medley Relay (Coghlan, Brian McElroy, Greg Eckman, John Hartnett)
First, 4-Mile Relay (Tom Gregan, Brian McElroy, Coghlan, John Hartnett)

1975 First, 2-Mile Relay (Phil Kane, Coghlan, Ken Schappert, Mark Belger)
First, Distance Medley Relay (Ken Schappert, Greg Eckman, Tom Gregan, Coghlan)
First, 4-Mile Relay (Mark Belger, Ken Schappert, Tom Gregan, Coghlan)

1976 First, 3200 Metre Relay (George MacKay, Phil Kane, Coghlan, Mark Belger)
First, Distance Medley Relay (Mark Belger, Greg Eckman, Phil Kane, Coghlan)
First, 6000 Meter Relay (Gary Trojanowski, George MacKay, Phil Kane, Coghlan)

EAMONN COGHLAN AT THE MILLROSE GAMES

Wanamaker Mile

1977 First

1978 DNR (competing in New Zealand)

1979 First

1980 First

1981 First

1982 DNR (injured)

1983 First

1984 DNR (injured)

1985 First

1986 Second

1987 First

1988 DNR (injured)

1989 DNR (injured)

1990 Fifth

Masters Mile

1993 First

1994 First

the record book stacks up

EAMONN COGHLAN'S 78 SUB-4 MINUTE MILES

ER = European Record WR = World Indoor Record MR = World Masters (over-40) Record 2K = Mile time in 2,000 metre race

1975

10 May Pittsburg	3:56.2
17 May Kingston (ER)	3:53.3
24 May Williamsburg	3:59.3
4 Jul London	3:57.78

1976

9 Jan College Park	3:59.7
13 Feb. Toronto	3:59.3
4 Aug Philadelphia	3:57.54
9 Aug Stockholm	3:55.07
20 Aug Berlin	3:59.85

1977

18 Feb San Diego	3:57.9
2 Jun Limerick	3:59.8
11 Jul Dublin	3:53.4
30 Jul Gatehead	3:59.7

1978

28 Jan Auckland	3:57.4
3 Feb Inglewood	3:59.6
17 Feb San Diego	3:56.0

1979

20 Jan Los Angeles	3:56.10
2 Feb Toronto	3:58.0
3 Feb Edmonton	3:57.7
9 Feb New York	3:55.0
16 Feb San Diego (WR)	3:52.6
6 May Los Angeles	3:56.91
12 May Philadelphia	3:56.34
21 Jun Cork	3:54.8
30 Jun Philadelphia	3:52.88
3 Jul Stockholm	3:56.24
17 Jul Oslo	3:52.45

1980

1 Feb Toronto	3:58.2
8 Feb New York	3:58.2
15 Feb Los Angeles	3:52.9
22 Feb San Diego	3:55.7
11 May Los Angeles	3:55.2
24 Jun Cork	3:56.42
17 Aug Nice	3:58.53
25 Aug London	3:55.74

1981

9 Jan Johnson City	3:59.10
30 Jan Los Angeles	3:54.3
31 Jan Dallas	3:55.55

1981 continued

6 Feb New York	3:53.0
13 Feb Toronto	3:55.63
14 Feb Ottawa	3:57.9
20 Feb San Diego (WR)	3:50.6
10 May Los Angeles	3:54.94
30 May Philadelphia	3:58.57
23 Jun Cork	3:52.11
11 Jul Oslo	3:56.50
14 Jul Dublin	3:58.47
17 Aug Tullyleash	3:57.8
28 Aug Brussels	3:53.30

1983

21 Jan Los Angeles	3:55.52
28 Jan New York	3:54.40
18 Feb San Diego	3:53.1
19 Feb Cleveland	3:57.23
25 Feb New York	3:58.5
27 Feb East R'ford (WR)	3:49.78
28 May San Jose	3:56.46
12 Jun Berkeley	3:52.52
16 Jun South Burnaby	3:54.04
9 Jul Oslo	3:51.59
11 Jul Dublin	3:53.48
23 Jul London	3:57.61

1985

18 Jan Los Angeles	3:56.34
25 Jan New York	3:53.82
27 Jan Rosemont	3:57.25
1 Feb Toronto	3:59.05
9 Feb East Rutherford	3:52.37
15 Feb San Diego	3:57.5

1986

17 Jan Los Angeles	3:58.55
14 Feb New York	3:56.34
14 Jun Villanova	3:56.88

1987

17 Jan Johnson City	3:56.59
30 Jan New York	3:55.91
7 Feb Dallas	3:56.59
14 Feb East Rutherford	3:56.83
21 Feb Inglewood (2K)	3:59.4
27 Feb New York	3:59.25
29 Jul Holmdel, NJ	3:59.90

1994

20 Feb Boston (MR)	3:58.15

Winning his first major medal, this one at the 1978 European Championships at Prague, where he finished second behind Steve Ovett with Dave Moorcroft (right) finishing in third. Old rival and friend, Thomas Wessinghage (522) finished fourth.

"Eamonn, look at you," he said. "You're only sixteen-years-of-age. You don't have a hair under your arm. Tony has a beard. He's physically matured earlier than you have, that's all. Just take your time, be patient, and I promise you that over the next year you're going to develop physically – and when you do have hair under your arms, and on your arse, believe me – you'll beat him. Not only that, when you fully mature you'll run for Ireland... and you'll win the Olympics."

Part

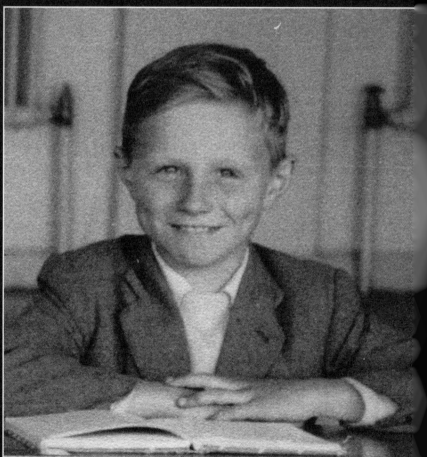

Eamonn at nine-years-of-age, photographed in his classroom at Drimnagh Castle during his primary school years. Despite his learning difficulties he was happy there – in marked contrast to his secondary school experience.

The wonder years

I was born on the 21st of November 1952 in Holles Street Maternity Hospital, Dublin. Weighing in at 7 pounds 6 ounces, I was the fourth child of William (Bill) and Kathleen Coghlan. My mother once told me that, while it was a normal birth, it was also the quickest labour of the five children. She says I was always in a hurry.

I was brought home to our house on Cooley Road in Drimnagh. It was a small, three bed-roomed, end of terrace house. I'd live there for the next eighteen years with my parents and siblings Ann, Bill, Brendan and Mary.

We were a typical hard-working middle-class family. My mother and father slept in the upstairs front bedroom, while the back room was for the three boys. Brendan and I slept on a bunk bed. Bill, the eldest, got the single bed. Ann and Mary shared a single bed, squeezed into a tiny box room.

My mother was a great cook. Her specialities were baked breads, home-made soups, and Christmas puddings. She'd get mad at me because, once I came off baby foods, I was an exceptionally fussy eater. In order to get the greens into me, she'd have to hide the cabbage or peas by mixing them into the mashed potatoes.

We were never short of her affection. If one of us caused a little trouble, she'd be sure to keep it from our father. She was our protector.

We never went on foreign holidays – there simply wasn't enough money. If we were lucky, we got a day-trip to Brittas Bay in Co. Wicklow. Chasing up and down the sand dunes playing hide-and-go-seek was my favourite. I could run forever, and I could stay hidden long enough not to be caught... or until the brothers got tired of looking for me.

If we didn't get to Brittas, a hose down in the back garden on a hot summer day was enough excitement for the kids in the Coghlan household.

A day trip up to the seaside resort of Skerries in North County Dublin was a real treat. Our 'rich' relations, Uncle Robbie and Aunt Cora, would rent a house in Skerries every summer.

Robbie and Cora lived on a substantial parcel of land in Shankill. Some Sundays, we would head to their estate and run wild over the land, chasing cattle and playing cross-country races. It was wonderful. We felt an extraordinary sense of freedom.

After tea, we'd crowd around the fire and sing songs, my mother or father accompanying us on the piano.

As a kid growing up on the streets of Drimnagh, I lived and breathed sports.

Though I wasn't aware of it at the time, I could run forever. I loved running, running, running.

At the back of the houses, across the street from where we lived, was a small park. About 400 metres around, it was known as The Field. My childhood pal Brian Kerr would later christen it, the "Field of Dreams." Brian would go on to achieve considerable success in his own right as manager of St. Patrick's Athletic Football Club – and eventually Ireland's Youth and Senior International soccer teams.

As little kids, the field was where we'd gather to play, morning, noon and night. We played soccer, Gaelic football, hurling and cricket. We relay-raced and had inter-roads' tournaments in all sports.

On the perimeter road around the field, we played a Dublin street-soccer game called lamp-ball. It was much like playing one-on-one basketball. You'd kick a soccer ball against a wooden post on one side, and a metal ESB lamppost on the other. If you hit the post, you scored a goal.

The field was the place where all the young boys and girls from the area grew up. It was where most of us got our first kisses, and later learned the facts of life.

If your parents were looking for you, they knew to look no further than the field.

If you'd asked what sports I liked when I was eleven-years-old, athletics wouldn't have made my top three. When I grew up, I wanted to play soccer for either Chelsea or Manchester United. When I was taking the throws, I'd go around holding my sleeves down like I was George Best or Ian Hutchinson. I played right half-back. While I was quick enough up and down the wings, I wasn't a stand out. My job was to take all the touches – and I loved it.

I could stand there on the sideline like Hutchinson and heave the ball right into the goalmouth... or so I imagined. I was only eleven and I couldn't, of course, but I pictured myself doing it. On reflection, the Field of Dreams was a wonderful place to have growing up. It taught us about sport. About winning and losing. It also taught us how to be tough – real tough.

At the back of my house was what they called The Clinic. It was an Eastern Health Board facility, with a concrete path surrounding it – about eight metres wide and almost 200 metres long. Sometimes we'd have races there. Relays, Round The Clinic races, what have you. Perhaps it was here that my proclivity for running on shorter, tighter tracks took root.

I'd race against the other boys of the neighbourhood. While I was one of the youngest of the gang, my speed meant I was usually first to be picked for the relays.

It hadn't always been the case. I was knock-kneed as a child. By the time I was four, my mother was sufficiently concerned that she took me to an orthopaedic specialist in Our Lady's Hospital, Crumlin. As a result of various accidents I had as a youngster, I was a regular visitor over the years. Later on, I'd return to Our Lady's to work as Director of Fundraising & Development for the Children's Medical Research Foundation.

Following a consultation with specialist Dr. Gerry Brady, I was fitted for corrective shoes. They cost my parents a little over £4.00 – an enormous sum at the time. I felt stupid wearing those shoes.

Everywhere I went I imagined people were staring and laughing at me. Over the course of a year or so, the awkwardness of my stance eased, and I was deemed cured. I don't believe anyone would have believed that this bandy-legged four-year-old would go on to become a runner.

My father used to call me "The Joiner": I joined everything. I joined the Boy Scouts, and then left. I joined the Knights of Malta, and left that too. I lasted a little longer at the local youth club – St. John Bosco's Boys' Club. Here you could do everything from play basketball, to arts and crafts, to watching newsreel films on the weekends. While I was going, a cobbler would come and teach the kids how to repair shoes. So for a short time, fixing up shoes became my speciality.

From the age of nine, I played Gaelic Football for Good Counsel GFC. Later I would play it at school for Drimnagh Castle. I also played hurling, but I wasn't especially good at it. When I got a crack on the head from a hurley, it dampened my enthusiasm for the game. It was around this time I started playing soccer with Rialto FC.

Brian Kerr and I had grown up together. We were inseparable. Our family lived at No.110 Cooley Road, and he lived across the street at No.93. His mother Margaret, and my mum, Kathleen, were great friends. When we were babies we'd be out in our prams together.

His Dad was the legendary Frankie Kerr who'd won the Golden Gloves boxing title. He was born and raised in Belfast. He moved south to work as general manager of Premier Tailors on O'Connell Street. Frankie was a legend. Businessmen from all over the country would come to Frankie Kerr for their suits.

When I was ten years of age, Frankie decided he would teach us how to box. I went down to Drimnagh Boxing Club to give it a try. It was easy for me to run around the ring and escape punishment, but I had nowhere to hide. On that very first night, I caught a right upper-cut that knocked me flat on the canvas – out for the count. After that, I never set foot in the ring again.

On weekends, or hot summer days, a gang of us would go to the Iveagh Baths in the Liberties area of Dublin. It was a tough neighbourhood, and we were always apprehensive – but that's where I overcame my fear of the water. I later became something of a water rat.

The part of Drimnagh we grew up in was a middle-class area in the southwest part of the city. Many families from the inner-city were relocated to Drimnagh following the demolition of their tenement homes. Others might have considered it a 'tough' part of Dublin.

It was tough enough, but even as kids we were under no illusions: We knew there were other neighbourhoods that were far tougher.

Some of my earliest memories involve fleeing kids from Crumlin or Ballyfermot.

We might be out playing football in the Field, and some young gurriers from Crumlin would come over with hurling sticks, bats, iron bars – even rocks – and attack us. We never knew when they were coming. When they did, they'd put us to flight. While some of the older lads were brave enough to stand and fight, I was terrified of getting involved in those gang wars. Usually, I was the first to flee.

A visit to the Star Cinema in Crumlin was another time you could find your life in danger. Instead of enjoying *The Lone Ranger* and a bag of popcorn, you'd sit there in fear of the Crumlin gang showing up. If word got out that the boys from Drimnagh were in the Star, the Crumlin gang would lie in wait and attack us.

Finding an escape route was always foremost in my mind. Most times I'd wait in the toilet until it was safe to leave. Sometimes the usher might force me out, and I'd scurry over the back wall into Pearse Park. Then I'd run, run, run for my life.

Sometimes, if they tired of waiting, the Crumlin gang would enter the cinema and start a riot while the movie was still showing.

Once again, I was usually first to run away. I didn't want to get into fights at all. Despite this, I soon fell foul of a young lad who would keep me on the run for years.

Sometimes the teenage kids would play poker in the Field. There might be five or six guys playing, but twenty or thirty more would stand around and watch. I was too young to join in, so I'd be standing and watching with the rest of them. Then one day, an older boy from Crumlin – I never knew his proper name – lost the hand.

He looked around and decided that I must have tipped off the winner – my pal Zip Nolan. He jumped up and tried to punch me.

As usual, I ran away. This time the respite was only temporary. For the next several years, this guy and his friends terrorised me. Even when I was older and working in Mittons – the local butchers – I'd have occasion to run from these guys. I'd like to say that I settled it myself, but it was actually my father who did that.

One winter's night, we were all watching television in the front room, when there was an explosion of shattered glass. The top of a car's petrol tank had been thrown through the window – hitting my mother on the forehead.

My father leapt out of his chair, grabbed a big stick from under the stairs, and chased a gang of them down the road. He was certain one of them was my tormentor.

I was frightened about what my father might do. If he had caught the lad that night, I suspect he would have done him some damage.

A year later, I was down at the Good Counsel Parish Hall. They'd put on bingo and various entertainments for the parishioners on weekend nights. My older brother Brendan and his friends were members of the Musical Society, and I was helping out with a production of *Oklahoma*. When it came time to go home, I stepped outside – only to spot my tormentor waiting with two of his henchmen.

One of the benefits of being the son of an electrician was having a phone in the house, back when most people in Ireland didn't. I went inside, rang home, and waited until I saw my father coming. Then I strolled out the door looking brave enough to face them.

My father was standing right across the street. When I pointed to the three of them, he went after them like he was running an Olympic 100 metre final. They had no head start, and I knew there'd be no getting away. When he caught up with them, he grabbed my tormentor by the throat, produced a pistol from his pocket, and put it against his head. He told him that if he ever came near me again, he'd blow his brains out. Then he raised the gun and fired two shots into the air.

The guy was rooted to the spot, paralysed by fear. Eventually, he ran off like a scared cat. He never came near me again.

I was probably more surprised to see my father with that gun than my tormentor was. On the way home that night, I learned this "weapon" was a starter's pistol he was minding for the Dublin County Athletics Board.

My father, Bill, was a product of inner-city Dublin. He grew up at No.16 South William Street in a top-floor, cold-water flat. It was across the street from what is now the Powerscourt Centre. His own father, Patrick, died from a stroke when my father was a toddler. His brother, Patrick Jr., died in infancy as a result of a bad vaccination. This left dad with his mother, Kitty, his Uncles Mick and Gerry, Aunt Molly, and his only sister, Cora.

Life was hard enough without a father, but the meagre living conditions, and a strict Catholic upbringing, made life lonely and miserable. It was common practice for him and Cora to attend Mass twice on Sunday in nearby St. Therese's Church. Then there would be Benediction in the evening. He was active in the church from a young age, and an altar boy for many years.

He went to Westland Row CBS and was a good student. While he had a keen interest in sports, he could not pursue it because of his home life. His favourite hobby was art and he became quite accomplished at it.

I remember, quite vividly, he'd take us to Mass in Clarendon Street, and then to my grandmother's for a greasy Irish breakfast. My younger sister, Mary, and I would count the steps as we climbed the five flights of stairs – all sixty-five of them. Then it was like stepping into a time warp: The flat looked as if it hadn't been painted or decorated once in the sixty years they'd lived there.

There was no hot water on that top-floor. In the kitchen-cum-living-and-sleeping-room, there was a wooden pedestal holding a basin. You'd bring the hot water from the gas stove, and pour it in to wash your hands.

Nor was there toilet paper. Whenever we were at Gran's, we'd use carefully torn-up newspaper that had been sewn onto a long string.

Mary and I would sneak downstairs while the adults drank tea and chatted. We'd look for 'secret treasures' in the lower basement – a scary place where you could hear the sound of mice scratching about. It was out of bounds, but we went anyway.

We were told that the basement was used as a "safe house" for the Old IRA during the Easter Rising, and that Michael Collins might have hidden there too. Our mission was to find guns and ammunition. We always went down there with great trepidation.

When my father left school, he became an apprentice electrician with Breen Electrical Co. – one of the most prominent contractors in the country. The owner of the company, Louis Breen, was Gran's brother. He took my father under his wing at the company's headquarters at Number 16 Dame Street.

It was there he became involved in athletics, through friends he'd met on the job. He fancied himself as a sprinter and – although he won a few cross-country races here and there – he never won anything at national level. He frequently challenged his fellow workers to races in the back lane. He joined Phoenix Harriers Athletics Club where he was a more effective administrator than competitive runner. Eventually, he went on to become the Honorary Registrar of the Amateur Athletic Union (AAU).

Once he met and married my mother, Kathleen, his interest in the sport dwindled. He did not compete beyond his twenties. Raising five children – all born in less than six-and-a-half years – did not give my parents much time to pursue hobbies or social activities.

They met in the Ierne Ballroom on Parnell Square – a dance club that was popular for many decades – and were regular visitors to the Theatre Royal, now gone. Once the relationship began, they were inseparable.

My mother, Kathleen King, was born in the top floor flat at No. 4 Adelaide Place, off Baggot Street. The flat was rented to the King family by the parents of the late Jackie Carey. Jackie was one of Ireland's international soccer legends, having played with Manchester United. Eventually, my mother's family moved to Derrynane Gardens, by Bath Avenue in Sandymount.

Kathleen lost her mother, Margaret, to cancer when she was sixteen years old. As my mother recalled "People didn't like to discuss cancer as it was considered a dirty disease."

She was left in a house with four men: Her father Christy, or "Kit", and three brothers, Kevin, Brendan and Christy Jr. Kit was a coach-painter with CIE on Spa Road. Kathleen went to Baggot Street School, and later to Haddington Road.

Kit took to the bottle after his wife's death, which brought much tension to the household. Kathleen was witness to many a fistfight between her father and her older brother, Kevin.

Kit's drinking became such a problem that he was eventually forced to leave the house. He lived out the rest of his days in a Rathmines tenement called Holyfield Buildings (where Martin 'The General' Cahill would later grow up).

The tension in the King household forced Brendan into the British army. He died in action while stationed in Florence during World War II. Christy Jr. headed to America to make a new life for himself. Kevin became a successful businessman and an administrator in the Irish Swimming Association.

Kathleen was a blouse-maker by trade, working for Wallpoles in Suffolk Street. It was handy for her, as it was only a few hundred yards from where my father lived, and not too far from Breen Electrical.

During their courtship, my parents would meet regularly after work. They'd go to the Carlton cinema, dance in the Ierne, or on special occasions attend a dance in Clerys. In those days, girls didn't have the opportunity to play sports. Kathleen's only participation was in school, where she played a little hockey and camogie.

Two years after meeting, they married on January 7th of 1947 in the Star of the Sea Church in Sandymount. Only the best man, Seamus Woods, my Dad's cousin, the bridesmaid Marie Foley, my mother's best friend, and their immediate families attended the early morning wedding. After a quick post-wedding breakfast, the couple sailed off to Holyhead, and on to London for their honeymoon. It was their first time out of Ireland.

The following day, Kathleen's father secretly married his new lover, Bridget – much to the disgust of the family.

When my parents returned from their honeymoon, they moved into a three-bedroom house on Cooley Road. It was there, nine months from the day they were married, that my sister Ann was born.

Because of the post-war depression, there were no electric or gas cookers available to purchase during the first year of their marriage, and cooking and water boiling was done on an open fire. It was on Cooley Road that my parents would raise their five children, and live the rest of their lives.

The area was a large housing estate, built between the mid-1930s and '40s. All the roads in the neighbourhood were named after Irish mountain ranges. Through his job at Breen's, my father had worked on the electrical installation of many of the houses in Crumlin and Drimnagh. At the time, they were fortunate enough to get the end-of-terrace house, which had just been vacated. They rented it from Byrne Builders for £1 and 1 shilling per week.

Their house was known as an Associated Properties House, to distinguish it from the nearby Dublin Corporation housing. Families who lived in the Associated Properties were generally regarded as being better off than those in Corporation housing.

Having served his apprenticeship in his uncle's business, Bill eventually became general foreman of Breen Electrical. The firm had major electrical engineering contracts all over Dublin. I remember tagging along with him to the American Embassy and Hume House when they were under construction. Breen's also had contracts to install and operate the sound systems at Dublin's premier sports venues. This included the RDS, Santry Stadium, Guinness Iveagh Grounds, Shamrock Rovers' grounds in Glenmalure Park, and the pride of them all, Croke Park – headquarters of the Gaelic Athletic Association.

Though not even the most die-hard sports fan could tell you his name, Bill Coghlan's face became a familiar one to GAA fans and television viewers alike. When it came time to present the Sam Maguire Cup or the McCarthy Cup to the All-Ireland champions, Bill was the man who would walk up to the microphone and say *"Testing, one-two-three-four-five…"* before handing over to the President of the GAA.

In that respect, Dad was sort of a fixture in Irish sport. The truth is, he loved doing it. I thought it was a big deal because my father was on television.

I would be particularly proud when I'd go into school on a Monday morning, and in front of the whole class, one of the Brothers would say "Oh, Eamonn, I saw your father on the television yesterday."

I loved accompanying him on his rounds. From the time I was eight or nine years-of-age, I would tag along, pulling on the wires, imagining I was an electrician myself. It made me feel important when I'd help set up the sound system, especially in Croke Park. I'd only be holding the wires, but that didn't matter – I was important.

I even had my own personal viewing spot at Croke Park. Whether it was for an All-Ireland final, a Leinster Championship, or a weekend game played by my beloved Dubs, I would routinely be found in front of a pillar right in the middle of the Ard Chomhairle – the VIP seating area. From my vantage point, I could watch the game without blocking anyone's view. The head stewards all knew me by name and would occasionally hand me a shilling or two to buy sweets in the shops below the stand.

From an early age, these Sunday forays brought me into contact with the country's best-known dignitaries and celebrities from the worlds of sport, politics, and the Church. Prominent figures like Eamon de Valera, Sean Lemass, Jack Lynch and even the Archbishop of Dublin, Dr John Charles McQuaid, might pat me on the head and say hello.

By the time I was 14, when I had begun to win league cross-country races, I was still going to Croke Park. My father would announce proudly that 'Young Eamonn is going to be a great runner one day.' That would drive me nuts. I hated him saying that – it really embarrassed me. I didn't want the recognition and I didn't like anyone knowing my business.

One day, I remember him saying that to Eamon de Valera, and the President of Ireland tapped my head and said "Then I'll be looking out for you, boy!"

The only place I wasn't allowed was the refreshment area at half-time on an All-Ireland day. This was located at the rear of the Ard Chomhairle where the VIPs would snack on tiny ham and cheese sandwiches and drink tea. It was strictly off limits for a young boy. On returning to her seat for the second half, Maureen Lynch – the then Taoiseach Jack Lynch's wife – brought me a sandwich wrapped in paper and a bottle of Taylor Keith orange.

As autumn gave way to winter, I would accompany my father on a job I found nearly as delightful as the weekend excursions to Croker. Breen Electrical also had the contract to install Christmas lights for the city of Dublin. As the holidays approached, I would tag along with my father as he oversaw the installation along O'Connell Street, Capel Street, Grafton Street, and Henry Street.

Because the installation couldn't disrupt traffic, it would start at 9.00pm and continue into the night. I would help replace the burned-out bulbs and untangle miles of wiring. When the time came to set the pièce de résistance – the star atop the display in the middle of Grafton Street – it was my job to pull the rope and hoist it into place.

Like many Drimnagh boys, I acquired early running experience legging it from the Gardaí. We weren't exactly hardened criminals, but a few times we'd get caught helping ourselves to apples from somebody's orchard – and we'd have to run like hell.

In my teens, I did have a more serious brush with the law. My father had forbidden me to go into, or be seen in the vicinity of, the snooker hall. He thought it was an inappropriate place for a young lad to be. In hindsight, he was probably right. But at the time being forbidden to be somewhere was, in my rebellious eyes, part of the attraction.

The result was that I fell into some particularly bad company in the form of two hard chaws. They had come to the attention of the Gardaí as being tough, adventurous petty criminals. I'd taken to hanging around with them in the snooker hall because they'd always have money to pay the table hire charge and buy cigarettes.

One particular night, the two boys decided they'd let me in on a plan to rob the car-wash at a petrol station. At first, I was reluctant to go along with their plan, but stupidly rose to the bait when they accused me of being a chicken. And so I went along as their Look Out Boy.

As we walked up the Long Mile Road passing our school at Drimnagh Castle, I was scared witless. We turned right onto Kylemore Road and headed for Smith's garage, at the intersection of the Naas Road.

Completely overwhelmed by fear, shame and false bravado, I waited outside on the footpath as the two lads headed for the car wash. In the thirty seconds they were gone, they managed to smash open the lock and grab the contents.

Off we ran into the dark of the night. We agreed to split up – I headed home to my house and them to theirs. My heart was pumping all night, a combination of the adrenaline rush of the crime and the fear of getting caught.

And caught we were. In jig time.

My partners-in-crime had left their fingerprints all over the scene, and it wasn't long before the Gardaí were knocking on the Coghlan's front door.

"I didn't rob any money! I was with them, but I didn't even get any money," I plaintively informed the Gardaí.

I'd been afraid to even share in the proceeds. But because I'd been part of the little gang, I was brought into the Children's Court at Dublin Castle.

I was lucky. My father refused to attend the court. He was well known and respected in Dublin Castle, where he had worked on many occasions. He wasn't about to let his brat of a son bring shame upon him. Instead, I was accompanied by my mother.

The judge accepted that, while I was party to the crime, I did not receive a share of the loot. As a first time offender he sentenced me to six months probation.

The incident was never again referred to in our house.

The joy of running

For as long as I can remember, I was always running. Along with a neighbour, Richard Holmes, I got involved in the weekly soccer pools around the streets of Drimnagh and Crumlin. He'd take one side of the street and I'd take the other, collecting a shilling on behalf of the Central Remedial Clinic. I made about five shillings a week for my efforts.

Richard would get annoyed at me because I'd go too fast for his liking. I'd run from house to house and instead of going in and out the garden gate, I'd vault right over the railings separating the houses.

I just loved to run and the faster I went the better I felt. The neighbours on Cooley Road, Mrs. Blake, Mrs. Carroll, Mrs. Holmes and Mrs. Donnolly, would regularly ask me to get milk, sugar and bread up at the shop. I'd set off across The Field and be back in no time, collecting an extra few pence if I was particularly quick.

The Kennedys of Castleross was my favourite radio soap opera. I'd run all the way home from school at lunchtime to make sure I heard it, and then race back to school when it was over. The lads were always amazed that I would run the mile distance home, catch the show, and make it back in time for class.

I also made a few bob on Saturday mornings. Our milkman from Merville Dairies would arrive with his horse-drawn milk float and I'd go running through the streets of Drimnagh delivering the milk. My pay for that was six-pence, and If Brendan was in good form, he'd let me ride the horse pulling the float along.

One summer, I got my first real job working as a "runner" for Brian Kerr's father. Many of the top Dublin businessmen would go to Frankie Kerr for their suits. Mr. Kerr paid me one pound, one-and-six a week to run the suits to various seamstresses for alterations. I'd be going from nine in the morning until six in the evening, Saturdays included. I'd fly around the city centre enjoying every minute of it.

One of the regular stops on my route was Crawford's Tailor shop on Fownes Street. Des Crawford's partner in the business was Joan Murphy – my future mother-in-law.

Every St. Stephen's Day, from an early age, I'd be up in Phoenix Park to watch the Waterhouse Byrne Baird Shield – a 10-mile race put on by Donore Harriers. Afterwards, everyone would head to Dillon's Black and Amber pub in Islandbridge for post-race refreshments and prize-giving.

Dating back to 1896, this annual event is the oldest cross-country club race in Ireland. After a number of years, my brothers outgrew the excitement. They had shown no particular aptitude for running. My father never pushed me or even suggested that I should take up athletics, but I was always eager to attend, and he was happy to bring me.

As I watched the likes of Eddie Spillane, Tommy Hopkins, Tom O'Riordan, Frank Cahill, Jim McNamara, Willie Dunne and the Reddigan brothers, Tommy and Maurice, racing through the mucky conditions, I recall telling myself "Some day I'd love to beat these auld fellows." At the time these guys were the legends of Irish running. Some of them had represented Ireland in the Olympic Games and European Championships.

In sixth class at Drimnagh Castle, I sat next to a boy named Jude Fagan. One day in October of 1964, Jude informed me that he'd joined Celtic Athletic Club. Jude was a quiet lad and running was something I never thought he'd be interested in – he seemed more into books than sporting activities,

It turned out a number of the lads from his street – Galtymore Close – were being trained by a man named Reggie Healy. Reggie played for the local Good Counsel hurling and gaelic football club and would have been considered one of their best players. He joined Celtic AC because he wanted to improve his running fitness and give himself an extra edge towards making the Dublin inter-county senior hurling team. He liked it so much that he encouraged the younger boys on the Good Counsel under-age teams to join Celtic and improve their fitness.

Reggie Healy was a kind man who couldn't bear to see young lads hanging about the streets of Drimnagh. He took it upon himself to do something about it. Reggie believed the more kids he could get to "try the running," the more kids he'd be able to recruit for the Counsel. Those who didn't have the stamina for running might yet have the skill to be a hurler. He was a smart man.

Jude invited me to come along the next Sunday morning. After nine o' clock mass, I headed off with Jude to Phoenix Park – where the Celtic Athletic Club trained on the Army Grounds. I was full of excitement, which wasn't in the slightest way diminished when I had to get changed outside while the adults changed inside their pavilion.

Not long after our arrival, a few elderly gentlemen turned up dressed in business suits. We gathered around an older, heavy-set man. This was Mr. Donnelly, who acted as the club's chairman. He told us that there would be a one mile league race and it would start over by the Dog Pond. The location could be identified by an old damaged tree, adjacent to the main road of the Park. It would commence in fifteen minutes and we were to go off and warm up. I didn't know anyone but Jude and I wasn't sure what to do. Jude and I walked over to the start area – the exact same spot I'd go to with my father to watch the Donore Harriers St. Stephen's Day race.

The race was a one-mile cross-country for boys thirteen and under. When the club officials called us to the start line, the new arrivals were asked to identify themselves and their ages. My hand was the only one raised. I said I was eleven, but would be twelve next month. Mr Donnelly replied "No, son. I don't think you should run in this race today. It's only your first day. You haven't trained and I'm afraid you might get lost."

I began to sob. "But I want to run!" I pleaded. "That's the only reason I came down here."

Mr. Donnelly relented. He instructed me to follow the older boys all the way around and not to let them out of my sight. He asked the more experienced boys to keep an eye on me lest I get lost in the woods.

The gun went off and I duly followed the pack. Halfway around the course, heading down the hills at the Khyber Pass, I moved up and began to run with the leaders. As I passed one of the older boys, I heard him shout "Hey Coghlan! Get back! Get back! You're going to get lost!"

"But I can't get lost," I replied cheerfully, "see, the red flags all along the course. I'll just follow them."

I continued along my merry way and won the race. Old Mr. Donnelly, Reggie Healy and the other officials couldn't believe that this skinny little kid who'd never raced before had won first time out.

"Jesus," I heard Mr Donnelly say to Reggie, "I think we've found ourselves one here."

When I came home and told my parents they were incredulous: "Sure you did, Eamonn." They thought it was just another fantasy of mine.

Over the next couple of months, the club continued to run the league races. I continued to win and my parents continued to disbelieve me.

I was still playing soccer for Rialto, and we were losing consistently to every team in the Dublin Schoolboy League. But there was something about running I loved. It became an expression of myself and it gave me a sense of confidence. I knew for the first time in my life that I was really good at something. It was me and me alone winning. It gave me a buzz like nothing else in all the activities I'd tried.

When the cross-country league finished up, I'd won the most points and was presented with the Celtic medal for being the top finisher overall. I remember the medal well – solid silver with a pure gold inset in the form of a Celtic cross. I was so proud.

I brought it home and reluctantly showed it off to my parents. I was bashful enough talking about my achievements and I wasn't sure if they'd believe me. But they did.

As it turned out my father had decided to pay a visit to the Park that morning "Just to see how good he really is," as my mother would later tell me. He hid behind a big chestnut tree on the main road opposite Áras an Úachtaran and watched the race unbeknownst to me.

I brought the medal home that day and announced to my mother "When I win fifty medals, I'm going to retire."

Following my conversion to athletics, my father decided I ought to wear his old Terenure AC track suit – partly for nostalgia's sake and partly so he wouldn't have to buy me a new one. It was bright orange, the ugliest thing imaginable. There was no way I was going to wear it. My running gear consisted of a white vest and shorts from Dunnes Stores on George's Street, and a pair of canvas shoes.

For Christmas my father bought me a lovely powder blue track suit and a pair of Blackthorn spikes with white stripes. I loved the suit – it was sleek and tight and it fit me well. As I ran around the house that Christmas morning, I felt as if I could cut right through the air.

My joy was short lived. Both parents decided that I'd only outgrow such a snug fit. Since they wanted to get a few years out of it, they took it back and exchanged it for a royal blue suit with white stripes on the chest. It was about three sizes too large and the most cumbersome thing I ever wore. I hated it, and was always embarrassed to wear it. But I had no choice.

I was a member of Celtic AC for less than two years when Gerry Donnelly died. With his death, the club dissolved, and so too did my nascent running career.

Some six months after Gerry's death, a fellow came to our home unannounced. His arrival, and our subsequent seventeen-year relationship, would have the most profound and lasting impact on me both as an athlete and a person.

No chance encounter

The man who came through the door that evening was Gerry Farnan. He had seen me race with Celtic AC and he wanted me to join a club he coached called Metropolitan Harriers AC. The clubhouse was located in Sarah Place – on the far side of Islandbridge, close to Donore Harriers.

From that day on, he was my coach, my mentor, my friend and confidant – right up until the day he died.

Michael "Gerry" Farnan was born in Artane on the Northside of Dublin. He moved to Palmerstown when he married his wife Sheila. He acquired the name "Gerry" from workmates in D.C. Cahill's, the pharmaceutical company – there were already too many Michaels on the job, so "Gerry" it was.

He had trained as a male nurse and worked for a time at St. Brendan's Psychiatric Hospital. He gave that up as there was so little money in it, and opted to become a fruit merchant instead.

At 5.00am each morning, he drove to the Dublin Corporation Fruit Market, just off Capel Street. He'd load up his Thames truck with fruit and vegetables, and deliver the produce to venues on the Northside one day, and the Southside the next.

Whilst Gerry was industrious and successful, his job was essentially a means of funding what he considered to be his true purpose: Overseeing the collection of young runners he had assembled.

Many running clubs around Dublin would sit back and await new applicants, but not Metropolitan Harriers. Gerry made active recruiting part of the process. He sought out promising youngsters from De La Salle in Ballyfermot, from Terenure College, Coláiste Mhuire and Oatlands CBS.

He had soon assembled one of the top collections of under-14 runners in Ireland. This included the likes of Jackie Smith, Matt Halligan, Davy Brien, Dennis McCarthy, Danny McGuire, John Lumsden, Derek Doran, Derry Dowling and myself – while I was still running for my school team at Drimnagh Castle.

Gerry was a keen student of horse racing, and he adapted the principles of the Sport of Kings in the coaching of his athletes. He borrowed from the techniques of the great thoroughbred trainers Vincent O'Brien and Robert Sangster.

The club's runners wore green shorts and a white singlet with a large capital M on the front. They trained three times a week. There was also a club crest, or Merit Badge, which incorporated a Phoenix Park reindeer. You had to win a Dublin or National title in either an individual or team competition before you could have one of those stitched to your vest. It was considered a badge of honour – one to be worn with pride and distinction.

From the very outset, Gerry made it clear to us that Metro had an ambitious, long-term plan. We started training together in late 1966. He pointed out that by the time 1972 rolled around, some of us might be ready to run in the Munich Olympics. He convinced us that we could be great runners, but time and patience were of the essence.

Gerry also studied the "Lydiard System" a method of coaching devised and named after famed New Zealand coach, Arthur Lydiard.

To bring this goal front-and-centre, Gerry christened one of the Phoenix Park training loops the Munich Lap – a three-quarter mile course beside the Magazine Fort.

The Munich Lap had a hundred-metre straight away, followed by six or seven short, sharp hills, before finishing back on the same straight. The starting point was identified with a big boulder rock. The team christened this the Rock of Hope.

Gerry's coaching philosophy was to continually break up our rhythm. If you go out for a five or six-mile run on a flat course, you'll inevitably ease into a pattern and not get much in return. In contrast, the Munich Lap worked on all aspects of our running armoury. It crucified your legs. It worked on every running muscle, pushed your lungs and tore the heart out of you. One of Gerry's favourite expressions was "You'll train here until you flatten the course." To psych us up when we were moaning about how hard it was, he'd say "Come on, there's gold in them hills!"

Gerry Farnan became my God. I idolised him and hung on every word of encouragement he gave me. He could read me like a book, and in many ways, understood me better than I did myself. He knew I didn't like to make a fuss of my achievements, and he knew that I was very sensitive. I could talk to him about anything and I trusted him deeply.

He became closer to me than my father.

Around this time I was still playing soccer. I had a decision to make when the under-14 soccer league was moved to Sunday mornings – which clashed with Metro's training time.

It wasn't a hard decision. I had never won a medal of any colour in all the years playing football. In running, I was getting close to the 'retirement number' of fifty I mentioned to my mother a year-and-a-half earlier.

From here on, *I was a runner.*

I never played another game of soccer.

Once I began to win races, my father's interest in the sport was rekindled. He bought a stopwatch and started coaching kids in Drimnagh Castle Athletics Club – which was now my secondary school.

Later he became Honorary Secretary with Metro. From there he went on to become secretary of the Dublin County Board. He was passionate about athletics. Sometimes, instead of going to work, he'd stay home all day and take care of the administration duties for the County Board. Frequently, I would come in from school in the evening and find him still working on athletics' affairs. The house was taken over with files — I thought it was a bit over the top at times. After a day in his "athletics office," he'd inevitably head out to an evening Board meeting.

He came to be known as an athletes' man, and an athletes' official. This was partly because I was doing so well – and there was a growing expectation that I might get a scholarship to an American University – and I might even go on to represent Ireland.

He became a very, very popular official – among the runners, if not his fellow bureaucrats. Years later, he became President of Bord Lúthchleas na hÉireann – the Irish Athletics Board – for an unprecedented three years in a row.

Despite his renewed career in athletics, he never once coached me. He knew where he stood. If I kicked up over anything, he'd let Gerry Farnan resolve it.

On Sunday mornings when there was no competition scheduled, Gerry would send his young charges out into the park for what he called "cat-and-mouse" games. Seven or eight mice would go dashing off toward the Furry Glen, about two miles from the clubhouse. Ten minutes later, the cats would be unleashed.

For all intents and purposes, it was a game of hide-and-seek. It would continue until the cats caught all the mice – whereupon they would reverse roles and start the chase anew. It was a welcome diversion from the more rigorous training on Tuesday and Thursday evenings.

Even at that young age, I realised Gerry harboured an ulterior motive: He was teaching us to run long distance – up and down hills, stopping, resting, sprinting over all kinds of terrain. It was meant to bring an element of fun and games into training, yet we'd be out for an hour-and-a-half, cover eight miles and be exhausted afterwards. It did the job.

I was only in Metro a few months when Gerry primed his charges for the Dublin under-fourteen cross-country championships. It would be my first county championship and it was something of a big deal. I would have to contend with my team-mates Matt Halligan, Danny Maguire, Dennis McCarthy – any one of whom could win. Then there were the runners from Phoenix Harriers, Raheny Shamrocks, Blackrock AC and Clonliffe Harriers. Metro were favourites to win the team title, but it was anyone's guess who'd get the individual honours.

I was still sneaking the odd cigarette, but the morning of the championship I decided I'd give it a rest. That afternoon, I made my way to Phoenix Park on the bus. I didn't mention anything to my family about the day's race. Our team met in the clubhouse, and as we changed into our gear, I could feel the tension. Usually we'd joke around and slag each other off – but this time it was different.

For the first time in my running life, I was really nervous. So were the others. I feared Matt Halligan the most. He was a guy with roaring red hair – a great sprinter, oozing with confidence.

As we left for our warm-up, and the start by the broken tree, Gerry called me back. Out of earshot of the others, he said "Cocko, I want you to win this."

"What about Matt?" I asked, "he has great speed and I can't keep up with him during the intervals."

"Listen to me. Matt has great speed over a hundred or two hundred metres. You have the stamina. You have the heart. If he pushes the pace, let him. He'll have no kick left in him by the time he comes off the last bend, and onto the Main Road."

I believed Gerry. Matt did push the pace all the way around the woods. He tried to get away from me up and down the hills. We had a huge lead on the rest of the field. Then, coming out of the woods and off the last turn, I moved past him and sprinted on to win my first ever championship.

The following day, the Irish Independent carried three photographs and a story on the championship. One picture of the senior winner, Tommy Byrne, one of Kevin Humphreys, the under-sixteen winner, and one of me. In the background, you could clearly see my father hiding behind a tree, cheering me on to victory.

He admitted later that "I thought it might upset you if you knew I was there." Metro won the team title and I got my Merit Badge.

Around 1967, there was talk of a possible merger in Irish athletics. I was too young to understand the bitterness of the politics that had divided the sport since 1932. All I wanted was to run. I didn't care about the arguments amongst the officials. Regularly, I'd hear my father debate The Split with other administrators. It was directly born out of the partition of the North and South of Ireland.

The Amateur Athletic Union (AAU) was recognised by the International Amateur Athletics Federation (IAAF) and the International Olympic Committee (IOC) as the official body in the Republic of Ireland's twenty-six counties for the promotion of athletics.

AAU athletes could represent Ireland in the Olympic Games and European Championships, while the National Athletics and Cycling Association (NACA) was not recognised, and its athletes could not "compete officially" in international competitions. The NACA wanted a thirty-two county body whose motives were more Republican than athletic. NACA athletes were confined to small towns and villages, along with a handful of Dublin clubs.

My club, Metro, was in the NACA. If I was to have any chance of becoming an international runner in the future, an amalgamation of the two bodies was important. Otherwise, I might have to consider moving to an AAU club.

Thankfully, the AAU and NACA later merged to form Bord Lúthcleas na hÉireann. Some die-hards of the NACA were none too happy with this outcome, and continued to meet "illegally" for years. To this day, there are dissidents unhappy with the set up of Irish athletics.

The Dublin Community Games were established by County Councillor Joe Connolly. It was a government-backed initiative that brought together children from the various resident associations of the city, and an opportunity to introduce them to sports. It was called The Mini Olympics.

The athletics were held in Santry stadium. This was my first official race in Santry. Previously, NACA clubs could not compete in the stadium due to "The Split." I won the mile race for under-sixteens and received the Evening Herald cup for my efforts. This was regarded as a big deal, and it received extensive newspaper coverage.

One year later, the Community Games introduced the mini marathon for boys under-seventeen. I was set to run in this event, when there was a protest from the Cabra Residents' Association. They complained to Connolly that I was a "professional," being a member of an established running club. They claimed it was unfair.

The truth of the matter was they had a runner fancied to win... if I wasn't in the race. A rumour spread that, if I was allowed to run, and was in the lead when the race reached Binns Bridge at Dorset Street, they would block my passage. Their complaint was dismissed and I was allowed to run.

Right from the starting gun, I was gone. I had established a lead of five hundred yards by the time I reached Binns Bridge. There was no sign of a protest by the Cabra people – the Drimnagh supporters made sure of that. They were there on the bridge to protect me "just in case." I went on to win by over half a mile.

These were pivotal wins in my young career. Senior members in Metro began showing me respect. The great Joe Cunningham (a champion miler in his heyday), Tommy Swift (a solid, reliable performer), and Gerry Carty were talking to me. I was accepted. Swifty even let me change into my gear in "his corner spot" on the days we met for training. Officials in the Dublin County Board also took notice as I was now set to be part of their team for the regional and national championships.

Athletics began to take over my teenage life. The pictures on my bedroom wall of my beloved Dublin football team: John Timmons, Des Foley and Snitchy Ferguson were replaced with runners: Kip Keino, Michael Jazy, Peter Snell and Ron Clarke. I began to dream that one day I'd be as good as they were. Although I struggled with my reading, I would pore over Arthur Lydiard's book and try to glean something from it that would make me a better runner.

Could I be as good as the superstars? When it came to the Leinster and National Championships, I couldn't even match the mighty "culchies." The lads from Wexford and Galway were bigger and stronger. I found it difficult to match them. I was reduced to an also-ran.

My confidence dwindled. Even in Metro, my reverie was interrupted when Gerry recruited a newcomer: Tony Carroll from De La Salle, Ballyfermot. Carroll was only six months older than me, but he was more developed. Even worse, he had a beard.

I had become accustomed to being top dog. Tony Carroll's arrival changed that. Just as I had destroyed other runners' confidence by imposing myself on them, Carroll would destroy mine.

As a regular practice after training on Tuesday and Thursday evenings, Gerry conducted what I like to describe as chin-wagging sessions. Gerry would take turns talking with whichever of the boys felt the need for an audience. Whether it was to talk over family problems, school problems, girl problems, or running problems, Gerry was there to listen and dispense advice. If a boy happened to be short of money, these audiences might even end with the coach slipping him a few bob to tide him over.

After you sat with Gerry in the confessional, you invariably left him in high spirits. Gerry had an even temperament, and an exceptionally quiet tone. You'd have to ask him to speak up, but whatever he did say, you knew he meant it. He had a wonderful knack for instilling confidence and self-belief.

On one of these occasions, I found myself in some despair. Tony Carroll was beating me like a drum in all cross-country races that year. I saw no likelihood of the trend reversing, so I turned to Gerry.

"Eamonn, look at you," he said, "you're only sixteen-years-of-age. You don't have a hair under your arm. Tony has a beard. He's physically matured earlier than you have, that's all. Just take your time, be patient, and I promise you that over the next year you're going to develop physically – and when you do have hair under your arms, and on your arse, believe me – you'll beat him. Not only that, when you fully mature you'll run for Ireland... and you'll win the Olympics."

I never forgot those words. I learned to be patient and I learned to trust in my ability. Of course he was right about Tony (although not about the Olympics.) Within a year it happened just the way Gerry had said it would.

By the time of the 1969 Leinster Colleges' intermediate cross-country championship, I had grown hair under my arms, and even a bit of stubble on my chin. I shocked the entire athletic community when I out-kicked hairy Tony Carroll to win the race at Belfield.

Brother Perkins was the hurling and football coach at Drimnagh Castle when I was at school there. He also organised the athletics team for inter-schools' competitions. He would go on to christen my blistering finishing speed as the "Cocky Kick." While it became the hallmark of my running, it wasn't something I was born with. Rather, it was carefully nurtured when I was a novice runner at Metro.

After John Whetton of Great Britain defeated Ireland's Frank Murphy to win the 1969 European 1,500 metres title, Gerry Farnan sat me down and the two of us analysed how it happened. Earlier that summer, in the British AAA championships, Murphy had beaten Whetton... but in Athens he lost because he was out-kicked down the final stretch.

Gerry outlined his concept and referred to it as Reflex Speed. "Frank Murphy," he explained, "doesn't have the ability to change from a middle distance runner's stride to that of a sprinter. It's too consistent and too single-paced. When you come off that final bend and make your move, I want you to feel like you're running on hot coals. Turn into a Jesse Owens: Turn into a sprinter."

As I trained over the next few years, Gerry would have me do "speed drills" – simulating the experience of coming off the last turn. We worked to change, not just my style, but also my mental outlook. I wanted to understand, and visualise, the process of switching gears instantly to that of a sprinter.

He had me sprint without using my arms – just my legs in high knee lifts. He used a whistle, and when he blew it, I had to react immediately. The reflex speed was mental as much as it was physical. He hammered that into me until I understood. The sudden change in gear would shock the opposition, and you'd be gone before they had time to react.

It was yet another example of Gerry's prescience and insight. I hadn't been a particularly fast half or quarter-miler. My times over two hundred metres were mediocre, and I didn't seem to have much natural speed. But his technique helped transform me. Eventually, I could run quicker over the last quarter, or two hundred, as I could in a once-off run. "Speed work," he would say "is over rated. If you are strong at the end of a race, the reflex speed will do the work."

As I progressed, along with the other boys from Metro, Gerry studied our individual temperaments. He wanted to get into our heads and find out who his runners really were.

By the time we were sixteen or so, he would hire some of us to help out with his route on the fruit truck. During the summer, or on weekends during the school year, I would catch the 23 bus to the markets first thing in the morning. There, I'd help Gerry load what seemed like tonnes of fruit and vegetables.

The market was a tough place. I'd watch Gerry haggle over the price of tomatoes, apples and oranges and not give an inch. The market workers were real down-to-earth Dubs who'd buy and sell you in a second. The only time I ever saw Gerry get mad was when some local hard man would slag off his runners. Gerry's face would turn redder than one of his tomatoes, and he'd explode in a verbal rage.

Once loaded, we'd spend all day delivering to the shops on his route. His customers knew him as Michael... but in athletics circles, he was always Gerry.

We'd work until seven in the evening, and then he'd drop me home. While I was happy enough for the few quid, I didn't realise his motive was to strengthen me up. We never did any formal weight training at Metro, but lifting all those boxes and sacks of potatoes accomplished the same goal.

I also came to realise he was applying a psychological approach in dealing with his young runners. By this time I was known to be one of his good prospects, and sometimes his customers would ask questions or offer words of encouragement. I was always embarrassed and didn't want any kind of a fuss made.

Gerry spotted this sensitive side of my personality. I'd get upset if my father made a big deal about my running, or make a joke of me in front of people. It would send me into a state of despair for days. At times we'd argue about it, but Gerry always knew how to handle my mood swings. He knew from our days working and chatting how sensitive I was behind the facade.

I never minded hard work and I had all sorts of jobs growing up. Besides helping out my Dad and Gerry, I worked for Mittons – a well known family butchers.

Mittons owned a number of shops around Dublin and as well as various odd-jobs in store, I would deliver meat to the locals on a bicycle with the traditional basket on the front. We never had one in the house so, for all intents and purposes, it was my first bike.

The real reason I loved working there was I got to wash Paddy and Maurice Mittons' fancy cars. The Mittons were well to do and had new car after new car. I learned how to wash and polish them correctly and was hugely proud of the sparkle I achieved.

I'd already learned to drive from going around in the truck with Gerry. I'd be up in the passenger seat and Gerry would teach me how to change gears. Eventually he'd let me take a short drive in a quiet area.

After I washed the Mittons' cars, I'd dry them with a drive through the streets of Drimnagh. I'd go for half-an-hour just hoping some of my friends might see me behind the wheel. It was pretty heady stuff for a teenage boy in those days. You might call it legal joyriding. Paddy and Maurice trusted me to have a gleaming car back by the shop door, safe and sound.

I'd often accompany them to Mondello Park for the racing. The Mittons boys always attracted a raft of attractive people to their post-race parties. It was glamorous stuff for a young lad and dreamed that one day I'd be "rich and famous" just like them.

Whilst my athletic career was taking off, my academic career was headed in the opposite direction.

I'd loved every minute of junior school at Good Counsel, and primary at Drimnagh Castle. I never missed a day in my life. Even if I was sick, I'd cry if Ma kept me home. I couldn't wait to get to school; I enjoyed it that much.

Brother Gordon in primary school was my great friend and confidant. We hit it off because of our common interest in Gaelic football. He was a young Kildare man with a soft manner, and he'd take the mickey if the Dubs lost a game. He knew I was finding it difficult to concentrate and absorb information. As I approached my entrance examination for secondary school, he gave me additional help with my maths and Irish.

I admired Brother Gordon. He understood my problems – problems that would affect me throughout secondary school, and which weren't identified until much later in my life.

When the new secondary school was built, the students transferred from a 16th century Norman Castle into a new, modern building. There was a moat surrounding the castle, and the old drawbridge was removed and replaced with a tarmac pathway. My brothers were among the first students in the new building.

To my parents' surprise – and thanks to Brother Gordon's help – I did pass my entrance examination. They were delighted. Now they could have their three boys attend at no cost. Prior to that year, the Castle was a fee-paying school. The Government had just introduced free second-level education, and this would free up an extra few bob.

Secondary school was where I began to have problems. Bill and Brendan were academically bright, but I ended up in D class: Where the less able students were dumped. I found the transition from primary to secondary hugely intimidating. I felt completely out of my depth. The absence of a figure like Brother Gordon added to my sense of isolation.

I managed reasonably well in geography and biology, but was completely at sea in maths and Irish. Unfortunately, both were compulsory subjects. Fail these in the Inter-Cert or Leaving-Cert, and you failed everything – no matter how well you performed in the other subjects.

In those days, corporal punishment was an accepted means of discipline. If your parents didn't give you the odd clatter, you could be sure that the teacher would. If you forgot your homework or misbehaved in class, you'd get six lashes across the palm of your hand with a black leather strap. If the teacher couldn't afford a strap, he'd use a bamboo cane instead.

I was at the receiving end of the teachers' leather on many an occasion. It was either for forgetting homework or causing a disturbance.

I became accustomed to, and somewhat immune to the pain. By the time third year rolled around, my confidence as a runner had grown. All I wanted to do was run. School did not matter to me one iota. The better I performed as a runner, the less I feared the 'leather'.

And then, half way through my secondary schooling, my confidence was completely shattered

Up to that point I thought it couldn't get any worse. But it did. In the form of a sadistic Brother nicknamed "Stoney" by the students – got this moniker from the TV western of the same name. To be a Christian Brother might be considered a calling from God, but this guy was sent by the devil.

His reputation was well known. He instilled fear into all his pupils. He possessed a leather a foot and-a-half long. If you stepped out of line, not only did you get it across the hands, you'd get it on your arse, back, legs and even over the head. Stoney seemed to take great pleasure in the beatings, and I was on the receiving end far too often.

He harassed and humiliated the weaker pupils in maths. Stoney insisted that the word "minus" was pronounced "mee-nus" because that's how they said it in his part of Tipperary. If you didn't pronounce it to his satisfaction, he might walk over and slap you right in your face.

If he was really angry, he'd grab you by the sideburns and lift you right off the floor. Sometimes he'd pull hair off in the process.

On one occasion, I stood my ground. I told him to "F*** off! We pronounce it 'my-nus' in Dublin – not the way you culchies say it in Tipperary."

He grabbed me by the throat, pulling the shirt collar tight around my neck. He pushed me hard against the back wall where I cracked my head on a sharp corner of a hanging crucifix.

I was sent out of class with blood streaming from the wound. I walked to hospital where I had three stitches inserted. In those days, you dared not curse at a teacher. In any event, nobody would have believed my story. Nobody would believe a Christian Brother could be so sadistic.

Faced with the prospect of Stoney, I found myself crying in bed every night. I became depressed and started to mitch off school.

At 9:00am, I'd go down to Noel Fitzroy's house on Galtymore Road. We'd hang out there all day, smoking cigarettes and playing cards. We didn't dare go outside for fear of being spotted. Noel's mother had died when he was younger, and his father would be out to work.

On one of my "days off", I went home at lunchtime, as usual. As I ate my sandwich and listened to *The Kennedys of Castleross*, I noticed my Dad's white Ford Cortina pull up outside. He never came home at this hour. I knew it wasn't a good sign. I immediately ran upstairs to avoid meeting him as he came through the hall door. I eavesdropped from the top of the stairs and could just make out his conversation with my mother. Scared of what he might do to me I climbed out the bathroom window and ran off to the safety of a friend's house where I hid until he tracked me down.

I was surprised at his tone when he confronted me. I was half expecting a thrashing, but he was calm and softly spoken. He told me he'd talked to my brothers, Bill and Brendan, and he knew I'd been absent from school. He also knew exactly what I had been going through, and what kind of a man Stoney was. We would go to the Principal the next morning and arrange a transfer out of his class.

I felt huge sense of relief. I was enormously impressed with how my father handled the issue.

The following day, we visited Principal Burke. He expressed his delight at how I had represented the school in athletics and he agreed to a transfer from Stoney's class. It was a lucky escape for me, though I did feel a bit guilty leaving my classmates behind.

The sisters and me

B y the time I turned seventeen, my circle of friends had expanded to include members of other clubs around Dublin. Through my friend and rival Frank Murphy Jr. (later a Villanova team-mate) I got to know some of the young athletes from Clonliffe Harriers and Greenfield Athletic Club.

Clonliffe was one of the oldest, most established clubs in the country. They had a 440 yards cinder track in their home base, JFK Stadium. It was there in 1958 that Herb Elliott broke the world record for the mile with 3:54. In one race, five men went under the magical four-minute barrier for the first time ever. I had gone there many times to see Billy Morton's international athletics meetings. I watched Snell, Keino, Ibbotson, Ireland's Noel Carroll and Frank Murphy Sr. all ply their trade. It was there I'd won many juvenile and schools races, and it would be my home training base when I became an international runner.

Clonliffe's runners were a strong presence in junior athletics. One was half-miler Jean Appleby, a niece of the noted Dublin jewellery family. Jean had a friend, Theo Byrne, a long-jumper and half-miler. My other Clonliffe friend, Matt Slattery was madly in love with Jean.

He would sometimes ask me to join him on a double date – him escorting Jean and me escorting Theo – as Jean would not be allowed out with Matt on her own.

As I was getting to know the kids from Clonliffe, I took notice of a striking young 400 metre runner named Patricia Murphy. She was a member of the Greenfield club: Traditionally their best athletes would move on to Clonliffe as they got older.

In the spring of 1970 I was nominated, along with several runners from other clubs, to represent Dublin in a triangular meeting against Liverpool and Manchester. The meeting would take place at a stadium in Salford, and a trip across the Irish Sea was an exotic prospect.

I spent most of the journey to Manchester and back trying to impress Patricia – without much success. She was a gorgeous girl, if a bit stand-offish. Of course, I didn't have enough sense to realise she just wasn't interested. I thought if I kept at it I'd eventually wear her down, but I got absolutely nowhere.

I didn't perform too well in my 1,500 metre race. It wasn't because my focus was on chasing Patricia, I just wasn't good enough to mix it with the English teams.

Shortly after that, the All-Ireland under-17 Track and Field Championships were held in Tipperary.

The standard arrangement was that the representatives of the various Dublin clubs would meet at Liberty Hall, and all would travel down together by coach.

I was just about to board the coach when the crew from Clonliffe arrived: Jean, Theo, Felicia Farrelly, and finally – Patricia. I almost went into shock when we made eye contact... but something about her had changed.

"Wow, Patricia! What did you do with your hair?" I found myself saying, "you look fantastic!"

"I'm not Patricia," she replied, "I'm her sister, Yvonne."

My heart leapt to my throat. I had fallen in love with this girl the moment I laid eyes on her.

Yvonne was also a member of Greenfield. She was friendly with many of the girls in the club, and she would go to all their meets and look after the gear while they competed. Sometimes she would be asked to do the long jump if the team was short a person.

All the way down to Tipperary I couldn't keep my eyes off her. She was reserved and quiet. She was elegant. Everyone was laughing and joking, but I just sat back and wondered how I might pluck up the courage to ask her out. I was besotted.

Over the next few months, I ran into her from time to time. I worshipped her from afar. She was never terribly receptive to my advances.

Some time later I discovered she had a boyfriend. When I heard she had broken up with him, I plucked up the courage to make contact with her. To my delight, she agreed to accompany me to a dance at O'Connell's CBS. The band at the dance happened to be Thin Lizzy, with the legendary Phil Lynott at the helm.

It was a wonderful night. We shared our first kiss at that dance, and I felt an extraordinary sense of elation and self-worth.

How had I captured such a stunning girl? Her Dad collected us from the dance and dropped me home. I was high as a kite, but nearly blew it on my first date when I said "Sorry, Mr. Murphy for dragging you over to this side of the city, it was Yvonne's fault we missed the bus."

From the moment we started dating, we were almost inseparable. Yvonne was everything in the whole world to me, and my parents took to her immediately.

My father was particularly pleased. He felt that I finally had someone to look after me and settle me down. Everywhere I went, Yvonne came too: Track meets together, cross-country meets together, she was always there. So much so that Joey Bridgeman, Honorary Treasurer to the Dublin Juvenile Athletics Board, would call her The Coach.

Both Joey and Bill Battersby, another athletics official, were great friends of my father. Between the three of them, they led the juvenile athletics programme in

Dublin. These two men knew me well, all my strengths and my failings. They liked Yvonne too when they saw how much I had settled down. As a matter of fact, it was Joey who gave me £20 to buy Yvonne a watch for her sixteenth birthday. He knew I'd no money, and he wanted me to give her something nice.

Yvonne and her sister, Patricia, were stylish dressers. They'd head off to Paris, Rome, Milan and London with their auntie Anne and treat themselves to the latest fashions; mini-skirts, hot-pants, tight jeans and leather boots.

Their mother, Joan, had a tailoring business in Fownes Street and Yvonne would help her take up the hems or repair the dresses. She even made her own dresses from patterns she saw in the shops. Her sense of style even had an influence on me and it wasn't long before I was dressing better.

Yvonne understood me well. She was able to handle my quirkiness and my moods. She could share in my athletic progress. Knowing my ability, she gave me the space to go do it.

It was always "You do what you need to do and I'll follow." There was never any selfishness on her part. Not once did she say "No, you can't train. I want to attend this dance." I'm sure we missed out plenty of the things normal couples did.

She might get annoyed when I got moody coming up to a race, but she always understood and supported me without fail.

We weren't into drinking at all. We had a simple life together as young teenagers. On Sundays, we'd meet under the clock at Clerys and head for the Dandelion Market to check out the latest rock bands.

We'd dance at Sloopy's or the Zhivago nightclub and we'd go to the cinema twice a week. Yvonne's family lived in Santry, so we were usually catching the last bus from O'Connell Street. I'd drop her off and then run all the way home to Drimnagh – a distance of eight or nine miles. Sometimes I'd even bring my running gear and change at her house. Other nights I'd just run home in my street clothes.

While my love-life prospered, my academic performance continued to cause great alarm. This was despite my transfer out of Stoney's class.

I was doing so well athletically, the prospect of going to America on a scholarship was a genuine possibility. But if I failed to pass my Leaving Certificate, there would be no chance of getting into a US college.

Before I sat the Leaving Cert, I was to have one more unpleasant encounter at Drimnagh Castle. It would ultimately see me expelled from the school.

I'd had an ongoing disagreement with one of the teachers. It led to the pair of us brandishing chairs and issuing all sorts of threatening noises.

It might have passed off had the whole scene not been witnessed by the principal, Brother Burke. He had no option but to send me home. Once there, I refused point-blank to even contemplate returning. With the Leaving Certificate fast approaching, my father and Gerry Farnan took radical action

They approached Brother Kevin Clonliffe, who was athletics coach in St Vincent's CBS in Glasnevin. After a meeting, he offered me a chance to do my Leaving in St Vincent's. "A fresh start," he said, "new teachers and new friends."

To everyone's surprise, I agreed. It was only for six months anyhow. My father offered to drive me to the other side of the city every morning, and I would get the bus home.

I agreed not just because I had to get my Leaving (and my ticket to America), but because Yvonne attended the Holy Faith Convent in Glasnevin, and this meant I would get to see more of her.

My days at St Vincent's were definitely more pleasant and less stressful than those at the Castle. I attended school every day as scheduled, and didn't mitch any more. I felt welcomed by my new teachers and classmates. I had no baggage there and I felt comfortable right from the start. I was training well too. Runs over the Munich lap were a little easier to handle. I even began to run around the Field a couple of mornings a week, before school.

I looked forward to lunchtime each day. I'd meet up with Yvonne, her friend Pauline Butler and Pauline's boyfriend Frank O'Neill. We'd sit on a wall and chat away without a care in the world. I felt so good about myself – free from the pressures that had previously beset me. Lunch break always passed too quickly. I wished we could stay longer. I just could not get enough time with her.

But Yvonne was the sensible one; she helped me to focus on school and she paced our developing relationship maturely. While I was due to do my Leaving Cert in a few months, she'd be doing her Inter Cert. She didn't want my obsession with her to be a distraction.

Within one month of the Leaving, I had no firm offer of an athletics scholarship from any American University. Everyone in Ireland assumed I would be heading off, but with nothing in the can, I was getting concerned. Even though school had improved, my attitude towards maths and Irish had not. I just couldn't get my head around these subjects, no matter how hard I tried.

I didn't panic. I'd taken the Scholastic Aptitude Test (SAT) in Rockwell College that spring, and found the multiple choice and reasoning test questions easier.

I got very good results – good enough to see me accepted into most US Colleges. It was a huge relief. When I eventually sat my Leaving, I said "To hell with it. Who in America cares about the Leaving and Irish?"

Despite years of listening to "You must pass your Leaving if you want to go to America." I'd decided I'd take my chances with the SATs.

I failed Leaving Cert Maths and Irish, as I had expected. Otherwise, I did well. At least I was through with school and I could begin to look forward to the next stage of my life. What I hoped would be a serious athletics career, with Yvonne by my side.

The Villanova connection

When a young Irish runner in the 1960s and '70s spoke of hoping to run in America, what he really meant was he hoped to run for Villanova University. I was no exception. Almost every Irish kid who ran track and field wanted to go to Villanova, which was founded by the Augustinian Order in 1842. This was because of Ronnie Delany and the legendary coach James "Jumbo" Elliott – a man who would play a pivotal role in my career.

Delany's triumphs in America had given this Philadelphia school (and Jumbo) a place of prominence in the world of Irish athletics, culminating in his Olympic gold in the 1956 Melbourne Games. But Villanova's Irish Connection went back even further than that.

Like most other American universities, Villanova's athletics programmes had been decimated by the Second World War. Jumbo had been among the first to recognise the problem. He set to remedy this, targeting returning war veterans to form the nucleus of his post-war teams.

One of his athletes, quarter-miler George Guida, had used just a year of his collegiate eligibility before signing up. He had returned a more mature runner and student.

Another, Browning Ross, was still in the Navy when Jumbo saw him win an indoor mile at the Knights of Columbus meet in New York. He offered Ross a scholarship, and persuaded him to enrol at Villanova after his discharge.

Guida and Ross would become national AAU champions. They formed the centrepiece of a Villanova team that quickly established itself as a national powerhouse. When the Olympic Games resumed in 1948 after a 12-year hiatus, the two Villanovans qualified for the United States team. They were the first of a seemingly endless list of Olympians developed on Jumbo's watch.

Guida was sixth in the 400 metres, Ross seventh in the 3,000 steeplechase. The pair stayed in Europe and ran in several post-Olympic events that summer. After one such meet in Ireland, the two men were joined for drinks by Jim Reardon – who had befriended Guida when they competed previously.

The faster the pints went down the more Reardon was intrigued.

"It's beautiful in the States," the Americans assured him, "and the best part is Villanova University in Pennsylvania. Jumbo Elliott is an Irishman just like you, Reardon! You'll do fine with Jumbo."

By the time they went their separate ways, Reardon was sold. When they got back to the States a few weeks later, Guida and Ross told Jumbo about this Irish Olympian who was interested in coming to Villanova.

Because the two athletes were older men with both a war and an Olympic Games behind them, Jumbo was inclined to trust their judgement. He contacted Reardon immediately, inviting him to Villanova.

When Reardon arrived in Philadelphia that autumn, he was the first and only foreigner ever to run for Jumbo. He didn't retain that distinction for long. Within a couple of months he was joined by John Joe Barry. Barry was the reigning Irish Mile Champion and he'd run against Ross the previous summer.

Barry was known as The Ballincurry Hare. He claimed to have run the first-ever sub-four minute mile, years before Bannister. Since this feat was accomplished in training, and before a paucity of reliable witnesses, it was regarded with some scepticism. Yet another Irish champion, the shot putter Cummin Clancy, soon joined the fold.

Thus started what was later known as The Irish Connection, a tradition that would continue with Delany in the 1950s, Noel Carroll in the early 1960s, steeple-chaser Des McCormack, Frank Murphy Sr. and shortly before my arrival, Donal Walsh and John Hartnett. Future world champions Marcus O'Sullivan and Sonia O'Sullivan would follow in their footsteps too.

I'm sure Brother Conliffe hadn't considered it when he suggested I complete my secondary school studies in St Vincent's, but the school was also to benefit. That year, I won the Irish CBS Championships at 800, 1,500 and 5,000 metres. My points were good enough to win the school the team championship. I also won the Leinster and All-Ireland Colleges Senior 1,500 and 5,000 metre races. St. Vincents had a well-respected athletics programme before my enrolment, but overnight it became the top school in the country.

Despite my success on the track, by July there was still no offer from Villanova. "Too late," I thought. Although I had been contacted by Portland State University, there was no solid offer. I had no real interest in going anywhere other than Villanova anyway. As the deadline for the incoming freshman class of 1971 approached, I wondered if Villanova really wanted me or not?

Jumbo already had another Irish runner in his sights – Tom Gregan – and it was unclear if there would be a second scholarship available.

Tom was regarded as the best of the Irish kids. He was a budding superstar who, at seventeen years old, had already run a 4:01.6 mile and 4:43 for 1,500 metres. Maurice Ahern, the former Lord Mayor of Dublin (and brother of future Taoiseach Bertie Ahern), was his coach.

Tom would usually hammer me over 800 metres or the mile. I'd have the upper hand over longer distances – 3,000 and 5,000 metres, or cross-country. But there's no question that his times were more impressive.

I'd been coached by Gerry Farnan to win, win, win. Times would come with your wins – essentially the same philosophy Jumbo Elliott espoused. But there's no way Jumbo could have known this. Without ever having laid eyes on either of us, our times were all he had to go by.

Changing school in my last year had given me the opportunity to do something no Irish schoolboy had ever done before: I'd won successive Irish Schools 5,000 metre titles for two different schools – Drimnagh Castle and St. Vincent's.

Tom had been recruited early in the summer and had long since committed to Villanova. Frank Murphy Sr. had just finished at Villanova and gone on to win the Silver Medal at the European Championships in 1969. He kept telling Jumbo and Jack Pyrah, his assistant "I think you might be better off getting this Coghlan kid too."

At this point, my only contact with Villanova had come through Frank. Jumbo had never approached me directly, nor had Jack Pyrah. They were still sorting out their budget and available scholarships and had yet to offer me anything. Whenever I got feedback, it was always "We'll just wait and see."

Frank counselled me to be patient. To be honest, I was beginning to have mixed feelings. Even though going off to compete in America would be the fulfilment of a dream, it would also mean leaving Yvonne. She promised she would wait for me, but I wasn't sure I could bear that separation.

Meanwhile, I had a summer job in the PMPA Insurance Company. I worked in the filing room with future Irish international rugby star, Tony Ward. I began to think that perhaps I'd be better off staying home and pursuing a career in the company – like my sister, Ann. She was secretary to the personnel manager, and he had suggested I could work full-time as an insurance underwriter.

In mid-August, Villanova came through with a full scholarship offer – at last! It consisted of tuition, books and room and board. Airfares and spending money were the responsibility of the family. In truth, I didn't know whether to celebrate or curse the offer. There was no choice. I had to accept the opportunity.

My family didn't have a great deal of money, and flights across the Atlantic were very expensive at the time. My mother had been involved with an Irish-American travel society. For years, she'd been putting money away so she could travel to America and visit her brother Christy in Chicago. She had accumulated enough credits in this scheme that she could get me a round-trip ticket to New York on a chartered flight in late August. It was a 21-day excursion ticket with a return date of September 17.

The word got around quickly that both Tom Gregan and I would be heading to Villanova. I was seen as being very much in Tom's shadow. The newspapers did feature stories covering our imminent departure. It was a big deal to get into Villanova, and the closer the time came to leave, the more apprehensive I felt.

Then tragedy struck. Just four days before we were due to fly out, Tom's father died. He was devastated, his world turned completely upside down. He ended up staying home while I headed off to America alone.

The departure from my parents and from Yvonne was every bit as tearful as you can imagine. I flew from Dublin, via Shannon, to Kennedy Airport. I had one small suitcase, £100 in sponsorship from Joe Moore, the managing director of PMPA, and £100 from my rich Uncle Robbie. I never had so much money in all my life – but this newfound wealth did not excite me one bit. The ten hours of the flight was a fierce melancholy existence. As I looked out the window, into the twilight zone, I felt as if I was travelling to the moon. I sobbed for the duration of the flight, thinking "I'll never see Ireland again."

I was met at Kennedy Airport by Jay Williams, a third year "walk-on" (non-scholarship) runner at Villanova. He had spent a few weeks holidaying in Cork with John Hartnett, and arrived back in the US an hour before I landed. Jay had agreed to wait for me and bring me to his parents' home in New Jersey – where I'd spend my first night on American soil. It was a huge culture shock. I was blown away by the intense heat and humidity, something I had never experienced before. It was like going into a steam room – ninety-two degrees Fahrenheit with seventy percent humidity. Sweat oozed out of me from the terminal to the parked car. I felt like I was in hell.

The following afternoon, Mr. Williams drove Jay and I to Villanova. Arriving at dusk, Jay took me straight over to the track office in the Field House. There I met Jack Pyrah, universally known as Mother Pyrah.

I noticed a gigantic framed photograph of Ronnie Delany on the wall. He was kneeling in prayer after his great win in the Olympics. Jack was assigned to look after me. He was Jumbo's Number One assistant, the man who took care of the runners' needs. I soon learned that Jumbo had very little day-to-day contact with his runners – Jack was the man front-and-centre.

If Jumbo got pissed off at somebody on the team, he'd get pissed off at Jack first. Jumbo would give him hell over any problem with the team. I would soon learn that Jack was a great, great man... and one you could count on to cover your ass.

Mother Pyrah was also a dead-ringer for Bob Hope – the same smile, the same hairstyle, even the same little pot belly – except that Jack was even funnier. His shirt pocket was his office. The pocket was always packed with notes, receipts, and useless pieces of papers. It bulged so much it would tear the stitching out.

Nominally, he was Villanova's Assistant Track and Field Coach and Head Cross-Country Coach. In reality, Jumbo coached the cross-country team too. Jack certainly had the credentials to get a head-coaching job somewhere, but I don't think he'd have enjoyed it. He'd rather be right where he was – working for Jumbo at Villanova. He loved Jumbo, respected him, and would do anything he asked. He might have been Jumbo's "go-fer," but to the lads on the team he was much more.

Jack had the utmost respect of all the athletes, perhaps even more so than Jumbo. Jumbo didn't have time for the weaker runners, but Jack had time for everyone. If you got yourself into trouble, you never went to Jumbo, you went to Mother Pyrah.

That first evening on campus, Jack walked me over to Sheehan Hall. This was the dormitory where Tom Gregan and I would share a room, located in an area called the quad.

The quad was an open courtyard that ran between Sheehan Hall on one side, and Sullivan Hall on the other. It was dark, and still very hot and humid. It was also quite eerie, as there were hardly any students about.

I was shown to my room at No. 251 on the third floor. Once inside, I switched on the light – nothing happened. It looked like the overhead light didn't work. I was so exhausted from the jet-lag that I just fell into the bed – hitting my head off the top bunk in the process. I fell fast asleep for the night. Fourteen hours later I awoke feeling hot, sweaty, groggy and hungry. I hadn't eaten since breakfast the day before.

I would soon learn there were few overhead lights in American homes or dormitories. Instead, the other students used plug-in lamps they brought from home. Of course, I didn't have a lamp. I didn't have anything except the small, shabby suitcase I'd brought from Ireland.

As I unpacked my few belongings, I looked out the window at the students returning from their summer vacations. The boots of their parents' cars were crammed with stuff – lamps, stereos, furniture, books, television sets, and suitcases full of clothing.

I'd gone to bed exhausted and homesick, and now I was awake and wondering what I'd gotten myself into. I missed Ireland. I missed Yvonne. I was in this strange and unwelcoming room where, for all I knew, I would spend the next four years. In the light of day, all I could see were four cinder-block walls and a solitary crucifix above the bunk bed. I might as well have been in jail. Instead of being excited, I was depressed and scared.

There were already a couple of great Irish runners on the team that year. Donal Walsh from Cork had finished second to Steve Prefontaine in the NCAA Cross-Country Championships the previous season. Donie was a senior on the team. He looked like a human version of a garden gnome, so they called him The Troll.

John Hartnett was the big star on the Villanova team. Another Corkman, he was two years ahead of me. He'd already been a junior international cross-country champion, and they called him The Duke.

Back in Ireland that summer, Hartnett and Walsh had filled me with stories about the Villanova athletic dorms being filled with wall-to-wall carpeting and colour televisions. This wasn't what I'd expected at all. All that fanciful bullshit turned out to be part of the initiation process... but only part of it.

They'd also warned me that "Mr. Elliott doesn't tolerate long hair. You better get rid of it before you get to Villanova."

I didn't want to start off on Jumbo's bad side. Just before I left Ireland, I swapped my shoulder-length Beatles like hair for a military style buzz-cut. Not only did I feel like was I living in jail, I had the shaved head to match.

After I got dressed that first morning, I met Jay Woods. He took me over to break-fast in Dougherty Hall cafeteria where I met some of the new recruits. Afterwards, we went to inspect the locker rooms and check out the facilities. Hartnett and Walsh had also told me of the beautiful new tartan track we'd be running on. To my horror and disgust there was no tartan track, just a grubby old grey cinder track. It was full of potholes and no better than what I'd been running on back in Ireland.

To make matters worse, when the team showed up at the track office, all of them had long hair! I couldn't believe it.

Hartnett and Walsh were there, laughing at me.

"Ha-ha!" they cackled, "we got you!"

There was nothing I could do but laugh back and think to myself, "F*** you guys. You got me, you Cork culchies." They'd pulled a good one over the Dub.

I'd never heard of the expression "ball-busting" before. Only later would I learn that the Villanova tradition was, if the guys like you, they bust your balls. If they didn't like you, they just ignored you.

I was issued my Villanova vest, shorts, tracksuit, and sweatshirt – number 123. I had seen pictures of Ronnie Delany, Noel Carroll, and Frank Murphy in the Villanova strip – and now I had my very own. I felt so proud. My dream had come true – I was now a part of the Irish Connection.

I'd soon discover the reality of the situation was totally different to the dream. Old Charlie, the equipment manager, warned us that if we lost the tracksuit, we were responsible for the $50 cost of replacing it.

"Jesus! Fifty dollars!" I thought, "it's not worth fifty bucks! It's an old, used tracksuit."

He was only busting my balls too.

I met Jake Nevin, the diminutive athletic trainer with whom I would spend a good deal of time over the next five years. In both appearance and demeanour, Jake resembled Grumpy – the elderly dwarf from Snow White.

I would come to understand that he was actually a lovable character, and his brusque manner was just his way of showing that he liked you.

Standing at four foot twelve – as he'd always say when asked – he'd flick the hot ash from his foot long Cuban cigar right onto your bare arse, as you stood naked in the locker hall. We'd come in from a ten mile run and he'd be there, smoking away. And he didn't give a hoot.

He was Villanova's head trainer. He taped the ankles of all the football and basketball players as well as attending to the track athletes. Jake was sometimes described as "the field house field mouse." It's fitting that the main athletic facility on campus is now called the Jake Nevin Field House in his honour.

Later that day, I put on my tracksuit and had my picture taken in front of the big Villanova sign, by the campus entrance. I wanted to send it back to Ireland as proof that I'd finally made it – onto the great Jumbo Elliott's Wildcat team.

Almost a week would pass before I got to meet the man himself. I'd just returned from a five mile run with some of the lads, when word spread that Jumbo was "back to work" – upstairs in the track office. He arrived unannounced, his green Cadillac Eldorado parked at the back of the Field House.

There was no formal meeting arranged for the newcomers to be introduced to Jumbo. It was suggested that I stop by the track office on my way to dinner and say "Hello."

I had mixed emotions. I didn't know if it was fear of the man based on what I'd heard, or just the excitement of meeting the legend for the first time.

He was sitting back in his leather chair, feet up on the desk as I nervously walked in. He rose quickly to his feet.

"Jeeesusus Chrriissstt! Ss-ss-s-so cha-cha-champ, welcome to Villanova." he stuttered, shaking my hand warmly. "How was your flight? How's Mom? How's Dad? How's your sisters? How's your brothers?" he asked.

"Fine, thank you," I said.

"Ss-ss-s-so, we start on the track tomorrow. I'll see you there wi-wi-with the boys. Be warmed up and ready to go at three-thirty. Don't be late. Oh, and make sure you study, you son of a bitch!"

I left for dinner not knowing quite what to make of Jumbo Elliott.

Like nearly everyone else, upon first encountering the legendary Villanova coach, I was stunned to find him relatively short in stature.

I'd always assumed that a man named Jumbo would be a giant of a man. I wasn't sure what I expected him to look like. I'd never even seen a photograph of him.

His friends had bestowed the nickname upon him when he was growing up on the playgrounds of West Philadelphia. At the time, the Philadelphia Phillies baseball team employed a journeyman pitcher called Jumbo Jim Elliott.

A left-hander, the original Jumbo stood almost 6'3", weighed 235 pounds, and was quite deserving of the sobriquet.

By 1934, he had been traded away to the Boston Braves, leaving his namesake the only Jumbo Elliott in town.

Born in 1915, Jumbo was raised in an Irish immigrant neighbourhood of Philadelphia. Its official name was Our Lady of Victory Parish. To most people, its residents included, it was known as Shantytown.

Jumbo's father had died when he was quite young. His mother raised him and a younger sister with the assistance of a doting uncle named Louis. It was remarkably similar to my own father's upbringing.

But it was there that the similarities ended. While my Da's uncle Louis Breen had been relatively well-off by Dublin standards, Louis Elliott was not. To help the family make ends meet, Jumbo had to work part-time at a Shantytown grocery store from the time he could walk.

He caddied at local golf clubs and was a scratch golfer when he was still a teenager.

Jumbo attended West Philadelphia Catholic High School for Boys. On the day of the school's first track meet, he was due to report to the store later that afternoon – so he entered the first event of the day – the 100 yard dash.

He won, only to discover it was only a preliminary heat. The final wouldn't be run until later, too late for him to make it to work on time. Instead, he entered the next event – the 440 yard dash.

"I can run that and then get the hell out of here," thought Jumbo. He proceeded to do just that, and won in 56 seconds flat. Later, he recalled "I had to crawl to the bus stop afterward."

For better or for worse, Jumbo had found his niche on the track. He would be a quarter-miler for the rest of his athletic career.

His prowess on the track was good enough to earn him a scholarship to Villanova. It was the one granted specifically for track and field.

In Jumbo's first year at Villanova, he ran a 51-second leg at the Penn Relays. The Villanova Freshman team defeated all comers to win the American Championship. He simultaneously served both as team captain, and coach of the university's golf team. He would go undefeated as a collegiate golfer for four years.

In Jumbo's sophomore year, the track coach was forced to abdicate for health reasons. Jumbo eventually took over as coach of the track team – the Wildcats. Aside from the years he spent in the Navy during World War II, he would hold the job until his death in 1981. Forty-six seasons, in all. He never coached anywhere but Villanova.

After graduating from Villanova, Jumbo continued to run competitively – representing the Shanahan Athletic Club of West Philadelphia. He ran both the 440 and 880 metres, and entertained hopes of qualifying for the 1936 Olympics in Berlin.

The American Olympic hopefuls spent much of that summer barnstorming their way through a series of meets across the country. For much of this period, Jumbo travelled and roomed with the Ohio State sprinter Jesse Owens. Owens would later upset Adolf Hitler's grand design by winning four Gold Medals at the Berlin Games.

Although the two would become lifelong friends, Owens was also indirectly responsible for Jumbo's failure to qualify. At Jesse's suggestion, Jumbo studied the training methods of the great Kansas miler Glenn Cunningham. Glenn won a record six Wanamaker Miles in Madison Square (a feat I would surpass half a century later).

"That's where I went wrong," Jumbo would later tell his biographer, Ted Berry. "Those exercises were okay for Cunningham, but they got me screwed up – for good. I pulled a leg muscle so badly; it was the end of the trials for me."

"I went home with a good lesson," he told Berry. "Every athlete is different. Each one has different training needs. Ever since then, I never expected a runner to work and react like any other runner."

Jumbo continued to coach both track and golf until the United States entered the

War. In 1942, he was commissioned as an Ensign in the Navy. In acknowledgement of his background, he was assigned as an athletic specialist.

In a 1943 dispatch, the Philadelphia Evening Bulletin related that "Lt. (JG) James (Jumbo) Elliott played an exhibition golf match with Jimmy Demaret against Byron Nelson and Jug McSpaden. Elliott scored a 69, McSpaden a 68, and Nelson and Demaret 70 each."

Jumbo continued to play the game at a high level throughout his life. He numbered the country's top pros among his best friends and sometime opponents. The noted course designer Tom Fazio was his son Tommy's godfather.

Jumbo married his wife, Kay, during the War. At its conclusion, he was discharged as a Lieutenant Commander, and he immediately resumed his coaching duties at Villanova.

He took a job as a salesman for Frantz & Company, a firm manufacturing earth-moving equipment. He was so successful that he eventually became a partner, then president. In 1970, he bought the company outright, changing its name to Elliott & Frantz. A self-made multi-millionaire, Jumbo declined to accept a salary for his coaching work at Villanova. Instead, he insisted the university plough the money back into its track programme. Jumbo managed his runners like he did his earth-moving company: Businesslike. No bullshit. Tough, hard, fair and honest.

There were no shortcuts to success, as far as he was concerned. "You just do the work and the success will come," he'd always say.

He took great care not to drink around his athletes, but it wasn't exactly a secret that Jumbo was fond of the gargle.

To say that my experience was a culture shock would be an understatement. Everything about Villanova was different. A lot of people in Ireland believed that when an athlete took up a scholarship to Villanova, all they had to do was run – that their grades would be handed to them, as long as they ran well. That was far from the truth. Villanova placed as much emphasis on the academic aspects of college life (if not more).

Back in Ireland, I'd managed to get by on natural talent. Even when I thought I was training hard, I wasn't really. Not compared to these boys. I was used to running thirty-five miles a week. At Villanova, it wasn't unusual to run one hundred miles a week. I quickly developed a terrible case of shin splints from the increased mileage.

The sessions on the track were far and beyond anything I had ever done. On my first official track workout, Jumbo had us to do twenty quarter-miles in sixty-eight seconds, each in a row. Seventy seconds rest over 220 yards jog in between. The most I had ever done in my life was ten. It was excruciatingly difficult, but I did it. The next morning, I was so sore I had to crawl backwards down the stairs of my dormitory. I couldn't run for days afterwards. Meanwhile, the older, more experienced guys would be out getting the five miles run in. They'd follow it with a ten or twelve in the afternoon. It was demoralising for me, mixing with these guys.

School was no easier. While I had my fair share of academic problems in secondary school, college proved to be just as tough. In secondary, it was more regimented – you would be missed if you failed to show up. Here, you could almost come and go as you pleased – as long as you completed the work. I had exciting new subjects: Economics, Sociology, Philosophy, and English. But I also had to do the dreaded Maths, and then there was Statistics – a new horror.

The professors would give their lectures, and it was up to the student to take notes. Being new to this approach, I found it hard to get the information down quick enough. All these new pressures made me feel terribly homesick. I began to wonder how on earth I would stay here for four more years, living in a room with bare walls, a crucifix and a borrowed stereo.

Tom Gregan came over a few weeks later. At least now I had some company in the dorm room. He had missed several weeks of classes, but Jumbo pulled a few strings and got him enrolled in night school. This meant Tom couldn't compete for Villanova, so he red-shirted that first semester. As it turned out, so did I, but for very different reasons: I was injured, and my grades weren't good enough.

After Gregan moved in, we decorated our room at Sheehan Hall in the basic style of the Homesick Irish Teenager. I had two calendars by my bed, both showing the days left before I went home for Christmas. I marked off one calendar each morning, and the other at night.

I spelled out Yvonne's name in black masking tape on my headboard. Tom had done the same, writing the name of his girlfriend, Lorraine. At night, the two of us would lie there with the lights out, talking about home and how much we missed our girls. I wrote a letter to Yvonne every day, and I'd be upset if I didn't get one back at the same rate.

I was so homesick those first few weeks that Christmas seemed an eternity away. I decided I wasn't staying any longer. I remembered the return flight on my ticket left New York on September 17. One night, I made the mistake of mentioning it to Ernie DeChellis, a 110 metre hurdler who lived down the hall. He was a crazy guy with a snake for a pet. We'd watch him feed the snake with a live mouse for entertainment.

When I told Ernie about the ticket back to Ireland, he acted as if he didn't believe me.

"September 17?" he asked, "that's impossible! Let me see the ticket."

So I went back to my room, got the ticket and brought it back to show my new buddy, Ernie. He looked it over and nodded thoughtfully.

"Yep, it says September 17, all right. How can you let this go to waste?" He grabbed the ticket and tore it up. "I guess you're not quitting school now," he said, tossing the pieces of paper out the window.

Despite the homesickness, the academic trials and the insane team mates, there was something special about being a track athlete at Villanova. At other American universities, the focus was on the football and basketball teams, with track and field regarded as a junior partner. At Villanova, the success of Jumbo's teams meant we held a lot more respect in the eyes of the student body.

Jumbo had coached more Olympic Champions than any other American. He was the Bear Bryant of Track and Field. In 1971, he had a stable of runners from which any number could qualify for the following year's Munich Olympics. At that point in my college career, the likelihood of me making the Games was less than slim. I'd have to work a lot harder to fulfil Gerry Farnan's expectations of me.

The football and basketball teams had their own training tables, and they took their meals away from the main student body. The track team ate with the rest of the students in Dougherty Hall. When you came down the ramp, into the cafeteria, there were two tables in the middle of the room. It was understood by all that was where the track guys ate. If somebody happened to be sitting at one of our tables when we arrived, they knew to move immediately. The area was unofficially reserved for the track guys.

The training tables were where we really got to know one another. Ball-busting was part and parcel of the team's make-up. Thursday nights we'd be in the Cat's Eye, Friday nights would be Kelly's Bar and Saturday nights would invariably be a student party. All of the these would be planned at the training tables.

Most days, after meals, the team would "chain-hang" outside Dougherty Hall. We'd sit on the chain fencing shooting the breeze, checking out the beautiful girls, and generally fooling around. On one of my first days chain-hanging, I had a run-in with team mate Kenny Schappert.

Schap was a great runner, and nationally ranked coming out of high school. Whatever I did, he didn't like it. He came chasing after me, looking to land some punches... but he couldn't catch me. I got away – back to the safe haven of my dorm room. Schap was an intimidating, loud-mouthed character. You'd hear him before you saw him. He was tough and street-smart: He'd grown up one of the only white kids in his Bronx neighbourhood, next to Yankee Stadium. He spoke in the vernacular of the ghetto, and if you closed your eyes, you'd have thought you were listening to a black guy.

The next day, Hartnett and other guys warned me "You'd better watch out for Schap. He's going to beat the crap out of you when he sees you."

I was afraid for my life, but I knew I had no choice – I'd have to meet him at three o'clock practice later that day. I was told "I better be prepared."

I was walking down the long corridor in the Field House when he jumped out of a locker and confronted me.

"You little Irishman! I got you now." I happened to be carrying a pair of scissors. I pointed them at him.

"What do you f***** mean!" I said, putting him on the back foot.

"Whoa, Bro, hang on a minute! Easy does it. I didn't mean it. I was only kidding!" he said, backing up further. "I was only taking the piss! Just to see how tough an Irish guy you really are. It's okay, cool down man!"

We became pals after that. For years since, Schap has been one of my great supporters – both on and off the track. We still keep in touch to this very day.

By now, I'd been accepted as one of the boys in the track team's fraternity. We had a great team to choose from: Hartnett, Walsh, Schap, Brian McElroy, Davy Wright and Gerry Bouma to name a few. But due to injuries, I could not compete on the Junior Varsity team.

This meant I had no distraction from the homesickness, and with school getting harder, I was soon depressed. If I could have run, I would have been happier – but without running I was a different person. I'd stay in my room all day, cut classes and smoke a few cigarettes. I couldn't deal with the pressure.

I was, once again, heading on a downward spiral.

By now, Gregan's love for Lorraine had dissipated and he was going out on dates. He'd have two girlfriends at any one time, and he always picked girls who were rich and drove expensive cars. There were times he'd have two cars for his personal use and we'd race them around the same running loops we trained on.

The odd venture off-campus would ease my homesickness some, but while my body was in Pennsylvania, my mind was back in Ireland.

One such venture was Marty Liquori's wedding. He married his high school sweetheart Carol, and it was great to get the invitation. Marty was ranked number one in the world in the mile, and a real American hero. He beat Jim Ryun in the Philadelphia Dream Mile years earlier and was a household name in the States. I was embarrassed that I couldn't afford to buy them a wedding present.

Money was in short supply. I'd go to the laundry room to wash my clothes and not put in detergent – so I could save the few quarters for something more important.

With the help of Jimmy Cipriano, I did manage to scrounge together a few furnishings for my dorm room.

Jimmy was a smooth character with a real Italian Mafioso look about him. He had a wardrobe filled with dozens of shirts, and about fifty pairs of shoes. He dressed for classes like he was going off to a ball. He and I connected almost immediately. I'm sure he felt sorry for me, since it was obvious that I had next to no money. He helped organise a stereo system for my room, along with other little touches that made it more liveable – and less like a prison cell.

I was a stranger in a strange land. I didn't even leave the Villanova campus on an overnight visit until late November. That was when Jimmy invited me to spend Thanksgiving weekend at his parents' home in Hazleton, upstate Pennsylvania.

It was a nice, relaxing weekend and my first real exposure to American life. We had a wonderful feast with Jimmy's parents. I hung out with him and his girlfriend Pam for the next few days. Jimmy's Dad ran a gas-station. In my first experience of an American snowstorm, I went down to the station to join Jimmy as he put in a few hours. I had no warm clothes, and my hands almost stuck to the petrol pumps when I went out to fill up a car.

Jimmy decided we should go shopping one afternoon. He spent $65 on an outlandish pair of those platform shoes that were in vogue. So what did I do? I bought myself a pair of platform shoes too.

They were navy blue and bright yellow, and they cost $39.95. I'd never spent that much on a pair of shoes in my life. To make matters worse, I'd only brought $40 to last me the whole weekend. I had a nickel in my pocket for the rest of the trip. Once Jimmy figured out I was broke, he started paying for everything.

"Look, you're my guest," he told me. Being homesick and penniless made me feel even more out of place than I already did.

That winter of 1971-72 was the unhappiest time of my young life there in Villanova. After spending my first Christmas at home, I didn't want to go back. But, I had no choice. My first semester's examination results were poor. I failed Maths and barely passed the other subjects.

Nothing seemed to have gone right. Technically, I wasn't in danger of flunking out, but my grade-point average was 1.2. According to NCAA rules, a student-athlete was supposed to maintain a 1.5 to retain his eligibility. Jumbo's standard was even higher – he insisted his athletes maintain a 2.0 Grade Point Average.

There was one uplifting moment which, in retrospect, gave me a glimpse into the future.

As a boy, I'd once seen a photograph in the newspapers of Noel Carroll anchoring Ireland's 4 x 880 yard relay team in Madison Square Garden. Noel had out-leaned his opponent at the tape, and the Irish team (which also included Ronnie Delany, Derek McClean and Basil Clifford) had set a new Irish record. That was the first time I was aware there was such a thing as indoor running. Until I went to the States, I'd never seen an indoor race – not even on television. It was only now I began to learn about how great Ronnie Delany was on the boards. He broke the world record for the mile twice, and he went undefeated in that distance forty-two times during his career.

At Villanova, I knew we competed indoors in the winter... but I'd been in school for several months before I realised that I'd never seen the indoor track.

As it turned out there was a good reason for that: There wasn't one. We had a banked, wooden indoor track, all right. It just wasn't indoors. It was stored beneath the stands at the stadium each fall – until the football season was over. Then it would be erected right on top of the practice football field. Only a couple of days were required to assemble the track, and it would stay up throughout the winter. There were often days when we'd have to chip away the ice and sweep off the snow before we could actually train on it.

One day that first year, I was returning to campus. As I passed the football field, there it was. As if by magic, the boards had gone up overnight.

It seemed almost incongruous, an apparition. If they'd installed a fully equipped, hardwood basketball court right there in the middle of the field, it would have appeared no more out of place.

It was noon and not a soul was about. I walked across the field to the track. There, in my street clothes, I started to jog around the banked oval. As I broke into a trot, it occurred to me that the all the great Villanova Olympic Champions had trained on this very surface.

It was my first time on a board track – and this was far from the greatest board track in the world. At 160 yards (or eleven laps to the mile) the banks were relatively shallow. The turns were very tight and the straightaways short. There were loose boards where you might trip or step right through them. Still, I was thrilled by the way it felt beneath my feet. By the way the springy pine boards responded to my steps.

There was a fantastic feeling of speed and exhilaration as I ran through the turns and off the banks. I knew there and then that the boards were for me.

As it turned out, more than a year would pass before I got to train on the boards, or run a competitive race indoors... but I remember walking off the track that day with one thought in my mind "I think I'm going to love this."

I continued to struggle with injuries. Unbeknownst to my team mates, I received an invitation to fly back to Ireland to join the National team for the Junior International Cross-Country Championships. They were being held that March in Cambridge, England. I was so eager for the chance to get home that I didn't bother to inform the BLÉ officials of the maladies that had curtailed my training throughout the winter.

I'd been telling them I was fit enough to compete, even though I wasn't. When it came time to go, I sneaked away from Villanova like a thief in the night. I went back to Ireland first to meet the team and then travelled to England for the race. I was in terrible condition, and I didn't run well at all.

The day after the cross-country championships, the BLÉ had arranged a friendly competition against a team from the London Irish Club. I was already well beaten and out of the running, when I came across my old friend Dessie O'Connor. Dessie, a Rod Stewart look-alike and impersonator, wasn't participating in the second-day competition; he was only jogging on the course.

On a lark, I gave him my race number, and he went on to finish the race in my stead. When Brendan Foreman, the BLÉ treasurer, heard what had happened, he was not amused.

What we did was wrong, no doubt about it. It was a stupid, childish thing to do... but it wasn't exactly cheating. I was so far back in the field that my place wouldn't even count in the score. Nonetheless, I had to write a letter of apology to avoid being suspended.

I went back to collect my gear, only to find someone had stolen the Villanova sweatshirt from out of my bag.

After my miserable cross-country performances in Cambridge, I announced to everyone's shock that "I'm not going back to America."

Yes, I'd been homesick – especially for Yvonne. But beyond that, I couldn't deal with school, I couldn't deal with the pressure of being away... and I was running poorly.

Once they realised I meant it, that I had no intention of returning to Villanova, my father was crushed. As was Gerry Farnan. Needless to say, Jumbo was furious. He'd put his faith in me, and I'd repaid it by sneaking off without a word.

Even Yvonne was devastated. She didn't want to be blamed for my having quit college. I applied for a job with PMPA, and I got it. I was an underwriter for new business. Basically, it was an entry-level position. I checked the new application forms, and if something was amiss, I would pass them on to someone further up the chain.

All my life I'd wanted to own a motorbike. In my newly liberated state, I purchased a used Yamaha 50 for £60, borrowing the money from a company society. I'd pick up Yvonne and we'd head off about town. On weekends, we'd jump on the bike and drive off into the country.

My parents were so pissed off with me at this point that they decided to ratchet up the pressure. They told me they didn't want Yvonne riding on the motorbike because it was too dangerous. I basically told them to get lost. That it was none of their business. I was 19 years-of-age and could do what I pleased.

My mother eventually contacted the Murphys and told them that "Under no circumstances should Yvonne be allowed to ride on the back of Eamonn's motorbike," and that she and my father "won't be held responsible for anything that happens to her."

It wasn't that they disliked Yvonne, or blamed her for any of this. On the contrary, they loved her. But they realised that, since I appeared determined to ruin my life, my relationship with her might be the only leverage they had.

Of course, I felt this was just their way of punishing me.

As it turned out, they had an ulterior motive. What I hadn't realised, was that Jumbo had been in contact with my father throughout the summer.

Jumbo's lifelong policy had been, that if a kid quit on Villanova, that was it. He'd never take them back. But for whatever reason, in my case he was ready to reconsider. He was willing to make an exception for me because of the circumstances. Moreover, he'd managed to cut through the red tape and make a special arrangement.

Since I hadn't competed at all that first year, by NCAA regulations it would count as a red-shirt year. That left me four years of eligibility. And because I hadn't completed any of my classes, Jumbo arranged for the entire year to be wiped off the books. I could start from scratch as an incoming freshman.

I was still hesitant. All the reasons I'd left school in the first place still seemed to be in place. My father sat me down for a talk.

"Look, Eamonn," he pleaded "I don't have much money, but if you'll go back to Villanova, I promise that I'll buy you a ticket to come home every Christmas, and every summer, for as long as you're there."

Gerry Farnan also sat down with me and explained "Eamonn, in life you'll come to many crossroads. This is one of those crossroads right now. You can either go left, or you can go right. You can take a left turn, and work in the PMPA making your few quid. And for six months you'll even think you're happy. But trust me, you'll eventually come to regret it. For the rest of your life – because nobody gets a second chance from Jumbo Elliott the way you're getting one now."

"Or," he continued, "you can make a right turn. If you do, you'll probably hate it for the next six months, or even a year. But if you do go back, I want you to focus on two things. The first is that running is the one thing you're really good at. Both Jumbo and I believe you'll be a world champion one day."

"You are still a young, raw talent. You're nineteen-years-old and now is the time to get going. It will be tough, but you will not regret it ever. The other is school. For the sake of these four years, focus on that too. Don't worry about Ireland, don't worry about me. Let Jumbo coach you, and four years from now you'll be in Montreal, running for Ireland in the 1976 Olympic Games. And another thing... stop smoking!" he gently whispered, knowing not to upset me any further.

"Shit! He knew!" I was too embarrassed to answer back.

The killer-blow came from Yvonne.

"If you stay here, I won't go out with you any more," she told me. "You've got to go back to Villanova. I don't want to spend the rest of my life being blamed for your quitting college. And I don't want to be blamed for the rest of my life for you quitting running. If you go back, I promise I'll wait for you and we'll see how things work out. But if you stay here, we're finished."

It took a minute for that to sink in. I definitely had no choice.

"Jesus," I said, "I guess I'm going back to Villanova."

CHAIRMAN O

MASTER OF T

Called to our marks, I remember thinking to myself "This is the biggest thing you're ever going to do in your whole life." I was aware that millions were tuned in on television and 70,000 people in the stadium were watching with incredible anticipation for this, the blue ribbon event of the Olympic Games.

I felt like a little boy amongst men. When the gun went off, I hesitated momentarily to let the others go so I could identify Walker's position and follow my plan. Dave Moorcroft took the lead, while I settled in third or fourth from last, with Walker right in front of me. Perfect, I had him in sight.

Part

THE BOARD

HE MILE

Return to Villanova

When I returned to Villanova, I knew what to expect. I wasn't going back to wall-to-wall carpeting and colour television in the dorm room, and I knew I'd be running on an old beat-up cinder track. But one thing for sure was that I knew, I was going back to become a real athlete.

I went back with a completely different and more mature attitude. I kept reminding myself that I'd been given a second chance and that I couldn't screw it up. By now I also knew most of the lads and there was a sense of respect shown that I was man enough to return. They believed I had talent, and they knew it would have been wasted if I hadn't come back. There was a feeling of acceptance all around. It was like "Great! Eamonn is back."

This was a critical period in my metamorphosis from suspect to prospect.

Jumbo clearly recognised my hidden talent and potential long before it really came out in a consistent manner. Without the confidence Jumbo displayed in me, I'm certain that I'd have ended up back in Dublin without completing my degree and would have become a mere footnote in the Villanova track annals – another kid who couldn't make the cut.

Success is a fine line comprising talent, hard work, circumstances, and key individuals who provide confidence and support at the right time. I had the good fortune to have these factors fall on the right side at the right time – and I wanted to make sure that I'd make the most of it.

My new room-mate was Frank Murphy Jr. who was called "Junior" to distinguish him from the Irish international who'd helped recruit me to Villanova, but the two weren't related. They were only about half-a-dozen years apart in age, but both lived in Drumcondra and had attended the same Dublin school – O'Connell's CBS.

Any residual homesickness I might have felt upon returning to college was also alleviated by the presence of another lad from my Dublin neighbourhood, Chalkie White, who had grown up on Benbulben Road in Drimnagh, although I had never met him up until that time.

I had known him by reputation for years. Chalkie had literally burst onto the Irish sports scene at the age of nine, when he beat a field consisting of mostly adults, to win the annual Liffey Swim.

When Chalkie won the Liffey Swim as a nine-year-old, it was considered truly amazing and received widespread media coverage. It would have been an even bigger deal in my own family, since my first cousin, Kevin King Jr., had won it several years earlier, and, at least until I came along, Kevin's success was renowned as the foremost sporting achievement in our family's history.

When Chalkie was recruited to Villanova, he became the first Irish swimmer ever to have been offered a scholarship to any American university.

We immediately hit it off becoming great pals and soul-mates. Night after night, we'd visit each other to talk and share our training experiences. His presence helped me the most to settle down at Villanova, and our relationship turned out to be one of those friendships that would last a lifetime. Chalkie's goal, like mine, was to represent Ireland in the Olympic Games in Montreal.

When Yvonne and I married years later, Chalkie was my best man, and when he married Val, I was his best man. Chalkie is my daughter Suzanne's godfather, and when his son Niall was born, I became his godfather.

While it was easier to settle down the second time around, I still found school tough to handle. But this time I had extra help. Jumbo made provision for special tuition when needed, and I could call on team-mate Gerry Bouma, a Canadian track scholarship runner on the team. Gerry was the Einstein of the team and amazed all of us with his depth of knowledge. While most subjects were manageable – Maths was still incomprehensible. I would go on to fail this subject three times before passing.

Jumbo always emphasised routine, routine, routine: "Live like a clock, get up at the same time, eat at the same time, train at the same time, study at the same time and God dammit, shit at the same time every day," he would remind us often.

And this was exactly how life unfolded for me over the next four years. Up at 7:30am. Run, breakfast, classes, lunch, class, run, dinner and study.

Right from the beginning, rather than trying to do the eighty, ninety, and one hundred miles a week that the lads might have done, I just gradually built my training mileage from thirty, to forty, to sixty and eventually seventy per week over the following months. It meant I didn't get injured, while at the same time propelling me up the team ladder.

The NCAA had amended its regulations that year to make freshmen eligible for varsity competitions, so I was in contention to make the cross-country team. Donie Walsh had graduated the year before and had returned to live in Ireland, but Hartnett was still there as the Number One runner. He was known as Duke and was the guy we all looked up to. His commitment to training was par excellence and while he was a quiet, low-key personality, he was usually the one who'd instigate the "misadventures."

I never made it to the Munich Olympics. Maybe it was just as well. The killing of eleven Israeli athletes and coaches by Black September and the subsequent killing of five of the eight terrorists, cast a pall over the 1972 Games. I remember watching the macabre events unfolding on television and feeling totally repulsed.

Hartnett and Walsh ran for Ireland, but Marty Liquori sadly missed out through injury. American television coverage was terrible with races interrupted with commercials. Still I got caught up in the excitement of Lasse Viren winning his double gold medals in the 5,000 and 10,000 metres, Valerie Borzov beating the Americans in the 100 dash, and Frank Shorter winning the marathon after an imposter ran into the stadium before him.

Looking at the games on television fuelled my ambition, and I knew in my heart and soul that I wanted to graduate from Villanova in four years' time and go to the Montreal Games.

Villanova had a great team, made up from the likes of Hartnett, returning from Munich, Bouma, Gregan, Schap and another new freshman Kevin McCarey, from Woodside, Queens. His parents were both from Ireland, and whenever he was around the Irish guys, he'd start talking in an accent even more pronounced than ours.

Kevin was a tough, hard worker. And we had smoothy Brian McElroy, who'd transferred from Kansas where he'd trained with Jim Ryun, to run for Villanova. There were several other pretty talented walk-on runners, Charlie McCarthy and Steve Dorsey being two, and I had my work cut out just to make the top five.

With the Vietnam War at its zenith, many of the guys spent their time worrying about whether they might get called up to serve. As it turned out none of them were, but the prospect hung over them like a pall during their time at Villanova.

Hartnett, Bouma and I became almost an inseparable trio that semester. My confidence grew as I managed to stick with the boys while out on five, ten and fifteen mile runs or when doing the twenty, quarter-mile repeats on the track. I began to realise that if I was patient, I could soon match their talent.

Camaraderie within the team was something Jumbo instilled in all of us. We ate together, ran together, studied together and partied together. We looked out for one another all the time and if you slackened off, it wasn't Jumbo who'd come running after you – it was your team-mates.

I began to monitor the behaviour of the guys off the track: I began to think like them, believe like them, knowing in time that I'd be able to beat them.

By the time the cross-country season finished, I was a regular on the team and, while not setting the world on fire, was learning all the time

I got my first taste of indoor competition ever on the boards, two days after I returned from spending Christmas at home in Ireland. Jumbo entered me in the Freshman Mile in Philadelphia's Convention Centre. The boards were similar to the antiquated ones we used in Villanova.   To everyone's surprise, including my own, I won in 4:18.

Though the time was slow, it was the start of an undefeated, four-year college career I would enjoy over the one-mile distance.

Jumbo never liked to push his talented guys too soon, but there was also the fact that we had a lot of good runners who were upperclassmen. Jumbo wanted to bring down my race distance. I came to Villanova regarded more as a long distance runner, but he wanted to get my times down over the 800 metres and the mile. So for the most part, I ran as a member of Villanova's 4 x 880-yard relay team in my first two years where I could hide and improve without anyone bothering me too much. The relay team was the best in the country and I gained a vast amount of experience travelling to and racing in places like Madison Square Gardens, Philadelphia Spectrum and Cobo Hall in Detroit.

Training on the 160 yards' lap boards was always an adventure. On bitter cold days, we'd sometimes have to scrape the snow and ice off the track before we could do the workout. We'd wrap up in heavy layers of clothing with our eyes being the only part of us exposed to the elements. We ran unconventional workouts. One lappers 160 yards, two lappers 320 yards, three lappers 480 yards where our times would not easily equate. We'd run them like clockwork, twenty, twenty, twenty seconds per lap and by the time we got to race in bigger arenas we knew what was required.

It would be so cold in the winters that the sweat would freeze on our clothing and around our eyes and ears. It was brutally tough. Jumbo would set himself up in a small wooden protective hut by the finish line and call out splits, "twenty, forty, sixty," as we'd file by. He'd roar us to, "relax, relax, relax," non-stop.

I once got pissed off with him when I passed him by because I was hurting so badly. I stopped and asked "How the hell can I relax when I am breaking my balls here and you are standing in there nice and warm out of this freezing gale."

"Le le le listen champ, I want y y you to th th think r r relax, relax, and believe me you will feel better and you will feel more relaxed," he stuttered out.

From that day on "relax, relax" became my running mantra. I understood exactly what he wanted me to do mentally.

I was consumed by the boards from that very first season and wished it could have lasted longer. But I'd have to wait another year.

During the off-season, I had too much time to think and the thoughts of Yvonne back home wondering what she might be doing made me feel lonely. But I discovered a cure.

There were no mobile phones and certainly no e-mails in those days and the cost of a call to Ireland was out of the question. NCAA rules did not allow the athletes make free calls home from the track office. It was considered a perk.

Quite by accident, I found a coin box under a stairwell in Tollentine Hall, which, if you hung it up just right, would return whatever coins you'd put into it. I'd go over there with a $10 roll of quarters, talk for as long as it would allow, and most days the money would come tumbling back out when I was finished, if I hung the phone up in a certain way.

I didn't want to screw up a good thing, so I never told any of the other lads about it. I got a couple of years out of the magic telephone, but eventually I messed it up. Nine times out of ten the coins came back, but when they didn't I would be out ten bucks. I knew that an Irish 5p coin was the same size as a quarter and would work. I brought a bunch of them over from Ireland. But when those 5p coins began turning up, Philadelphia Bell sent somebody around to fix it, and the magic disappeared.

After the indoor season, Frank Murphy Jr. decided to quit school. Frank announced that he didn't like Villanova and was going to visit friends in Canada. From there he proposed to enter Clonliffe College seminary back in Ireland. He had earned himself something of a reputation as a ladies' man during his brief time at Villanova, and of all the guys on the team, he seemed the least likely to become a priest.

He broke the hearts of half the girls in Dublin too, including that of Yvonne's sister Patricia when he enrolled in the seminary. Before the year was out, he decided that he wasn't cut out to be a priest after all.

His departure didn't help and I had to keep reminding myself of the crossroads that Gerry talked about and mentally switched to looking forward to the outdoor season, the Penn Relays as well as my final first year examinations.

All our training took place on the battered old cinder track. The new tartan track was not laid in Villanova until well after I graduated. It turned out that Jumbo wasn't in a hurry to get the modern synthetic rubber surface installed. He preferred us to train on the cinders. He believed that if we could roll off fast 200 and 400 metres on a crap surface, that we'd really fly when we got to race on the rubber. Besides, he believed we'd be more susceptible to injury training on rubber.

Jumbo toughened me up on the track that first outdoor season.

"You'll do, quarters, quarters, quarters, 'til they come out of your ass," he'd say, when anyone would question theory.

Every workout we'd either do twenty of them at a modest pace or ten at a much faster clip with less than a minute to recover between each. And, it was almost every day. He taught us to run with rhythm, style and grace.

"Run like you're ten feet tall, keep the head up and relax those Goddam shoulders," he'd continually roar.

We'd hit each one within a tenth of a second of each other. Running in Indian file, ten or twelve of us would hammer around the track, pulling and encouraging one another until we'd almost drop with fatigue.

He raced me a lot – more than I'd ever done in my life. Week after week, I'd run on relay teams as well as double in one and three mile races. We were always on the go. Jumbo made us feel like champions, Jumbo made us act like champions. He insisted that we wear jacket, shirt and tie and that we had respectable hair-cuts when we travelled to meets. He was just as much interested in being "The maker of milers as well as the maker of men."

On a number of occasions, I'd tell him I had no money for a hair-cut and he'd throw me a $10 bill and say "Get the Goddam thing cut." I'd then have one of the lads in the dorm do it for nothing and delighted to be a few dollars richer.

The Penn Relays somewhat grandiosely called its marquee relay races The Championships of America, and while that claim might not have carried a lot of weight outside the state of Pennsylvania, Jumbo always placed a premium on those championship titles.

His teams had won more titles in the history of the meet. Tens of thousands of spectators would pack Franklin Field every year to watch and cheer on the best talent in high school and college athletics in America. It was like the relays were more important to Jumbo than the Olympics. He seemed to specialise here and he got more physically nervous at this meet than any other. The Villanova track teams were regarded as invincible. And if an athlete made one of Jumbo's teams, he had to be good.

Just before a big race Jumbo would pull a bunch of hundred dollar bills out of his pocket and wave the money around in the other coaches' faces, saying "Come on, a thousand dollars, my boys against the f-f-field!" He knew well the other coaches couldn't afford the money to take up his bets.

While our team would invariably screw up at other relay events in Tennessee, Quantico or Iona, we always got it right for Penn.

I got my first taste of Penn that year as a freshman when Jumbo selected me to lead off the 4 x 1 mile team which included McElroy, Schappert and the almighty

Hartnett. I passed over the baton in first place running my lead-off leg in 4:09 and we went on to win.

It was my first Championship of America and I would go on to win nine titles during my college career and be voted Outstanding Athlete of the Championships on two occasions. This was my first taste of big time athletics in front of sixty thousand fanatical fans. I was now considered one of Jumbo's big boys. I finished up my year passing my exams and left for Ireland for the summer holidays a new runner and a new man. I couldn't wait to get back for more. I had taken the right turn.

That summer I took up my summer job in the PMPA and ran a few races for Metro. I won the George V Ryan Invitational 800 and 1500 metre titles as well as my first Dublin Senior Championship 800 and 1500 metre double. That season was curtailed by tiredness and injury. I severely pulled a muscle in my quadriceps which bulged up like a golf ball and I found it difficult to walk, let alone run.

From the time I was 13 years of age until I went to college, Barney Crosbie was my physiotherapist. Barney was a former Army private and had a massage therapy practice located in his converted garage in Walkinstown. Barney was strictly an old-school sort and he had hundreds of patients queuing for his services. For his rub-downs, he used a special recipe which blended poitín and olive oil. He also used to advise me to take a hot bath with a quart of malt vinegar thrown in "And by Jesus, it will make you run forever." I never liked doing it too much because it didn't do much for Yvonne.

But try as he might, he couldn't fix my muscle.

Yvonne had just completed her Leaving Certificate, so we headed to New Jersey for the remainder of the summer. My father was not too pleased to see me head back to America so soon. He thought he'd get to have me around a little longer, especially after paying the airfare to get me home. But, by now, America was in my blood and the prospect of a hot summer and having fun with Yvonne away from the scrutiny of my parents, was more appealing.

We stayed with her aunt Mae and her uncle, Charlie Connon, in Hackensack, New Jersey. The Connons had emigrated to New York years earlier, but then moved to Canada. When their two older children grew up they returned to the New York area with the two younger ones. They effectively became our godparents for that summer and for many years to come.

I got a job working at a nearby lamp factory. It was boring, assembly-line work, and I hated doing the same thing, day after day, but it was a job. Yvonne found summer work as a checkout girl at a local Woolworths, and between us we had real money to spend for our first summer holiday away together.

Charlie and Mae's son Sean came down from Canada with one of his friends, so the four of us decided to go camping to Seaside Heights on the Jersey Shore over the weekend. We had a fantastic time, camping by the beach, playing guitars, singing and just unwinding.

That Sunday afternoon, the other two lads and I were knee-deep in the surf, playing ball. Yvonne isn't a swimmer, but she walked out to join us. Suddenly a huge wave broke right over her head. When we looked around she was gone.

By the time we spotted her, she was several yards away and being pulled out to sea – disappearing from sight under the waves. We scrambled and managed to pull her out – barely conscious – and I had to do mouth-to-mouth resuscitation to revive her. The episode scared the life out of us and we immediately headed back to Hackensack.

The following morning she was very sick, her body completely destroyed by sunburn. There were blisters all over her face, her body, her arms and legs. I phoned Woolworths to explain that she wouldn't be coming in to work, but forgot to phone the lamp factory to say I wouldn't be in.

The following morning I walked in the door and they said "Hey, Coghlan, you're fired!" No opportunity to explain, nothing. "We don't take excuses, you are fired," the young supervisor said, pointing his finger to the door.

Yvonne recovered and returned to Ireland, and I headed back to Villanova for my sophomore year. Thankfully my injury had mended and I was able to get straight back into action.

Since Frank Junior's departure, I once again found myself in search of a room-mate, so I moved to Sullivan Hall in the Quad and shared a room with Jack Nash.

Jack had kind of a squeaky voice and was from Friday's Harbour in Washington State. While he was a walk-on with the track team, he was at Villanova on a Naval ROTC scholarship and sometimes had to wear his uniform to class. He and Russ Ebbets, another walk-on, started calling me "Steamin' Eeemin," and other times it would be "Flamin Aimin," because of the new found speed I had gathered. I had the kick, which Gerry trained me to do, but now my times were coming down over the 800 metres and mile.

Sullivan Hall was a zoo, like something out of the movie Animal House. There was always music blaring away, morning, noon and late at night. It was no dorm for an athlete. But there were athletes. Not just runners, but swimmers and football players too. You'd pass by certain rooms and the smell of marijuana would blow you away. I was a bit naïve at first and didn't know what the smell was and besides, I was so straight I never even had taken a beer and I was now twenty-one. But that would soon change.

After a decent cross country season when I'd won a couple of local duel meets on Fairmount Park's tough hilly course, I was invited up to Newport, Rhode Island, by Phil "Tiny" Kane to spend Thanksgiving with his family. Tiny was the newest scholarship freshman on the team.

Schap was invited along too and we agreed to make two stop-overs on the way to Rhode Island. The first was in Schap's parents' apartment in the Bronx and the second would be in Schap's brother's house in Upstate New York.

I had my first beer in the Bronx. Between us we drank a case of Budweiser. I was sick as a dog when I eventually crawled into bed. The weekend trip to Tiny's house ended in a bit of a whirlwind and one I said I'd never do again.

I was so sick from alcohol, it was a week before I recovered and was able to train properly.

Moving up a gear

I got my first opportunity in February 1974 to run in the CYO meet in Cleveland Ohio. With my level of training now up with the best lads on the team, Jumbo believed I was now ready to be tested against the big boys. He entered me in an open mile, in a field that included Dave Wottle, the defending 800 metre Olympic champion. Wottle was more or less on his own home turf, so the rest of us were rightly considered also-rans going into the race.

Before I departed, an injured Brian McElroy jokingly asked "So, Eamonn, how do you like your chances against Wottle?"

I smiled back and said nothing, because in my own mind I was going out there to beat Wottle – and I still think I did on that night.

The race came right down to the wire, and Wottle won in a disputed photo-finish – we were both timed at 4:03.9 – my best ever mile. To the judges, it appeared that he'd out-leaned me at the wire with the peak of the famous blue baseball cap he always wore, but I swore that I'd gotten to the line ahead of him.

He got the win, but the newspapers the next day showed that my torso was definitely ahead of his crossing the finish line. It didn't matter then, I was satisfied. And by the time I got back to Villanova, I found that I commanded a new respect.

"Jesus Christ," the boys were saying, "Eamonn's after running Dave Wottle to the wire!" Now they were ribbing me, asking "Aren't you ever going to break four minutes?"

My response was always the same as what Gerry and Jumbo preached "My times will come with the wins."

Apart from that race against Wottle, I'd mostly been used on relay teams, but when the IC4A Indoor Championships in Princeton rolled around, I got another big break. Ken Schappert was injured and unable to run, so I was entered in his place in the 880 yard run. The favourites were a couple of half-milers, Cliff Bruce of Manhattan College and Reggie Clark of William & Mary who were faster and more experienced than me.

I came out of nowhere and blew them all away to win in my fastest time 1:51.7. Thirty minutes later, I ran 1:53 on a relay leg. I was ecstatic with the wins and the confirmation that with a combination of correct training and my natural talent, I could become a real champion.

"I knew you were a tough son-of-a-bitch, that's why I ran you," Jumbo said as we left the arena.

My sophomore outdoor season was another stepping stone and I climbed closer to the magical four minute barrier running a best time of 4:00.9. Jumbo got me to race in anything from 880 yard races to 3 miles. I won a fair few of my outings including the IC4A 3 miles in record time.

Another year over at Villanova, and I was now almost on top of my running game. School too was going great. I went back to Ireland for the summer with a new found confidence and looking forward to a few months with Yvonne.

Jumbo would be over for a visit too, and I was looking forward to him meeting my family and Gerry Farnan.

When I got back, I found that things weren't the same in Metro. Most of the lads had moved on and I had less training partners to run with. I decided to transfer clubs and moved over the Liffey at Islandbridge to Donore Harriers, so that I could train with more seasoned runners.

In hindsight, it was a selfish move. I also dropped Gerry – though he wasn't coaching me at that time. Donore had a great team made up of Tony Brien, Tom O'Riordan, Jim McNamara, Willie Smith, Tony Murphy and the Reddigan brothers. Eddie Hogan was their highly regarded coach and I felt I could only get better training in their company. It was good for me then, but it was something I regretted over the following few years.

Every time I'd see Gerry, it was hard to look him in the face. He had done so much for me and I left him and it hurt him very much.

That summer I won the Dublin Senior 10,000 metres and then my first All-Ireland Senior Championship in the 800 metres beating one of my hero's, Noel Carroll, in 1:50.2. I considered that to be the biggest scalp I'd ever taken because of my enormous respect for that great champion.

But I missed the qualifying time for the forthcoming European Championships by 2/10th of a second in the 1,500 metres, when I finished second to Hartnett in a meet against Portugal in Belfield. I ran 3:41.9, my best ever time. I was only a stride behind Hartnett, but believed my breakthrough was right on course.

While disappointed to miss the European time, I was selected to run for Ireland in my first senior international in the European Cup B meeting in Bielefeld, West Germany. It was an adventurous trip which would introduce me to one of the great characters in the history of Irish athletics who would go on to become both a soul-mate and confidant until his tragic death twenty one years later.

Long before I knew Fanahan McSweeney, I knew of him. But then nearly everyone in Ireland did. From Castletownroche in County Cork, he was Ireland's greatest-ever 400 metre runner. He was also a formidable sprinter who could also win at 100 or 200 metres.

Fanahan McSweeney. I'd always loved the name, which, along with his physical demeanour, always reminded me of Fionn MacCumhaill. Like MacCumhaill, Fanahan truly was a larger than life character, dashing in a rough-hewn sort of way.

There was a rough edge to his running style as well, but he was as naturally gifted a runner as ever laced on a pair of spikes.

He attended McNeese State University in Louisiana on a scholarship, and had won back-to-back national indoor titles there. In 1970 at the Houston Astrodome, he ran a 46.3 400 metres that stood as a European record for sixteen years, and he owned the Irish record for the distance right up until the day he died.

He was a National Champion in Ireland a dozen times, and at his hometown meet, the Cork City Sports, he was undefeated for sixteen years. When he was in America, he set South Louisiana records for every distance from 100 yards to the mile. When it came time to select the "Cajun Sportsman of the 20th Century" in various sports, Fanahan was the unanimous choice in *Track & Field*, even though he was technically only an honorary Cajun.

In my teenage years, I'd have known him only as a great Irish athlete. When I met him in 1974, we became firm friends. He was a flamboyant, outgoing, and happy-go-lucky character.

A life-long pioneer, Fanahan managed to exude confidence and happiness to anyone who was around him. He also had a rebellious, anti-establishment streak running through him, which he kept in check remarkably well.

The team had arrived late in the afternoon, and after checking into our accommodation at the University, Fanahan and I decided to go out.

We went off to a nightclub that night and didn't return until around 11.00. Eddie Spillane was waiting up for us. I guess he'd heard we'd been spotted sampling the town's night life and couldn't imagine what else we might have been up to. He proceeded to read the riot act to the pair of us.

Eddie was the team manager and was a member of my new club, Donore Harriers. In his youth, he'd been a pretty decent cross-country runner in his own right. He seemed to be taking this quite seriously and reamed us out. He reminded us that we were there to represent Ireland, that we'd behaved disgracefully, that we shouldn't have stayed out so late, and that we should have been in bed long ago.

He was even harder on Fanahan than he was on me: As an experienced international competitor, he was supposed to be setting an example for the rest of the team and that the misbehaviour would be reported back to the Federation on our return to Dublin.

The next day the 400 metres was the first race on the card, and Fanahan won. Then an hour or so later I was running the 1,500 metres. Since it was my first event ever as an Irish International, Fanahan was worried that I'd mess up and he'd be blamed. When I went through the first 400 metres he was there on the inside of the track urging me on "Come on boy, don't let me down."

When I came around for the second time, I winked at him, more or less to say "I'm okay, I'll win." I went on to win the race – we were the only two winners on the entire Irish team – and we never were reported.

That summer Jumbo came to Ireland at the invitation of the Olympic Council of Ireland. Although his Irish Connection had been in operation for over a quarter of a century by then, Jumbo had never travelled to Ireland; but this time he reckoned he had two good reasons for going.

The first was that, since he would be addressing a seminar hosted by the Olympic Council, the trip would be free. The other was that he hoped to personally recruit John Treacy, who was the hottest runner coming out of the Irish school system that year.

Jumbo usually left the recruiting to Jack Pyrah and to his extensive Villanova alumni network. Treacy, however, was the first athlete, other than Carl Lewis, he had ever personally travelled to recruit. Treacy ultimately became the first Irish runner ever to turn Jumbo Elliott down when he accepted a scholarship to Providence College and Lewis headed to Houston, Texas.

At the seminar in Dublin, the legendary coach took questions from the audience, including one from Brendan Foreman, who asked him to discuss the role of the manager when it came to international competition.

Since Foreman was an official of both BLE and the Olympic Council, and had been named manager of Irish teams on several occasions, he was asking a question to which he already knew the answer. Presumably he was hoping that Jumbo might toss a bouquet in his direction with his response.

What he didn't realise was that he had stumbled into a semantic minefield. In the American collegiate system, a coach is THE COACH, while a "manager" is generally an undergraduate assistant not good enough to make the team – but who functions as a gopher for the coaches and athletes.

Foreman, looking very pleased with himself, eased back into his chair.

"G-g-god-damn managers!" stammered Jumbo. "All they're g-g-good for is washing s-s-socks and j-j-jocks!"

Late that summer, the BLE decided that they'd send me to the European Championships. Though I hadn't qualified, the BLE were entitled to enter one athlete in an event without achieving the necessary time provided no other Irish athlete had qualified.

As a result, I was entered in the 5,000 metres because they believed it would give me enormous experience at this level. When I arrived in Rome, I was simply in awe. It was my first major championship, and I walked around the hotel housing the athletes in a daze: Lasse Viren, Valery Borzov, Brendan Foster, Ian Stewart, Guy Drut – all the great champions from Europe there to compete.

For the first time I felt I was in the club, albeit as a decidedly junior member. I was competing in the European Championships, and while I hadn't got an infinite chance of beating these guys, I knew I wanted to be one of them.

This was the first time that it ever struck home with me that I really wanted to be a top international athlete. I loved the buzz of the track, I loved the buzz of the hotel, and I even loved the buzz of the restaurant, sharing the same table, rubbing shoulders with some of the best champions in the world and being part of this elite international scene.

While I ran in the 5,000 metres, I didn't come close to qualifying for the finals. I simply wasn't good enough – yet. I left Rome after this wonderful experience telling myself "This is it, this is what I want – to be a champion."

I vowed that my next goal would be to break the four minute mile and to run in the Olympics two years down the road in Montreal.

When I went back to Villanova that September, I put my head down in earnest, determined to become a real world-class athlete. For the first time in my career, I began to think about times. I now had my own single room in Austin Hall. Austin was considered the best dorm on campus and one had to have pull to get in here. I now had the wall-to-wall carpet and black and white TV and all the comforts that a leading athlete on campus would want. Though I was now in my third year and regarded as one of the best athletes on the Villanova team, I still had not won a major college title.

In the privacy of my new single room, I'd scrawled a number – 3:53.5 – on the back of the mirror. That would be my goal for the coming year. I filed it away and never said a word to anyone.

Pay for play

Although Marty Liquori had graduated the year before I came to the States, he was that rare exception – a Villanova athlete who stayed in the area to avail himself of Jumbo's tutelage. He had by then beaten Jim Ryun and become America's Golden Boy, but despite his accomplishments, I was surprised to learn that he was relatively quiet, almost bashful. Marty was very astute and listened very carefully to Jumbo.

He was always ambitious, and having seen what Jumbo had made of his life as a businessman, Marty wanted to learn from that, too.

Mentally, he always seemed to be one step ahead of the rest of us, particularly when it came to money. Even when he was an undergraduate, he and Ron Stanko (who would later become Liquori's agent and, eventually, a meet promoter himself) were wheeling and dealing, selling stereo systems and stuff to the other students.

They were entrepreneurs even when they were in college, and when the running boom exploded a few years later, Marty was there to cash in by founding the Athletic Attic, a chain of stores which sold running gear and apparel.

But Liquori was always generous with his advice and counsel to the younger athletes, and it didn't seem to matter to him whether you were a big-time runner or a struggling walk-on. Even though I was by now running against him and might have been considered a rival, he had taken me under his wing and was very helpful to me.

My constant exposure to Liquori and the other senior athletes dragged me up both physically and mentally and I began to think that they were no different to me.

At 22-years-old, I was considered a good college runner, but not yet a world threat: That was around the time when Liquori phoned me with word of an opportunity to make some money by serving as John Walker's "rabbit" in a mile race at the Maple Leaf Games in Toronto.

With his long, flowing mane of blond hair and his all-black gear, the New Zealander looked more like a rock star than a runner, and was well on his way to establishing himself as the sport's first sex symbol.

Lean, powerful, and barrel-chested, he exuded a confidence that bordered on arrogance.

Liquori outlined the terms of the deal: There was no question about who the star of the show was supposed to be that evening, but for every second under three minutes I could bring the pace through the three-quarter-mile mark, I was to receive $100.

The track at Maple Leaf Gardens had extremely sharp turns, and the starting line for the mile was near the end of the long straightaway. Almost the instant the gun went off, Poland's Henryk Szordykowski tripped and we all went down like a pack of cards.

They called us all back to the starting line, the gun went off, and BANG! We were all down in a heap again.

When the gun sounded for the third time, I was left standing in my tracks. For the first few laps I was breaking my ass to try and catch up on those tight turns, and by the time we hit the half-mile mark I was still lying fifth or sixth.

"Shit," I was thinking, "I'm not going to get any money here."

So with that I put on a big burst, shot into the lead and by the three-quarter mark I went through in 2:57. The crowd went crazy.

Walker went on to win the race in 3:57 and while I actually finished, fading to something like 4:06, I'd done my job. But I had no idea how I was to collect the promised money.

Jumbo hadn't ordered me not to run in Toronto, but he hadn't been exactly enthusiastic about the idea, either. That night I figured out why. The meet promoter, Ken Twigg, hosted a big party afterwards, and coaches from all over North America traditionally got together there each year to renew acquaintances and toss down a few drinks. Or in Jumbo's case, many of them.

When I was on my way into the party that night, I crossed paths with my coach – who was being carried out the door, feet first, in a tired and emotional state.

"Now you know the secret," Schapp said when I told him later about the bizarre scene. Jumbo obviously wasn't going to be much help, so I had to track down Twigg on my own. I saw him in conversation with Walker, and finally summoned up the nerve to approach him.

"Mr. Twigg," I timidly asked, "do you think maybe I could get my… uh… money now?"

"Money?" He looked at me as if he had no idea what I was talking about. "What do you mean, kid?"

I told him that I was supposed to get a $100 for every second under three minutes.

"Were you even in the lead at three-quarters?" he asked.

Clearly, he hadn't even noticed.

"Yeah, he was," chuckled Walker, coming to my defence. "Go on, give the kid his money!"

With that, Twigg peeled off three new $100 bills. Never mind that it was Canadian money, it was my first ever pay-day. I was delighted with myself.

It was also my first encounter with the great John Walker. A year later we would meet again in another Canadian city under very different circumstances in the 1976 Olympic Games.

My four years at Villanova were now almost two-thirds of the way through and life could not have been better. Hartnett had graduated the previous year and I was now regarded the best miler on the team after winning my first NCAA Indoor Mile Championship in Detroit. But I still hadn't broken the four-minute barrier.

While we trained hard twice a day, six days a week and ran a twenty miler on Sundays, we found plenty of time to party during the off-season. We certainly weren't what you'd consider track nerds.

The record book says that I broke four minutes for the first time on May 10, 1975, but that was only the first "official" one and it might never had happened at all.

Two weekends earlier at the Penn Relays in the presence of my visiting father, I'd been clocked in sub-four not once but twice.

In a torrential rain storm with hot and humid conditions, I ran 3:56.2 in a relay leg so it didn't really count, when Schapp, Greg Eckman, Gregan and I broke the world record for the Distance Medley Relay. My time that day turned out to be the second-fastest relay leg ever recorded at the Penn Relays. Only Jim Ryun had a faster one.

The following day I ran 3:59.7 as our four-mile relay team Mark Belger, Schapp, Gregan, and I won. I also ran the second leg on the two mile relay team. This time it was Tiny, me, Schapp, and Belger. We won all three Championships of America races, and I was voted the meet's Most Valuable Athlete. The lads were amazed that I could run so fast in such difficult conditions. But, I had moved the bar up and it seemed that after all the waiting and "Let the times come with the wins" the four minute mile was easy.

I was supposed to go to western Pennsylvania for the Pitt Invitational in Pittsburgh one week later – but I got into a barney with my Dad before the race.

I was getting uncomfortable with him living in my dormitory room. He chose not to stay in a hotel because he wanted to enjoy the fun with the team – as if he was one of the boys. Hanging out on the chain, eating in the cafeteria, he began to think he was a kid again and the lads enjoyed his presence.

He thought it was cool. I thought it decidedly uncool. I'd end up sharing with Chalkie or whoever had space, night after night for two weeks.

Eventually, I snapped and told him he had overstayed his welcome and that he had caused me no end of frustration and embarrassment. Stressed, I went AWOL for two days. I figured I'd get my own back on him and decided to skip the trip to Pittsburgh.

When I returned, my old man was waiting for me. The team had already departed on the four hour car journey.

"You're a bloody disgrace, and you've let the team down," he said in a vexed voice."

Another heated row erupted until we finally became too tired to argue any further. He told me that Jumbo had informed him "If he doesn't get his sulky ass to Pittsburgh, he can forget about going to Jamaica the next week."'

It was a big stick – Filbert Bayi was supposed to be going for a world record in what they were calling the Dream Mile in Kingston, and I'd been invited to be part of the field.

"Come on let's get to Pittsburgh," urged my Dad.

We took a flight from Philadelphia and arrived before the team. I won the One Mile Invitational in 3:56.2 – exactly the same time I'd run in the Penn relay race a week earlier. It was the first sub-four minute mile ever run in Western Pennsylvania, and Jumbo was so happy he forgot all about me nearly ducking out of the meet. Two hours later I won the three miles.

Jumbo received a Driving While Intoxicated (DWI) arrest earlier that year and he wasn't even supposed to be behind the wheel of a car, but he'd driven to Pittsburgh. He knew I had an international driving license, so going back he tossed me the keys and said "S-s-so, ch-ch—champ, you d-d-drive the c-c-car."

I'm driving this beautiful new blue Cadillac Eldorado with a white leather roof with Jumbo, my father, and Tiny and Gregan as passengers. On the highway, Jumbo says "G-g-go ahead, ch-ch—champ. P-p-put the b-b-boot down."

He was aware that I had a heavy foot and he was anxious to get back to Philly so he could meet up with his drinking buddies at Jerkey's Saloon.

Then I heard the siren and saw the flashing lights through the mirror. When I showed my international licence to the cop, he hadn't a clue what it was. I tried to explain that I was from Ireland, a student at Villanova and that my licence allowed me to drive in any country. Jumbo got out of his car to come to my assistance, when suddenly the police officer pulled his gun and told him in no uncertain terms to get back in the car.

Then a light went off in the cop's mind.

"Ireland? Villanova? You aren't by chance that kid who ran a sub-four minute mile at Panther Stadium today?"

He grinned and said "Nice race son. I am a track fan and I was impressed with your time. It's your first sub-four." He then told me to go ahead and take it easy on the way home. I was thrilled – people were beginning to recognise me – and Jumbo couldn't believe my luck. As I got into the car, another speeding car flew by. It was Schap and a few of the boys. The cop took off in pursuit and he ended up with a ticket.

A week later, Jumbo let me to go to Kingston, Jamaica. The meeting there had been organised by a Philadelphia promoter named Bert Lancaster, and the word was that Bayi was going after Jim Ryun's world record 3:51.1, which had stood for nearly eight years.

Before I left Philadelphia, Jumbo pulled me aside and told me I was ready to run a really fast time.

"I think so, too," I told him.

Lancaster was a wheeler-dealer promoter from Philadelphia. He'd devised the International Freedom Games in honour of Dr Martin Luther King, which had taken place previously in Oslo and Philadelphia but was now moved to Kingston.

The field included not only Bayi, Marty Liquori, and myself, but also Rick Wolhuter and Tony Waldrop, who was then the indoor mile record-holder, Reggie McAfee of North Carolina, Walter Wilkinson of England, and Sylvan Barrett of Jamaica. With the exception of Walker and Ben Jipcho, just about every top miler in the world was there.

Schapp and Belger were running in the 800 in the same meet, so the three of us flew down together.

It was a hot, steamy evening in Kingston with a crowd of 36,000 people in the National Stadium. When the gun went off, Bayi took off the same way he'd done when he'd set the 1,500 metre record at the Commonwealth Games the year before. (In that race he did something no other athlete had done, going out in 52 seconds for his first quarter – it changed running forever.)

This time, Filbert ran the first quarter in 56.9 opening a big gap on the rest of the field. I was running second about fifteen yards back and hanging on for dear life. Bayi went through the half in 1:56.6 and by now I was closing in on the king.

Bayi twisted around in a sort of golfer's follow-through, to see how far he had got ahead, but I was right with him now going through the three quarter mile in his 2:55.3 to my 2:55.7 with Liquori in third place. 36,000 spectators were up on their feet cheering us through the turns.

With 250 yards remaining Bayi fought off my challenge and made his decisive move. I tried to force Liquori wide as we entered the home-straight and caused a bit of elbow rubbing. My legs began to wobble under me like never before as Bayi went on to win in a new world record 3:51 flat, breaking Jim Ryun's eight year old mark of 3:51.1 with Liquori second and me coming in third, delighted with myself.

I knew it was the fastest I'd ever gone, but I had no idea how fast until the results were announced. In reverse order the announcer started off... "In third place, with a new Irish and European record…"

I couldn't believe my ears when I heard I was credited with a time of 3:53.3. "Holy shit," I said to Schap who was standing beside me. I am now the European record-holder and eleventh fastest ever on the world all time list.

"You sure are man and you deserve it, well done," he said as he gave me a big hug. What I didn't even realise at the time was that the record that I broke was Michel Jazy's 1965 clocking of 3:53.6, which had at the time been a world record.

In the space of three weeks, I'd taken almost eight seconds off my personal best. I'd gone from being a novice 4:01 miler to a world contender. Jumbo had called it right. I couldn't wait to get back to Villanova to check the goal time I had written on the back of the mirror in my room. I got a huge kick when I discovered I'd beat that prediction by 2/10ths.

No one would had believed me if I told them the goal I had set for myself the day I left Rome the previous September.

The following week I made the cover of *Sports Illustrated*.

From the world spotlight in Jamaica to the Wildcat Meet of Champions at Villanova, I was supposed to be matched against not only Liquori, but the legendary maverick, Steve Prefontaine, as well.

Pre, as he was known, was scheduled to run, and I'd looked forward to meeting and running against him. I'd always loved his cocky attitude and his lack of fear for the competition – he had also finished fourth in the 5,000 metres Olympic Games in Munich. I was disappointed when opted to stay in out west coast and attempt to break the US three-mile record in the Oregon Twilight meet – which he did.

A day-long downpour had turned the cinder track into a soupy black muck, and the weather kept most of the anticipated crowd away as well. Only 2,300 were on hand when I defeated Liquori for first time in the Villanova race."

Only afterwards, I learned that Pre had been killed in a car crash that same evening. He was a legendary party animal, and it was no surprise that alcohol had been a factor. He had had several beers at a party that evening and lost control of his car driving home. He wasn't wearing a seat belt, and after the impact, his chest had been crushed by the roll bar of his sports car.

The spring of 1975 was my breakthrough season – but it had been an exhausting one. From the onset of the cross-country season, the previous autumn through the indoor and spring outdoor seasons, it had been a long, continuous grind.

On June 8, on a damp, rainy day in Provo, Utah, I capped off the college year by adding the NCAA outdoor mile title to the indoor. In keeping with what was becoming a trademark modus operandi, I allowed Waigwa to take the early lead and then out-kicked him over the final lap to win.

ABC had televised the meet, and in interviewing me afterwards, a young sports caster named Jim Lampley wondered whether the almost mile-high altitude had affected me during the race.

"Altitude?" I hadn't even been aware that I was running at an oxygen-depleted 4,500 feet.

"At first, I found it hard to imagine that his coach wouldn't have warned him about the altitude," said Lampley, "then I remembered who his coach was. That was classic Jumbo Elliott. He probably figured if Coghlan knew beforehand it would have given him one more thing to worry about."

Three days later I arrived unexpectedly in Dublin. Only my father knew I was en route.

It didn't take long for the word to spread that Ireland's newest athletics hero was back. I guessed my father was so proud of my latest achievements that he must have told newspaper reporters.

When I went for a jog in College Park that afternoon, I was met by reporters Tom O'Riordan and Jimmy Meagan. I had deliberately chosen the site for the rendezvous because I knew Yvonne would be there at on her lunchtime break from the Bank of Ireland and I wanted to surprise her. I couldn't believe the photographers were in waiting to capture our hugging and kissing for the following day's papers. To be honest I found it all a bit unsettling.

Bone-weary, I entered a few races in Ireland that summer, winning both the Cork City Sports and the Morton Mile at Santry, but apart from a 3:57.78 clocking at London's Crystal Palace in a 4th of July meet, in which I finished an exhausted third, the new European record-holder performed without distinction.

Opting to take an overdue break from competition, I headed off to Spain with Yvonne that August with at last a few quid in my pocket. Even there I couldn't escape the attention of the newly-growing legion of fans.

A few Irish holiday-makers recognised me one morning at breakfast, one of them called me from a nearby table "Hey, Coghlan, did you hear the news – John Walker just broke the world record. He ran a 3:49.4!"

"Well f*** it," I remembered saying under my breath "He got the 3:50 barrier before me." While Gerry Farnan was no longer my official coach, he would still meet me and lend his voice of encouragement and say "Don't worry about Walker, you'll get him next year and you can run the 3:50 indoors."

I had still regretted leaving Metro and still believed every word out of my mentor's mouth.

It was hard leaving Yvonne to go back for my final year at Villanova. We had fallen further in love and talked about marriage. We had no money, but that didn't matter. All I wanted to do was to marry her. Throughout my years in Villanova, she'd waited for me and that was enough to convince me that I wanted to spend the rest of my life with her.

But before we could think seriously about that, I had to graduate from college. And I had the Montreal Olympic Games to prepare for in ten months time.

Olympic countdown

From the moment I arrived back in Villanova, I never saw a day beyond the 31st of July 1976. It would be the day of the Olympic 1,500 metre final and I had every intention of winning it and emulating Ronnie Delany's triumph twenty years earlier.

I spent the autumn gradually building up my runs to ninety miles a week and carefully plotted the course that I hoped would bring me the success I now believed was in my grasp. I was slow to get going and was not concerned about my poor cross-country results. My goals were bigger and my plans long term.

Schap, Tiny, Belger, Bouma, Canadian quarter miler Glen Bogue and 400 metre hurdler Greg Eckman also had their sights on the games. We trained well together and when things were going bad on some of the days we were great for motivating one another.

The beauty about Villanova was that we thought big, we acted big and we all wanted to be great. There was no room for negative thoughts.

"Be positive, be positive, relax, relax," was Jumbo's mantra. I started to do a lot of weight lifting to build up my upper body strength. I used to see Tiny work out so well with the weights and I thought this would help – but I got hurt lifting and was out of action for a week with a back injury.

When Jumbo heard why I was missing the track workouts he went crazy. "Goddam, Irishman," he said. "The best weight training for running is running, up and down hills, you need the strength in your legs not in your arms."

Of course he was right. When I'd question him about diet, stretching or other principals he'd rebut "God-damit, be like a horse, you just do the running and I'll do the thinking, you never hear of a horse thinking about the training or racing, the trainer does all that and the horse does not worry."

From my elevated status to European record holder, I was now a prime candidate to be pursued by representatives of the shoe companies. Schapp was sponsored by Puma and initiated an arrangement with Art Simburg of Puma to sponsor me.

Week after week, boxes would arrive on campus and I felt like a star in my flashy gear. But there was no money on the plate for college runners. It was against NCAA rules to accept money. The top runners out of college were receiving under the table payments and I'd have to wait before I could get a slice of the action. The only thing I received at that time was a long leather jacket.

Christmas was approaching and my father booked my flight home. However, days before my departure Pyrah informed me that an invitation had arrived for me to run in the open mile at the CYO Invitational in Maryland in early January.

"But, I can't Mr. Pyrah, my ticket back to the States is after that date," I said. Next day, Pyrah came back to me to say, "Mr. Bob Comstock, the meet promoter said he'll buy you a new ticket if you can make it back."

"Ok, but the cost of the ticket is $1,000," I responded, "and I'll need the money to bring back to Ireland to buy it over there."

Money in hand, Yvonne and I got engaged on Christmas Eve 1976 and I made it back to Maryland in January and beat South African Daie Malan to the tape despite the worry of having the flu.

That indoor season went well – I won a series of miles in Philadelphia and Toronto beating a New Zealander in the process. But it was the "wrong Kiwi," not Walker but another Olympic hopeful for Montreal, Rod Dixon. My indoor season wrapped up successfully by defending my NCAA indoor mile in Detroit.

The outdoor track season was approaching and Olympic nerves were gathering. All the talk was "How do you think you'll do in the games." I kept trying to ignore the whole ordeal.

My Penn Relays career finished out with nine wins in ten relay races after anchoring Villanova wins in the 3,200 metre and 6,000 metre relays and gaining another 'Outstanding Athlete of the Meeting Award'. And in May I added another double winning both the 1,500 and 5,000 at the IC4A meet in Philadelphia, the latter amidst controversial circumstances.

The race was contested in what was supposed to be my "hometown." I inspired a chorus of boos from the stands when I paused to wave to the crowd with three laps to go in the 5,000. I was in third place at the time I made my gesture of confidence, and it appeared to be a case of unnecessary show boating.

In fact, I made a number of fast surges throughout the race trying to pick up the pace to help pull John Treacy to an Olympic qualifying time and the newspapers got it a little wrong.

According to one newspaper account "Coghlan had toyed with fellow Irishman John Treacy of Providence before sprinting to a ten-yard win in the final 50 yards, leaving Treacy exhausted and heartbroken."

I was accused of "hot-dogging" in more than one newspaper headline the next morning.

"The boos don't bother me," I replied, "it was so boring running around in circles. Nobody was cheering, so I thought I might as well do something to create a little excitement."

Elaborating, I revealed to Paul Zimmerman of the *New York Post* that the move was not without its psychological impact, making, as it did, a statement to the other runners in the field.

"To be honest, I wouldn't have given the signal if I didn't have the confidence that I was going to win. I just wouldn't do it otherwise," I explained. "It's a psych-out move, too. It psyches the other guys out when they see it. I was actually thinking of waving with four laps to go, but then I thought it might be too early. I didn't want to wake any runners up."

I met Ronnie Delany back in Dublin over the previous Christmas holiday and we had discussed this very subject. They booed Ronnie because he only ran to win, because he'd wait until the end of a race and then kick, because he didn't care about times. One thing Ronnie and I agreed on, though, was that it can be a good thing. It can stir you up. Whether they're booing or cheering, it's all action. The worst thing in the world is to hear nothing at all.

There would be one more race for Coghlan in a Villanova singlet. On the first weekend in June I successfully defended my collegiate championship in Franklin Field, Philadelphia winning the 1,500 in 3:37.1 – an NCAA and Irish record. My college career ended, I graduated with a degree in Marketing and a minor in Communications and I became the fastest Villanova runner over the 1,500 and mile distance.

Shortly afterwards, a trip to Los Angeles to race in the American AAU Championships also indirectly led to a relationship that would endure for the rest of my career and beyond.

As a young runner in Ireland, I'd always been impressed by Frank Murphy's warm-up gear. Murphy Snr. had been part of the national consciousness since 1969, when he won the British AAA title and then came second to Whetton in the European Championships 1,500 metres in Athens. When Frank returned to Ireland from Villanova on his summer holidays, he'd always be wearing this fantastic looking red track suit with 'NYAC' emblazoned on the front.

I didn't know anything about the New York Athletic Club, but I certainly fancied the gear.

Then, once I'd begun to run for Villanova I'd hear more and more about the NYAC. While in Los Angeles, Schap introduced me to Jimmy Rafferty and Ray Lumpp.

Ray, who'd won a gold medal as a member of the US Olympic basketball team in 1948 and also played for the New York Knicks, was the athletic director. Jimmy was the Chairman of Track & Field for the NYAC and a former winner of the Wanamaker Mile in his heyday.

The NYAC identified potential national and Olympic champions, by recruiting them as they came out of college and help them financially with the transition. They wanted to continue the NYAC's ethos as the amateur club with the best reputation for producing more Olympians than any other club in the world.

I won the 1,500 metres in LA and became the last foreigner to do so. I got stranded there after the race as the club I represented, the Penn AC, went bust and could not afford my return ticket to Villanova.

Jimmy asked me to join the NYAC, and promised to look after me. I made it back to Villanova thanks to the NYAC. That was thirty-two years ago, and today I'm still a member and Co-Chairman of Track and Field.

While most eyes were fixed on the showdown between Bayi and Walker in the upcoming Olympics, some experts, noting the dramatic ascent of my learning curve, were touting me as the potential spoiler in the 1,500 metres. I had, after all, come from relative obscurity of a 4:01 miler, to become the European record-holder in a single year, and, given my meteoric rise over the previous year, it was apparent that my limits had yet to be tested. Who knew what race I might yet harbour inside me?

"This," opined one analyst, "might be the guy to separate Walker from Bayi."

The sport's so-called Bible, *Track and Field News*, still operating on the assumption that both Walker and Bayi would run, had picked me for the bronze medal, but in a guest column in The Irish Times that spring, Ronnie Delany had cautioned his countrymen to be reasonable in their expectations.

"Realistically, the best we can hope of Coghlan at this stage is a bronze medal," wrote Delany.

I returned to Villanova from Los Angeles where I put the final touches to my training on the old cinder track. Sadly, Schapp, Belger and Tiny failed to make the US Olympic team but they stayed around to work out with me. School was out and it was quite boring around campus. All we did was train, eat and sleep. I had too much time to think about the games; the training I was doing and the political controversy hovering about a possible African boycott.

It was now time to sharpen the edge on the blade with speed work. I trusted I had all the strength I needed for the 1,500 and in the final run-up I wanted to concentrate on my 800 metre speed.

Day after day, session after session – all we did was 400s, 400s, 400s. Eight, ten, twelve in times between fifty-three and fifty-eight seconds each. Then in a concerned state of mind I questioned Jumbo. "Why can't we do some 800s or even 200s," I asked.

Jumbo was more blunt. "Gg-gg' God dammit it, I don't like 'em 800s, they tear the mind right out of you," he replied. "You'll b-b-be running quarters, until they c-c-ome out your ass."

Rhythm, rhythm, rhythm.

The next day we arrived at the track and Jumbo announces "Ss, ss, so, champ, I think we'll do a few 800s today." He had obviously taken into consideration my concerns.

But storm clouds of a pan-African boycott were gathering during the spring of 1976. I was among the first to recognise that while I would face Bayi or Walker in Montreal, I almost certainly would not race against both.

Three decades later the reasons underlying the boycott of the 1976 Olympics still seem hopelessly complex, but the matter was rooted in the political dynamic of the era.

South Africa, which still clung to its racist apartheid policies, had become a worldwide pariah, and had been barred from international competition at any level since 1964. Then, in the early summer of 1976, in defiance of the ban, New Zealand's national rugby team, the All-Blacks, had arranged a tour of South Africa, at the risk of having New Zealand's athletes, including Walker, declared personae non-gratae when it came to Olympic competition.

The moral issue was clouded by the fact that New Zealand had been far from the first nation to flout the ban: Sports teams representing more than two dozen nations had competed against South Africa since the ban had been instituted, and none of them had been threatened with Olympic expulsion. Still, the timing of the All-Blacks tour could not have been worse. To outward appearances, the New Zealanders appeared to be thumbing their noses at world opinion.

Widespread condemnation was quickly forthcoming, but the International Olympic Committee distanced itself from the issue. Its contention was that since rugby was not an Olympic sport, it was powerless to discipline New Zealand, whose Rugby Union functioned as an autonomous body and had nothing to do with the Olympics.

The African nations, understandably, did not view the situation in the same simplistic light, and when the IOC failed to act, twenty-six countries, Tanzania among them, withdrew from the Games on the eve of the opening ceremonies. Twenty of the twenty-six delegations had already arrived in Montreal by the time the decision was taken. The athletes, many of them in tears, sadly packed their bags and went home.

"Principles are more precious than medals," said Kenya's Foreign Minister James Osogo in announcing his country's enlistment in the boycott. Osogo said that by refusing to sanction New Zealand, the IOC would give "Comfort and respectability to the South African racist regime and encourage it to continue to defy world opinion."

When the Tanzanian withdrawal became official on July 14, John Walker commiserated with his arch rival Bayi.

"I feel sorry for Bayi," said Walker, "the Olympic Games are the ultimate thing.

I'm very disappointed. I think millions of people would have liked to see the clash. Also, for the last year I've been planning to run against him and I think we would have had a world record."

On the surface, it seemed to be one more unfortunate example of politics interfering with sport and on the other hand, I'd be less than honest if I said I was sorry to learn that Bayi would not run – just because it was one less formidable rival I'd have to beat. But I did feel particularly sorry for personal friends of mine like Mike Boit and Henry Rono, who were also being denied a chance to compete for an Olympic medal.

By now I had put the final touches to my preparation with one last 800 metres time trial and clocked 1:48.5. While I wasn't as fast as my potential Olympic competitors over this distance, I was pleased I could go this fast in a workout on cinders. I was content.

I didn't plan to leave Villanova for Montreal until two days before the heats of the 1,500 metres began. I purposely stayed there to relieve the pressure I suspected would accompany any Olympic Games. Being cooped up in the concrete jungle of an Olympic village with 6,000 athletes and officials wasn't my idea of preparation.

Instead, I chose to stay in my relaxed haven in Villanova to conserve mental energy and it would be only a short flight up to Montreal anyway. It was so surreal and I was happy to be detached from the hype.

As events unfolded on television, I listened to the boycott controversy and the protests about Queen Elizabeth who opened the Games. She was entitled as the official head of state to do so, but the French Canadians of Quebec were not pleased about this "outsider" coming in to perform the ceremony.

Further controversy arose when female athletes were subjected to sex tests – except Princess Anne of Great Britain who would compete in Equestrian. Then it was reported that the true spirit of the Olympic movement was being undermined by the growing commercial influence on sports. I didn't know what they were on about – all I was getting was a few free pairs of shoes from Puma.

Then a young Romanian, Nadia Comaneci brightened up the games when she mesmerised the world with seven perfect tens in gymnastics and won three gold medals.

Then track and field commenced. Even though I was in a different world miles away from Montreal, I could feel the tension build within me. Then there was a rumour that John Walker, who had pulled up in the 800 metre heats with an Achilles injury, might not make it to the 1,500 metres start line.

By now I was ready to head north to the Olympic Games in Montreal – fit, healthy and perfectly prepared to win.

Before I went though, I threw a massive wobbly. Harry and Ina Long were relatives who lived in North Conshohocken, Pennsylvania, not far from Villanova. From the time I'd arrived for my freshman year they'd adopted me and helped alleviate my homesickness.

I usually didn't mind being the centre of attention after a race, but I had come to value my privacy before one.

Before events I became moody and irritable – not the kind of person you'd want to be around. It was always just nerves kicking in as I narrowed my focus. Those who knew me gave me a wide berth at these times, knowing that I was like a volcano on the verge of eruption.

By the time I left Villanova I already had my game face on – completely focused on the task at hand. I just wanted to quietly get on the plane and get to the Olympics. I was in my zone.

Harry and Ina always used to boast of how proud they were of how their "nephew" was doing, and this time when I got to the airport they had organised a big send-off. They were there, along with their children and a bunch of their neighbours with tri-colour flags and banners. It was the last thing in the world I wanted at that stage.

I was furious and to their shock and amazement exploded in anger and frustration, verbally abusing them and generally acting the boor.

Once on the plane, I was overcome with shame that I tried to put out of my mind; but the guilt I felt over my behaviour that day was a weight I carried to the Games. To this day I feel a pang of remorse about my behaviour to those wonderful people.

Montreal... and bust

Arriving in Montreal was both nerve-wracking and exhilarating. I was about to go onto the biggest stage in sports and I could already feel the weight of expectation. When I got my first look at Stade Olympique, I was thinking "Wow, this is awesome! When are they going to finish building it?" It was eventually renamed the Big O because the city owed so much for it many years beyond the games.

The facility had been six or seven years in the making, but the Montreal

Olympics had run way over budget and many aspects of the venue weren't completed in time for the games. The track and the spectator seating areas were there all right, but a planned retractable roof never did get finished. There were cranes still in place, and you had the feeling you were in the midst of a construction site.

Because of the events at Munich four years earlier, security was much tighter. And most of the talk was still about the African boycott, with politics once again threatening to overshadow the Olympics.

As was the drugs issue. The word around Montreal was that the Eastern Bloc countries were systematically providing their athletes with steroids. Years later, the extent and magnitude of this particular drugs scandal would be revealed to a shocked world.

In Montreal, they won every women's event in track and field. In swimming there was also something fishy – there were twenty-one records broken by Eastern Bloc swimmers.

At the time I believed that the runners who I would race against were clean. Drugs never came up in conversations at Villanova. We knew nothing whatsoever about them. The nearest we got to drugs would be a B12 shot in the arse from Dr. Boyle in the college infirmary when we were run down from exhaustion. This was the Olympics and it is the loose talk that confuses the mind of an athlete.

"But hey," I thought, "I'm finally here, forget all the rumour and innuendo and just get on with the job."

We stayed in the newly constructed Olympic village. It was a large pyramid type structured building where all the athletes lived. It was a great feeling to walk around and soak up the atmosphere.

Here was I coming from being a college athlete one week, to an Olympic contender the next. In the cafeteria, I saw the great Alberto Juantorena who'd just won the 800 metres in world record time and Lasse Viren who successfully defended the 10,000 metres he'd won four years earlier in Munich: He'd be going for the double in the 5,000 metres days later.

Then when I saw Nadia Comaneci in the queue right in from of me I was in awe – amazed by the size of her tiny framed body. I thought it incomprehensible that such a slight little fourteen-year-old child could possess such magnificent power and grace.

And then there was an opportunity to make some money. The athletic shoe companies, Puma and adidas in particular, were working at the Olympics trying to get athletes to wear their shoes.

It was – and still is today – a big deal to have as many medal winners in their shoes. While I was a Puma man, I had no formal contract with them. Adidas were pursuing me to switch to switch to them. They had most of the top 1,500 metre runners on their books and wanted me.

When I let it be known to Peter Purcell, the Irish agent for Puma, that adidas were trying to poach me, he quickly took me to the Puma office to meet Derek Ibbotson, a former world mile record holder and Puma's number one guy, to get me "all the shoes I wanted." I said I wasn't interested in shoes, that money talks now.

We struck a deal. I'd get $10,000 for gold, $6,000 for silver and $4,000 for bronze. It sounded great, but I still wasn't happy.

I wanted a guaranteed payment to just wear the Puma shoes, on top of the offer for my finishing position. After much debate behind closed doors, they came out and handed me my shoes.

Inside one of the pairs was stuffed $4,000 in crispy new $100 bills. It was going to go a long way towards my wedding.

When I'd been back in Ireland the previous Christmas, I'd had a long talk with Ronnie Delany whose advice I respected. "Don't take any chances," he told me, "make sure you win your heats, make sure you win the semi-final, qualifying is most important and be ready to go in the final."

I took that advice to heart. I won my preliminary heat easily in 3:39.7 after a slight mishap with Canadian runner Dave Hill who'd clipped the back of my heel. I bolted out of trouble and ran thirty-eight seconds for the final 300 metres.

The luck of the draw put off the Walker-Coghlan confrontation for another day. My semi-final included Wolhuter, Wellman, Van Damme, and Britain's Frank Clement, while Walker's competition would come from Wessinghage, Hill, Britain's Steve Ovett, the Aussie Graham Crouch, and another Belgian, Herman Mignon.

When I ran in the semi-final, I put on another great kick and won that, too, in 3:38.6., though there was a momentary fright when it looked like I might be trapped coming off the final turn.

The charge was another thirty-eight seconds over the final 300 and in retrospect I had shown my aces too soon. John Walker won both his heat and semi-final in slower times than me – and there was no sign of that rumoured Achilles problem.

The Irish media went into a frenzy. I was being chased non-stop for a sound bite. Irish team manager Padraig Griffin did his best to protect me. For the media it was the first time in twenty years since Ronnie Delany won 1956 that Ireland had a genuine chance of striking gold.

Back in Dublin a banner headline in the *Evening Press* proclaimed;

"NOW FOR CLASH OF GIANTS"

After my semi-final qualification, I met Gerry Farnan and my parents outside the stadium. Gerry pulled me aside.

"So, Eamonn," he asked nervously, "what's your plan for tomorrow?"

I told him I intended to stick right behind Walker all the way and do my usual kick at some point off the last bend.

"That's all I needed to hear," he said, "no need to talk about it any further."

When I left Gerry that afternoon, I was still brimming with confidence. Then I went back to my room and planted the first seeds of my own self-destruction.

When I returned to the Olympic Village I decided to experiment. Over the years at Villanova, I'd had spent most nights in conversations with Chalkie White about training and racing techniques in our respective sports. One of the things that had always fascinated me was when he talked about "shaving down" for a big race. Swimmers are always looking for any edge, and removing body hair to decrease water resistance was one of them.

The way he described it, the process sounded almost exhilarating: Chalkie said when you shaved down for a big race you could just feel yourself get faster when you dived into the pool and you'd just glide through the water. I'm sure part of the perceived boost was psychological. He made it sound like an adrenaline rush as you rose to a new level.

I'd filed that information away and told myself that if I were to ever 'shave down' it would be for the final of the Olympic Games. Sadly, Chalkie didn't get selected to swim for Ireland in the Games. While I was disappointed for my friend he was devastated – he was so close to the qualifying times and I knew how dedicated he was and hard he had worked.

I'd assumed that the shaving process would take fifteen or twenty minutes, half-an-hour at most, but late that evening I was still in the bathtub, hacking away at my bloodied legs. It had taken over two hours and I'd nicked myself countless times.

And the worst part was still to come. Once I'd finished the job, I didn't realise that you were supposed to apply some cream. Now I was lying there in the bed, itching and scratching as the bed-sheets rubbed against my dry skin. I hardly got any sleep.

On the morning of the Olympic 1,500 metres final – I was a walking rash. Over breakfast I was rubbing and scratching and didn't even have the sense to tell the team doctor about what I'd done and the discomfort I was in.

My focus was on the cuts and not the race. My mental energy was being misdirected. I got to my room after breakfast when the phone rang. It was Jumbo. I couldn't tell him what I had stupidly done the night before.

"S-s-so, ch-ch-champ. H-h-how you feeling?"

"Oh, I'm grand," I lied.

"W-w-well, l-l-listen," he said, "I'm just l-l-looking at the field, and there's a lot of fast half-milers in here. Walker, 1:44, Van Damme, 1:43, Rick Wolhuter, 1:43. If the p-p-pace is slow, b-b-be careful. D-d-don't let the pace be too slow."

I got confused. Until the moment of Jumbo's call I'd never even thought about the pace being slow. All I'd thought about as I envisioned the way the race would unfold was running, sitting, and then kicking. That had always been my stock in trade. In virtually every race I'd run since I'd come to college I'd kicked from behind, whether it was with 150, 100 or 50 yards to go. I'd always been able to summon up that finishing burst.

Usually it was good enough, sometimes it wasn't, but until that brief conversation with Jumbo I'd never considered trying to run the race tactically any other way.

It was one more thing to think about. And with the final scheduled for that afternoon, I had too much time on hand to think as I lay around the room before I left for the stadium.

That afternoon I piled onto the athletes' bus for the Stade Olympique. I chose to go over alone as Danny McDaid, Neil Cusack and Jim McNamara my Irish teammates had already left to compete in the marathon. I felt they'd be better off having the assistance of team management.

The first person I ran into on the bus was Nadia Comaneci, riding over to watch the athletics finals. Guy Drut was also on the bus. The Frenchman was about to compete in the 110-Metre hurdles final. He was in the seat in front of me, smoking a cigarette. I was shocked. Here we were on our way to run in the Olympic final and I remember thinking "How can he be smoking?" Drut won gold that day.

Once we arrived, I went inside the stadium to taste the atmosphere. I was overwhelmed – almost numbed: Something I had never experienced before and would never experience again at the same level of intensity.

I kept thinking "This is my final day of judgement, What if I win and, what if I lose?"

Confusion crept up on me. I felt it running deeper and deeper in my thought process and felt myself swamped with a myriad emotions, ideas, strategies and worries.

I had a brief respite from the panic as I watched the American Dwight Stones compete in the final of the high-jump. Earlier in the week Stones had described the

Olympic organisers as rude and ignorant.

By the time the French-language press got through translating his remarks, Stones had also supposedly said he despised all French-Canadians.

Although he denied ever having said such a thing, he was the focal point of attention as the crowd heaped abuse on him all afternoon, booing loudly each time he removed his warm-ups to show off his Mickey Mouse tee-shirt. He threw petrol onto the fire by blowing kisses to the spectators.

It was no doubt distracting to all of the athletes, not just the high-jumpers, and the biggest cheer of the day came when he crashed out on the rain soaked run up area settling for bronze. The Canadians got what they were looking for.

I headed of to the warm-up area to relax and refocus for the final. But instead of concentrating on what I should have been doing, I was starting to feel a bit of awe as I watched the other runners jog around. I began to attach the names to the faces. I'd look at Walker and think "1:44," at Van Damme and think "Wow. 1:43."

I knew all about Walker, but I'd never laid eyes on Van Damme before. He wasn't the prettiest fellow you've ever seen, rather a fierce intimidating looking man with his beard, moustache, and long blonde hair. I'd already beaten him in the semi-final, and normally he wouldn't have been someone I feared. But after Jumbo's warning, I found myself wondering and thinking too much for my own liking.

Eyeballing the competition was something I'd never done before and in the "calling room" I was far from happy. Usually, I'd think about my own race – what I was going to do – not about the other competitors. Looking back at it, the indecision and the fear of failure was what I brought to the start line.

Once we were on the track, I removed my warm-ups just beyond the starting line. The others looked deadly serious. Meanwhile I was scratching my legs, which, despite the itch, did feel cool and light as the air hit them. I did my last couple of warm up strides and was ready to go.

Called to our marks, I remember thinking to myself "This is the biggest thing you're ever going to do in your whole life."

I was aware that millions were tuned in on television and 70,000 people in the stadium were watching with incredible anticipation for this, the blue ribbon event of the Olympic Games.

I felt like a little boy amongst men.

When the gun went off, I hesitated momentarily to let the others go so I could identify Walker's position and follow my plan. Dave Moorcroft took the lead, while I settled in third or fourth from last, with Walker right in front of me. Perfect, I had him in sight.

As we passed through the first quarter, Jumbo's warning flashed in my mind as I heard the split being called, 62.8 seconds.

"Shit!" I thought, "it is slow."

If it had been 58 or 59 seconds, I'd have stayed right where I was, but this seemed unconscionably slow. Then it was as if I turned on an electric switch. In one sudden gush of energy, I shot from the rear of the pack to the front over the length of the back straight. Now leading, I took a quick glance behind, and who was there but John Walker.

At that instant, I realised that I might already have set myself up to be the sacrificial lamb.

"Shit," I told myself, "you've become Walker's rabbit again."

For the next two-and-a-half laps, I was cursing myself and praying for somebody to go by.

My old mantra "relax, relax, relax," became "panic, panic, panic." Nobody would pass, no one else was that foolish. I didn't even increase the pace to break Walker or Van Damme's speed.

Instead, I cruised through 800 metres in 2:03. Walker forced me along. He was in control pushing me a little through the 1,200 metres in 3:01.

As Walker tried to pass me at the bell with 400 metres to go, I managed to hold him off and made him run wide of the curb. But, with 300 metres remaining, Walker made another big, big long run for home, and this time he got by. I tried to stay with him, but I was already sprinting just to stay with him. I was in top gear too soon.

Then 200 out, Van Damme went past me. Once again, I moved wide on the turn to try to establish a position coming into the stretch run. Wolhuter tried to pass me, but I held him off on the final turn.

As we hit that final straight, I moved wide still entertaining hopes of making a last big run at Walker and Van Damme on the outside. They weren't getting away from me – but I wasn't making up any ground on them, either. Then, with about 30 metres to go, Wellman came up the gap I'd opened on the inside lane and caught me on my left.

"Shit! Shit! Shit!" I was cursing myself as the race began to go away from me.

I knew I was running out of space and, as we came to the finish line, I frustratingly leaned too quickly and broke my momentum. We all went over the finish line in near-lockstep: Just three-tenths of a second separated first from fourth.

"F***, f***, f***," I screamed to myself.

I finished in fourth.

I misjudged Wellman who sneaked up on the inside to snatch the bronze. The last 400 metres were covered in a shade over fifty-one seconds.

The world had ended for me. I threw myself down on the infield of the track sobbing in a daze of disbelief. Every dream, all my expectations, everything that had ever seemed important had been drained right out of me there and then.

I was utterly crushed, humiliated by my naivety, utterly bereft of any feeling expect for the waves of self-pity that engulfed me.

I lay there on the infield thinking I'd never feel this badly again.

I was wrong.

Moments later I watched the medal presentation take place and felt a huge emotional sense of loss. I didn't want silver, I didn't want bronze. I wanted the gold. And I had just handed it to Walker on a plate.

To make matters worse, Lord Killanin the new President of the International Olympic Committee, presented the medals. An Irishman, it was pretty obvious that he expected to be placing one of those medals around my neck.

But Walker deserved it. He ran a brilliant tactical race and probably had to overcome greater pressure than I – such was the weight of expectation on his shoulders.

All I could do was shake his hand and say "Well done."

When I faced the Irish media, I could feel their disappointment. I had anticipated being pilloried by the Irish media after the final, but for the most part people were both understanding and kind

I knew they had built me up as the man who might beat Walker, and if I didn't, that I might at least get a medal of another colour. It was like a shared moment of respect. All I could do was bravely hide my disappointment and say "There is no use in complaining, I did what I had to do and finished fourth, a medal is not everything, life still goes on."

Back in Ireland, I learned that the media had staked out both my family's house and the Murphy's too. Cameras were rolling in anticipation of capturing the glorious moment on their faces as they were glued to television sets. Instead of ecstasy, they got agony. The nation had apparently come to a standstill. Weddings were delayed, workers came off the job, pubs packed with people all waiting for the gold. The national build up turned out to be a national set back.

"Coghlan couldn't do it when it really counted."

I would go on to hear that refrain for many years to come.

A couple of hours after the final Gerry Farnan tried to console me, even though deep down inside I knew he must have been as bitterly disappointed as I was. He'd truly believed that this had been one we were destined to win.

He decided the best thing we could do was get away from the Olympic Village as quickly as we could. We went off to find something to eat and try to get my mind off what had happened.

We walked into an Irish pub, and ran into a group of people drinking down at one end of the bar. When they spotted me, one of them looked up and shouted "Hey, Coghlan, what the f*** happened to you today? I lost ten dollars on you!"

Gerry exploded. His face turned crimson – I thought he was going to throttle the guy.

He finally spluttered "You can f*** off yourself!"

Then he grabbed me and marched me out.

We walked around Montreal that evening, passing pub after pub filled with Olympic revellers. We wandered around the subway area, talking about everything except running. There was no use crying over spilt milk and beside in all the years he mentored me, we never discussed a race until days after it had passed, good or bad.

At the end of the night, just before he left me back at the Village, Gerry said "Eamonn, what we'll do next is plan for Moscow in 1980. You'll train for the 5,000 metres, but you'll race the mile."

I discovered that my Dad – a pioneer all of his life until that point – had that night after the final, gone out and got royally pissed.

I should have too.

Home for the wedding

I wanted nothing more than to get back to Ireland to rejoin Yvonne, my family and friends, but one piece of unfinished business remained: I had committed to run in another Dream Mile in Philadelphia's Bicentennial Meet of Champions. The meet was being organised by Ron Stanko and had the financial backing of Rocky Aoki, a young Japanese entrepreneur.

I flew to the meet on a chartered plane along with Walker, Dixon, Quax, Stones and a host of other medal winners. I was amazed Viren was going to run in Philadelphia because he had not only won both the 5,000 and 10,000 metres but had also finished fifth in the marathon. But money was talking and the athletics' carnival I was soon to be a part of, was now on the road.

I felt lost and out somewhat of place. All these guys were upbeat while I was still distressed over my loss.

I stayed in my Villanova room to clear out the last of my belongings before moving home to Ireland for good, while the athletes stayed in a hotel. My remaining hours on campus were a tough ordeal.

If anyone made an attempt to come near me, I'd walk off rather than talk to them. I simply couldn't face anyone and talk about the race. The more I was reminded the more upset I got. I got an urge to smoke a cigarette and went off and bought a twenty pack of Winston. It was four years since I had one. I locked myself in my room and smoked them all.

The Bicentennial race was a real anti-climax for all save Walker. He won handily ahead of Wellman and Rod Dixon while I struggled in fourth. This time I had a good excuse.

I was sick as a dog and puked my guts up having overdosed on tobacco.

After the race, I was approached by Bill Twoomey, a former Olympic Champion and world record holder in the decathlon. Bill was heading up the World Track Association (WTA) that was trying to turn athletics into an open professional sport. He wanted to recruit me to the WTA and handed me a cheque made payable to Eamonn Coghlan for $10,000. It was impressive and enticing. I had never seen so much money in my life.

The WTA had haphazardly promoted professional indoor meetings for the previous couple of years and had recruited such athletes as Jim Ryun, Dave Wottle, Kip Keino and Ben Jipcho as their marquee names. WTA were in complete opposition to the amateur ethos of IAAF. They'd use strobe lights beamed onto the track and timed their movement to shine in front of the runners set at world record pace. While at first the audiences liked the idea it soon proved a dead duck in the making and a bit of a farce. The athletes were getting too old and no records were being broken. I told Twoomey that I'd think about it and get back to.

Nearby, Dave Wottle saw I was in conversation with Twoomey and later approached me with his advice. "Hey Eamonn, you're a great runner, you have the world right at your feet right now. Don't get involved in this WTA shambles." "Besides," he said, "there is more money in amateur track."

Six days after the Olympic final, I returned to Dublin. I was excited on the one hand that I'd see Yvonne, on the other hand I still felt humiliated. I didn't relish the prospect of being in Ireland and being seen as a failure.

There were quite a few placard-bearing friends and relatives and scores of well-wishers waiting when I came through customs at Dublin airport. I didn't know what to expect. I didn't know whether there was going to be cheering or booing. I could feel the warm welcome home and I knew these people were trying to help me to pick my head up again. Time to get on – nothing would bring it back again.

Following the round of hand-shaking, back-slapping, photographs and autograph signing, I looked up and sheepishly wondered "What would have happened if I'd won?"

The press assembled at the airport appeared to be nearly as interested in our wedding date as they were in the Olympics.

"Before the year is out, I'll marry Yvonne," I promised, "but before that happens I have to look for a job."

I had agreed to run in a series of post-Olympic events in Europe over the next several weeks. It was an opportunity to make some badly needed cash. With the Puma guarantee I got in Montreal and the series of races in Europe, I figured I'd have enough to start a new life with Yvonne by my side.

One week later, I beat Walker in the World Games meeting in Helsinki. It was my first time to beat him, but the result did not really matter. It wasn't the victory I wanted.

In between the European meetings, my father reminded me that I would have to run in the BLE National Championships in Limerick "No matter how much money you are getting elsewhere," he ordered me.

I was reluctant to leave the exciting continental race circuit but he went on to say "You promised me a long time ago that you'd compete in Limerick, and I don't think the fact that you're my son really enters into it. You know that you owe a lot to BLE and you have to be there."

I had no choice. I flew in to Limerick to compete in the Nationals, but he wasn't happy at all. Yvonne and I arranged to meet up in Limerick. She drove down a passenger with my father. After completing the heats Yvonne and me headed off to check into our hotel.

My father had pre-booked two rooms. A double and a single. We took the double and left him the single. Soon afterwards, we were snuggled up, snogging away, when there was a loud knock on the door.

"Eamonn, are you in there," my father shouted. "Yes," I said.

"So open up the door and let me in," he responded.

"No, this is Yvonne's and my room, you're in the single," I answered back.

Even though I won the National Championships to please him, he was so pissed off he wouldn't talk to either of us for a week. He could not accept his son had grown up and moved on.

Before I flew off to race in Europe again, I earned a few quid one afternoon with a personal appearance at Arnotts department store on Henry Street. I posed for photos and signed autographs for a seemingly endless queue of fans.

That meet-and-greet session provided the occasion for an interesting tête-à-tête encounter whose significance wouldn't come to light until two decades later.

In 1985, Yvonne and I were invited backstage following a U2 concert at the Meadowlands, in the same arena in which I had broken my own world indoor mile record two years earlier. We were chatting away with band members Larry Mullen and The Edge when Bono himself approached.

"Eamonn, you probably won't remember this," he said, "but when you came to Arnotts after the Olympics in 1976, I was one of the people queued up to get your autograph. I was carrying my young nephew on my shoulders. Of course you wouldn't have known who I was then. You were the star."

"You were really there?" I exclaimed, with a good reason not to remember.

Back then, Bono was still going by his given name of Paul Hewson, and his band was called Feedback, soon to be changed to The Hype. They didn't become U2 until 1978.

"Jesus, Bono, but look at you now. I used be the Irishman to rock the Meadowlands, now you are," I laughed.

Years later, Yvonne was rummaging around through volumes of old clippings which my mother had saved since I was 14-years-old, and discovered a tattered *Evening Press* newspaper photograph of the nascent rock star with the young lad perched on his shoulders, waiting to get my autograph.

I was done with competition for the summer, and with each day Montreal seemed to recede from everyone's memory save my own.

While I wanted to be a professional runner, there were no guarantees. I needed to get a full-time pensionable job with security for our future. With all the hype I got from Montreal, offers began to come in. The first was from Michael Fingleton, the Managing Director of the Irish Nationwide Building Society. I interviewed at their offices on Camden Street, but decided it wasn't something I wanted to do.

The next offer came from Tom Cavanagh, a very successful Ford dealer in Cork and member of the Cork City Sports committee. Tom wanted me to come down to Cork to work as a car salesman in his Fermoy dealership. Although he had wonderful powers of persuasion, he wasn't able to convince me to move to Cork.

Then I got a call from a merchant bank in Dublin, Equity Bank Limited. I was interviewed by them and got the job, and the appointment was immediately covered by the press.

They were only a small outfit at the time, just starting off, and operated out of offices in Grafton Street in Dublin. The most attractive aspect of the job was that Gerard McCarthy, the Managing Director, agreed that I could have six weeks off to go to the States for the indoor season. The expectation was that I would utilise my contacts with some of the other runners and persuade them to invest their earnings with Equity Bank. Interest rates on savings in Ireland were high and most attractive for the athletes to set up non-national accounts.

My title was Marketing Manager and my job was to drive around the country making calls on prospective clients. I'd drop in on office equipment supply companies and car dealerships, to sell the bank's hire-purchase services.

Now secured, in early September we decided to get married – in October. I was only 23 years of age and Yvonne was 21. Her parents were overjoyed and put everything in place at such short notice to make sure we had a great celebration. We had little money, but that didn't matter. Yvonne had faithfully waited for me to graduate from Villanova and to pursue a career as an athlete. Now she'd be my wife and we could look forward to a life together.

On the 28th of October we married in the Church of Our Lady of Dolours in Glasnevin. As she walked down the aisle, I was never so nervous in all my life. This was no race, this was not the Olympics. This was going to be the biggest step we were about take in our young lives.

When her Dad, Jim, handed her over to me, I looked into her beautiful eyes in awe. She looked stunning. I was a happy man, happier than ever before in all my life.

The media were out in their droves to capture the occasion and over a hundred and thirty family and friends attended the reception in Fitzpatrick's Killiney Castle Hotel. It was a marvellous occasion for us – described as the "wedding of the year," in the social columns. Chalkie White was my best man and Yvonne's sister, Patricia, was her bridesmaid. People came in from America and a whole range of athletics stars and media folk added to the glamour.

It was the happiest day of our lives and we'd be together forever to share the emotional ups and the downs that would surely follow.

After a brief honeymoon in County Kerry, we rented a small "luxury" apartment in Rathgar. My parents couldn't believe I was spending £85 a month in rent, but we felt we owed it to ourselves, and, since I was getting a company car for nothing, we convinced ourselves that we could afford it.

CHAIRMAN O
MASTER OF T

took a quick glance over my shoulder and saw the rest of the field were a long way back. There was no danger at all from behind. I was dying to go by him. It was a real temptation, but I forced myself to wait until we were coming off the final turn, at the exact spot I'd pointed out the night before. Then, reaching the spot, I drew abreast of Dimitriyev, turned, glanced at him, and when I saw the look on his face I knew I was about to be the World Champion. I clenched my fists, smiled and said "I got it. I got it. I got it for you guys."

Part

THE BOARDS

E MILE

Eamonn meets with Yvonne (right) and children
Suzanne (left) and Eamonn at Dublin airport
following his victory in the 1983
World 5,000 metres Championship at Helsinki

The running pro

I had no real background or training for my job in Equity Bank. Every time I'd go into a dealership they'd be delighted to see me. They'd want to talk about the Olympics and ask all sorts of questions "What happened to you in Montreal. What's John Walker really like? What about Filbert Bayi, do you think he'd have beaten Walker? When are you running again?" It was punishing stuff.

And when it came time to do business, they'd invariably say "Oh sorry, we already have a contract with the Bank of Ireland for that business, but perhaps you could come back in a few years." It was rejection after rejection and as Christmas 1976 approached I knew things weren't going well.

I could sense the Managing Director, Gerard McCarthy who had high hopes for me wasn't too happy with my results. I began to wonder if I had made a big mistake by taking the job in the first place.

My failure at the sales game was compounded by an unfortunate car accident in Dalkey, which left my shiny, new, white Fiat Mirafiore – a prized possession in those days – a total right off.

By now I had set up my races for the forthcoming American indoor season. I reminded Mr McCarthy of our agreement that I could take time off to race, and gave him my six weeks' schedule. Permission was refused and I had to make a choice. Professional runner, or failed banker? The decision was easy. I was either going to be miserable selling hire purchase agreements for £60 a week or be happy in America earning $1,000 a race. Without rancour, we agreed to part company.

In January, Yvonne and I were leaving Dublin for New York. My first race was against Marty Liquori in the Philadelphia Track Classic at the Spectrum the following weekend. Sean Diffley was the only journalist there to see us off, and wanted to discuss my forthcoming indoor racing campaign. I filled him in on my schedule and my ambitions for the races ahead. Then he said "Eamonn, isn't it wonderful to be getting time off from the bank to go over to America and compete on the indoor circuit?"

Since he'd put it like that I decided to be truthful, and explained that I wasn't actually being given the time off, but that I had resigned from the job. Then we hopped on the plane and away we went for the first time together to enjoy the excitement of the American indoor season. It was funny too, Yvonne had been working in the Bank of Ireland and she was given the time off to travel with me.

The next day the front page of the *Evening Herald* had a massive headline that could have been announcing World War III:

"BANK SLAMS IRISH OLYMPIC STAR"

It was my first experience with tabloid journalism. I had now moved from the sports pages to the front pages. I was angry and embarrassed by the headline. I hadn't said it in any sort of vindictive way. It had merely been a matter of setting the record straight.

Equity Bank, needless to say got a lot of publicity – but not the kind they wanted. They took a lot of unnecessary flak over the issue as the media tore into them. They defended themselves in a dignified manner and I kept my mouth shut when other journalists tried to probe deeper. I wanted to be a runner and not a banker.

My return to America represented my first taste of indoor athletics outside of college. The prospect of travelling the United States with Yvonne by my side made everything that much more exciting and adventurous. I had meets lined up in Philadelphia, New York, Los Angeles, San Diego and Toronto, and for the first time in our lives we would live like royalty. The mere thought of getting paid for doing what I loved to do since the days I ran around the streets of Drimnagh, seemed like a dream come true.

My first race, would be a rematch against Marty Liquori at the Spectrum in Philadelphia. Frank Murphy Jr. came over from Dublin to be the rabbit. Frank stayed with me and Yvonne at the house Schap shared with Steve Dorsey out on one of our old Villanova training loops, and I would use this as my base for the season.

It was freezing cold and hard to run on the roads with all the snow which had fallen, but it was great to be back on the old hunting ground of Villanova and I knew I could get in good track work-outs with the boys.

Ron Stanko was once again the race promoter, and he'd built up the whole event as a mano-a-mano duel between the new kid on the block – me – and the representative of the Old Guard, Marty, but since Stanko had a vested interest in Liquori, there wasn't much doubt about who he expected to win.

Frank didn't perform his paid job as expected, or at least he didn't do what he'd been asked to do with the pace. I won the race, while Stanko was pissed off and blamed Frank for Liquori's defeat. "The green rabbit," he told the Philadelphia press afterwards, "turned out to be a yellow chicken."

That year was to see me run in my first Wanamaker Mile in Madison Square Garden – a venue that would provide its fair share of drama in subsequent years.

The Millrose Games had been contested annually since 1908, the most storied event in indoor track and field, the Wanamaker Mile was named for Rodman Wanamaker, son of John Wanamaker the founder the turn-of-the-century Philadelphia department store. Employees of the department store had a club called the Wahna Athletic Association and they changed their name to the Millrose Athletic Association in 1913.

The Wanamaker family lived on the Main Line in Philadelphia coincidently close to Villanova. One could credit the department store owners as being the first company to promote corporate fitness. They installed a track on the roof of their store so employees could exercise on their lunch breaks.

Before the advent of television, the Wanamaker Mile was broadcast live on the radio by the legendary sports announcer Ted Husing. In the early days, its start was traditionally set for 10.00pm to coincide with the beginning of the nightly news programme, and New Yorkers who weren't there at Madison Square Garden would gather around their radios to listen to the race.

From 1916 to 1925, the race was contested over one and a half miles before changing to the mile distance. Some of the former winners included Paavo Nurmi, Glen Cunningham, Don Gehrmann, Ronnie Delany, Tom O'Hara, Kip Keino, Filbert Bayi and Marty Liquori. The Millrose Games, as the meet is called, is to athletics what Broadway is to theatre. It's the greatest indoor track meet in the world for a runner to tread the boards. The meet is action-packed and the most nerve-tingling event in which I have competed.

The track's outer lane reaches right up to the spectators who could touch the athletes as they fire around its bends. It's more akin to a gladiator stepping into the Colosseum than an athletics meet. In a word – exhilarating.

Before the start of the mile, the crowd are brought to a silent hush as the Star Spangled Banner is sung. Before its end, you can sense the anticipation of the audience as they begin to clap and roar and then the announcer proclaims, in a slow, deep, bold, voice "Ladies and Gentlemen. The Wanamaker Mile."

I faced a formidable array of opponents in my 1977 début: The field included former world record-holder Bayi, the Kenyan Waigwa and Paul Cummings, the defending champion who liked to run from the front.

Cummings immediately went ahead and took the field through splits of 59 seconds and two minutes flat for the half-mile, at which point Bayi passed him to seize the lead and then, almost immediately, deliberately attempted to slow the pace.

The Tanzanian was plainly struggling, and midway through the third quarter, Cummings retook the lead, followed in short order by myself and Waigwa.

With a lap-and-a-half to go, I moved into position and then shot past Cummings as the gun signalled the final lap. With all the tricks I honed on the old Villanova boards, I used the force of the steep banks to catapult me off the turns and onto the straights to move away from a chasing Waigwa and win in a slow tactical time of 4:00.5 while Bayi, who described himself as "very tired," got up for third.

I was ecstatic – fired up by my victory, fired up by the crowd, fired up by the realisation that my win was going to open up an awful lot of doors across the USA. I completed the season undefeated and much richer than I would have been had I'd stayed working in the bank.

Back in Dublin on a break from the indoor track circuit, I was approached, not for the first or last time, by Noel Carroll.

Noel was a Villanova alumnus who'd preceded me there by a decade. He had run for Ireland in the Olympic 800 metres, both in Tokyo in 1964 and in Mexico City four years later. As the Public Relations Officer with Dublin Corporation, Noel was by now a well-entrenched behind-the-scenes mover and shaker with connections in government circles.

Noel knew that I was out of work and passed along word that there might be a job available at Bord Fáilte – the Irish Tourist Board.

Noel had spoken with Joe Malone, the Director General of the Board. Noel and Joe became friends through Noel's wife Deirdre O'Callaghan who, as one of Ireland's most famous harpists, performed in Bunratty Castle and did some work for the Irish Tourist Board.

Arrangements were put in place for me to meet with Niall Miller, the board's new whiz-kid, at the Shelbourne Hotel to discuss the offer. I concluded that the position would be right up my alley and would provide Yvonne and me with financial stability. I accepted.

I was summoned to the Board's swank offices on Baggot Street Bridge. I had heard of Joe Malone by name, but I had never met him personally. I was suitably impressed; he reminded me in some ways of Jumbo Elliott. Joe was a very dapper man, every inch the gentleman with the most engaging warm smile, while at the same time he was a man of action and didn't put up with any nonsense.

He gave me a title – Youth and Educational Representative. The proposition was simple: Promote Ireland and use every opportunity to get Ireland's profile up there and to attract visitors to the country. It was a fantastic arrangement for me; it gave me a steady income stream, tapped right into my need for a flexible schedule to accommodate my training and gave me a real sense of purpose that I was doing some good for the country.

I took it with relish.

With the security of a full-time job, we could afford to move out of our "luxury flat" and buy a new house at Kingswood Heights in Tallaght. The location was ideal. It meant I could do most of my training on nearby Newlands Golf Club and close enough to run my 20 miles on Sundays in the Dublin Mountains.

I was clearly focused on my running career too and a forthcoming major event in Irish athletics, The Calor-Kosangas International meet that coincided with the launch of the country's first-ever tartan track at Belfield on the campus of University College Dublin.

The construction of the track was a by-product of the 1976 Olympics and an attempt to get athletics out of the doldrums since the death of legendary meet promoter, Billy Morton, who died in the most bizarre of circumstances.

Walking out of his local public house after his usual few pints on a Sunday night with his pal Matty Heuston, Billy fell down an unguarded construction hole. Nobody ever figured out whether he had a heart attack and fell in, or fell in and then had a heart attack. But when Billy Morton died, athletics seemed to die with him.

The Calor-Kosangas International attracted many of the world's top athletes and 10,000 piled into watch them in action and to see me and my arch enemy, John Walker, battle it out over the mile.

It was a fascinating duel with Walker out-kicking me on the straight to win in 3:53 flat to my 3:53.3. It was the fastest time run in Ireland for nineteen years, eclipsing the All Comers record of 3:54.5 that Herb Elliott had achieved in the legendary world record race back in Santry in 1958. Somehow Walker was always able to pick himself up for the one he really wanted – and that was to beat me on my own turf.

Down Under against Walker

I made my first trip to Australia and New Zealand in January 1978 to compete in their outdoor track season – opting to forfeit the early part of the US indoor season to experience life down-under – and besides they were offering better money.

I also thought it would give me a chance to gain revenge over Walker on his home turf. Yvonne decided to leave her job in the bank in order to accompany me. It was a relatively easy decision for her to make – I was now in a job and earning decent money as a runner. And we didn't want to be separated for two months.

With time off work not an issue with Bord Fáilte, I came up with an idea and suggested that I'd wear green t-shirts emblazoned with a shamrock and the slogan Discover Ireland on the front and "It's Great... It's Green" on the back.

I didn't wear them racing, but I'd wear them out and about and when I was warming up for races. More often than not a photograph would appear of me wearing one of my creations – all grist to the mill for Bord Fáilte who took advantage of my presence to build a marketing campaign around me.

It was the height of summer in Australia, and the heat and the humidity we experienced on arrival in Brisbane overwhelmed us. Yvonne and I could barely leave the hotel, and I wondered how I was going to be able to run at all.

With the new job and the move into the new house, my training was a little on the poor side and I didn't know what to expect.

To my surprise I won my first race, at 3,000 metres beating Dave Moorcroft and Jos Hermans, and then moved on to win a two-mile in Melbourne breaking the Irish record and beating Dixon and Quax. These were big scalps to take before I met Walker.

While in Melbourne, Yvonne and I took a side trip over to the Cricket Grounds where Ronnie Delany triumphed in the 1956 Olympics. Two decades later, the track had been dug up and grassed over, but I felt great pride standing on the spot where Ronnie had won his gold medal.

As I stood there, I couldn't help but think back to Montreal. It was still hard to let go the dreaded memory of defeat and the sense of disappointment that I continued to shoulder.

My first run against Walker was scheduled for Sydney. Up to then he chose to run in 800 metres races for speed work, while I went with the longer races for strength and conditioning.

My strategy worked and I beat him in the mile, then moving on to Christchurch in New Zealand, I beat him again over the mile. He was far from a happy camper. John was a huge star in New Zealand and beating him at home wasn't something he took well. But, he had other ideas for revenge. We avoided one another in Wellington where I won the 3,000 metres and he the 800 metres, with the final battle scheduled on his home soil in Auckland.

Even though John was only a year older than me and we'd raced against one another several times, I still looked up him as a hero.

I was thrilled and somewhat in awe when he invited Yvonne and I around to his house to meet his buddies and his fiancée Helen, to whom he had only recently become engaged.

I soon discovered there was a different side to John to that of his public image.

John came across as brash, arrogant, and almost pugnacious on the track, but I discovered he was actually sort of quiet and bashful.

He had a very business-like approach to the sport. When he became the first person in history to break 3:50 for the mile he was credited with a case of beer for his bonus. Now, as the Olympic champion he wasn't fooled.

Our era in athletics was the breakthrough period for earning decent money. We were the pathfinders. There were no agents to look after our every whim as there is today. We were our own agents and we had to talk for ourselves with tough, business-minded promoters who'd always be on the look out for a bargain.

Promoters could be intimidating and would make you feel less than important so they could get you on the cheap.

As we travelled around the circuit, our conversations over meals weren't confined to athletics, but would be about the stock market, interest rates and property. Walker and a number of other athletes were astute businessmen and I would learn much from being in their company.

We all trained hard to succeed on the track – and after racing we would party hard. We developed a strong bond and would become one another's best advisers.

My final encounter of the tour was going to be at Mount Smart Stadium and I could tell Walker wanted to win this one. There was a huge media build up to the confrontation. I had gone undefeated on the tour and beaten Walker twice, but this time he got me.

His pride was at stake in front of his home fans and yet again he had an uncanny ability to get up for the one race he really wanted to get up for. I ran 3:57.4, but this time he nipped me at the line. All I could do was laugh. The whole experience had made me a better and tougher athlete on and off the track.

As my personal respect for Walker grew, I recognised that he was a bit of a moaner when things weren't going well for him.

The day after the race, I flew from Auckland to Dublin to accept the Texaco Sports Star of the Year Award for 1977. The following day I was on a flight from Dublin to Los Angeles to compete against him in the Los Angeles Times Invitational in the Forum.

It was my first experience of Hollywood. The stars were out in force to watch the meeting, which passed in a whirlwind of limousines, press interviews and exotic parties. It was a fantastic experience and I remember thinking "If the Mittons could only see where I've gotten to now." It was great stuff.

I caught Walker off the final turn as he forced me wide over the remaining forty yards and with what seemed to be a giant leap over the finish line by the two of us

I managed to hold him off.

He was mad as hell. At the press conference afterwards he said he hadn't been at his best because he'd flown all the way in from Auckland the day before.

I turned around and said to him "Walker, you big moaner, you flew from Auckland to California? I flew from Auckland to London to Dublin and then turned around and flew to LA, I'm the one who should be knackered, you've no excuses!"

It was the first time I felt that I had his number.

Moscow in mind

A year before I left for Villanova the first time, Gerry Farnan tripped over a piece of rope hanging from the back of his truck and took a bad fall. Unable to move, he was taken to Mercer's Hospital in Dublin. During the course of his rehabilitation, he was diagnosed with a serious heart malady – the source of his chronic angina.

I was sworn to secrecy. Gerry didn't want the boys in the club worrying about him. For the rest of his life he sustained himself by popping nitroglycerine tablets like popcorn.

Gerry always said "Let Jumbo coach you," and remained in the background until I returned to live in Ireland after the Montreal Olympics.

Though I continued to run for Donore Harriers, my relationship with Gerry as coach blossomed again as we prepared for the Moscow Olympics. Gerry said "Mystery is Power. Keep racing the mile and we'll train for the 5,000 metres and then unleash a big one in the Games."

He was concerned about my strength and conditioning for the 5,000 metres. With Moscow in mind, as there would be three 5,000 metre races in four days and we decided that I'd have to increase my training to one hundred miles per week.

It would mean training twice per day, six days a week, and running up to twenty-three miles on my easy Sunday run in the Dublin Mountains. The Munich hill training would increase from six by three quarter mile intervals to eight, as well as doing four by two miles laps with short rests between each on alternate weeks.

On cold, wet days Gerry would meet me in the Park for a Munich session and invariably have to pop the pills just to get up the short walk to our meeting point.

He would always dismiss his condition and make some joke about himself. As I got stronger, another Irishman, John Treacy, came on to the scene and would go on to have a distinguished career in athletics.

John Treacy surprised the nation when he won the World Cross Country Championship in Glasgow. John didn't possess the body of an athlete; he was skinny and scrawny and had an unorthodox running style. Yet John had the engine, the heart and lungs of a champion and, more importantly, he had the desire to succeed at the highest level.

John's great win inspired me and my successes inspired him too. While I somewhat dismissed John as a threat in the past, now I had a fellow Irishman by my side to keep me focused. I didn't want to lose my title as the best runner in the country.

Over the course of the following years we would often break each other's Irish record for the 5,000 metres. There was never jealousy on either part, but pure respect for each other's talent. John knew where he was going while my path was over different distances.

After John's victory in the World Cross Country Championships, my focus shifted to the European Championships in Prague late that summer and in particular to beating Steve Ovett in the 1,500 metres event. Ovett had emerged on the world scene with a phenomenal string of victories over 800 and 1,500 metres and had a lethal kick. The consensus was that no-one could match him over the last lap.

From his bed in the Mater Hospital, where he had undergone triple-by-pass-surgery, Gerry Farnan had other ideas. Gerry believed that the reflex speed I had mastered over the years would be good enough to beat Ovett.

He had studied Ovett's races and identified that he made his move with exactly 230 metres remaining. It was a sudden burst and, if I was prepared for this move, he believed I could out-kick him over the final seventy-five metres. I just could not afford to let Ovett get away, he rationalised.

I spent the summer working at my job for Bord Fáilte, while periodically jetting off to the continent to participate in selected races – but I knew my main task ahead was the confrontation with Ovett in Prague. Sebastian Coe, was also just emerging on the world scene. He would become Ovett's bitter rival but in Prague, Coe would limit his participation to the 800 metres.

When Prague finally came around, I reflected that four years earlier I had competed in these championships as a mere boy looking for experience. Now I was in the world rankings and looking to win the gold medal. No Irishman had ever won a European gold and I was desperate to change that statistic.

I qualified easily for the final, and going into the 1,500 I knew my tactics; relax, sit and wait for the 230 metre mark when Ovett would go with his traditional burst.

I just had to time myself to go with him and kick off the last turn.

I had visualised this move so often in training that it seemed it would come naturally when needed.

From the off in the final, I held my position up near the front tucked in a relatively slow race. Nobody was running away with it and somehow, I found myself in the lead with about 420 metres to go. But I wasn't prepared to make any move for home.

Then, as we crossed the finish line with exactly a lap to go, the whole field swept by me on the outside and I found myself completely boxed in. As we went around the turn the journey seemed to take forever – I knew I couldn't get out and there was no gap emerging. I knew what was going to happen next, but from where I was that knowledge was damn all use to me. Great in bloody theory, the practice was something else.

I could see Ovett in control of the pack, completely out of trouble.

I panicked and began to nudge other runners in an attempt to create some sort of a gap, some sort of an opening that would at the very least allow me to stay in touch. We were all bunched up too tight, tripping each other up and getting in each other's way.

At the 230 metre mark, Ovett took off leaving me stuck in the pack, seething at the injustice of it all.

With just 135 metres to go, a small chink of light appeared and allowed me to force my way out of trouble. I surged past Wessinghage and Moorcroft and went off in chase of Ovett who was at that point out of sight and a shoo-in for gold.

Crossing the line in second, I threw my hands up in jubilation and relief. I mightn't have won gold, but at least I was going to go home with silver and not have to suffer the ignominy of finishing outside of the medals. My first medal in a major championship – better than nothing at all. Redemption – to a point.

I didn't have too much time to dwell on what might have been due to the birth of our first child, Suzanne, shortly afterwards. We were thrilled; the birth was relatively straightforward and as first-time parents we were both astounded and overwhelmed by the responsibility that faced us.

The new threesome took leave of Ireland and headed back to the USA and my new training base in San Diego. So taken were we by San Diego the previous year, that we decided to spend the winter months there and race promoter Al Franken found us a wonderful condo right on the bay on Mission Beach.

Training in the Mission Bay area was incredible. With the Pacific Ocean one side and the Bay on the other, I had endless miles of pathways on which to run. I got myself into great shape and for the first time in my career I began to think about racing against the clock.

Gerry had inspired the goal to break the indoor mile world record and here in San Diego I felt I could do it. Almost out of nowhere I had people to train with. I met Neil Finn, a retired Naval Officer who began running with me.

He spread the word and soon I had a strong group of local athletes lining up each day outside my house. While they couldn't keep up – they were great company. As were Bill and Suzi Johnston who were so welcoming to us, and who would go on to become very close and lifelong friends.

Each evening after training, I'd head to the ocean with Yvonne and baby Suzanne. I took walks in the cool water to ease my aching muscles and we'd watch magnificent sunsets over the Pacific Ocean.

Most days we'd come across a strange looking fellow who would invariably be eating a bag of popcorn and drinking a Diet Pepsi. Curiosity eventually got the better of me, and I started up a conversation.

His name was Mike Long, and he didn't have a clue who Eamonn Coghlan was, and cared less about athletics. Over the years we became great friends, and as Suzanne grew older and learned to speak, she'd always refer to him as Popcorn Mike.

Popcorn Mike was a stockbroker with a very soft and quiet temperament. It was refreshing to have someone who didn't want to talk about running. Mike became my diversion off the track and would eventually become my stockbroker and investment adviser.

While I was making money from running, I hadn't a clue how to make it work. Mike had been through a recent divorce and, through our friendship, he formed an interest in running and began to work out himself. As our friendship evolved, he became more involved in running, eventually retiring from the financial industry to take a job with Elite Racing in San Diego. Mike would go on to become one of the most respected good guys in the world of athletics. He formed an Eamonn Coghlan fan club, calling themselves the "'Flamin' Eamonn Track Club of San Diego." At indoor meets in California, they'd show up in there droves wearing their Kelly green tee shirts.

That indoor season, things started to click. Kenny Moore writing in *Sports Illustrated* said "Eamonn Coghlan proved himself to be the finest indoor miler the world had ever seen," following on from my victories which included a win in the Wanamaker Mile where I just missed out on a new record.

But it was in my home from home, San Diego, that I was to really up the ante on a track that was noted for its speed – and one where I felt a new world record was definitely "on."

Al Franken was promoting the meet and started to beat the media drum loudly predicting a major showdown between myself, John Walker and Wilson Waigwa. It was the first time I had ever set out to consciously break a world record and despite the presence of some of my family from Ireland, I could feel that extra bit of pressure coming to bear.

Two days before the event, Walker and Waigwa withdrew. Franken may have been annoyed, but I was silently relieved. I figured that without them I could get on with the business of watching the clock rather than watching the men.

Just before the start, Steve Lacy approached me to say "If you ran 3:55 in New York, Lord knows what you'll run here!"

There was no rabbit as such, but all running logic pointed to Paul Cummings assuming the role as the early pacesetter. Leading from the gun was always his style.

That assumption went right out the window as soon as the race started. Attempting to free himself from the tangle of bodies massed on the line, Steve Scott elbowed me, I crashed into Cummings who, knocked off-stride, was immediately passed by most of the field.

Steve Tyler took the early lead and passed the first quarter in 58.5. Cummings had recovered and moved into second place, trailed by Scott and me.

When we hit the three-quarter mark in 2:56.5, it was already apparent that whoever won this race would own the new world indoor mile record. At that point I eased past Cummings into the lead, and shortly thereafter I felt Lacy coming up on my right shoulder.

The cheer from the crowd of 12,000 in the sold out Sports Arena was electrifying. These fans knew their sport and were well aware that we were on schedule. I got such a lift of adrenaline from the noise that I exploded leaving the rest of the field in my wake. Scott overtook Lacy heading into the last lap and I could sense him vainly attempting to close in on me. But I had another gear left and bolted the final lap of the oval track as if I was on fire.

My time, 3:52.6, didn't just break Dick Buerkle's world record, it fairly obliterated it, shattering the mark by nearly two and a half seconds. It was a magical feeling. I was now the World Record Holder for the Indoor Mile. In the end, it seemed to have come so easy. With post race interviews out of the way, the thought of what I had just accomplished was hard to sink in. But it did feel a lot different to any other race I had previously won.

Later that night, we partied into the small hours in a San Diego pub. The pints were flowing and everyone was so happy. Half-smashed, I hoisted a pint and offered a toast of to my fellow competitors Scott, Lacy, and Cummings who had each in his own way made a decisive contribution to the record run. On his way out the door, Steve Scott stopped over to me and said "Eamonn, if it could only be someone else other than me to break the world record, I'm really glad it was you."

Kenny Moore from *Sports Illustrated* came over to me and said "Eamonn, do you know your world is going to change after this?" I had no idea what he meant at the time, but soon after I'd find out. I had just became public property!

Sports Illustrated made it their cover photo-story the following week with a one-word caption: Begorrah!

I left for Ireland with Yvonne and Suzanne with a slight hangover the day after I broke the world record and arrived in Dublin on the Sunday morning. I was whisked immediately to Multyfarnham in County Westmeath to run on the Donore Harriers team in the BLE National Inter-Clubs Cross-Country championships.

What a contrast, from the sunny climes of California to the freezing cold of Ireland, wet and extremely muddy 12,000 metres cross country course. I don't know how I did it, running in muck knee deep I managed to finish in sixth position helping Donore to the team victory and I qualified to run on the Irish team in the forthcoming World Cross-Country Championships.

The European Indoor Championships in Vienna were a week later. It was hard to pick myself up psychologically for the meet, but I managed to win the European 1,500 metres in a slow tactical race beating John Robson of Scotland and Wessinghage. It was Ireland's first gold medal in the European Indoors since Noel Carroll had won the 800 metres back in 1968.

Cross-Country had never been my forte, but to make the Irish team for the World Cross-Country Championships being held at Limerick's Greenpark Racecourse was meaningful for other reasons. It marked the most important achievement of my father's tenure as President of BLE. As head of the organising committee, he had brokered a deal for Kerrygold to sponsor the Championships, the most significant international sporting event to have taken place in Ireland in over a decade.

It was also an opportunity to showcase John Treacy who would be defending the title he'd won the previous year in Glasgow. Ireland had a great team lined up. Treacy, Danny McDaid, Tony Brien, Mick O'Shea, Eddie Leddy, Gerry Deegan and myself – but I was only considered a back up man.

On the day of the race, there was a torrential downpour. The rain didn't stop the 35,000 punters who'd travelled to the course to be part of Irish athletics history.

Though mud-splattered at the end Treacy defended his world title successfully while I finished in 70th position to earn a silver team medal as Ireland took second place. The championships proved to be a huge financial success for the BLE. My father, along with his committee, invested the profits by purchasing a house on Prospect Road in Dublin which would become the official headquarters for the Federation.

My new found fame as a celebrity runner got me invitations to all kinds of events from charity dinners to the opening of new night clubs in Dublin. I got tickets to Broadway shows and always got a good table at restaurants.

One in particular was an invitation from Trans World International to take part in *The Superstar* broadcast by the BBC a made-for-TV trash sport competition.

It was the modern day version of reality TV.

My opponents included the Spanish golfer Manuel Pinero, who had finished fourth in the European Tour Order of Merit the previous year, and Police Constable Geoff Capes, the burly, bearded British shot putter.

I was not allowed to participate in the running event, but nonetheless held my own, winning the soccer skills and cycling event, while coming in second in swimming. My last-place finish in weight-lifting essentially eliminated me in the overall order of finish, which was won by the Dutch speed-skater Hans Van Helden.

The highlight of the Superstars came for me in the last event, in which I was pitted against Capes in the shooting competition.

This was at the height of the Troubles in the North of Ireland and I'd always fancied my self as a good shooter ever since I learned to fire a rifle as a young boy at the rear of the Church of Our Lady of Good Council in Drimnagh when Father Andy Sheehan thought me how to use a gun.

Being a cop, Capes obviously fancied his chances too. Just before we positioned ourselves on the firing range, he waved his gun around and acted as if he was a cowboy in a western movie, ready to draw his gun. He look me straight in the eye and said "I got you on this one Irishman," as if he was trying to intimidate me.

We took our aim and fired off our ten rounds at the target. It was hard to tell from a distance, but both of us appeared to have close to perfect scores. The judges took the cardboard targets down and carefully checked the pierced holes. When they announced the results, I had won by a single point.

Capes protested and called for a recall. The judge showed him the target board and said "Sorry Mr Capes, Coghlan won." He was pissed off and couldn't believe that I had beaten him – particularly at this discipline.

In June of that year, Ron Stanko had organised a big international meeting calling it the Brooks Meet of Champions in Philadelphia. The mile was to be a heralded meeting between me and Sydney Maree.

Sydney had come to Villanova after I'd graduated, though I'd heard all about his developing exploits when he was a junior runner growing up in South Africa. Bert Lancaster first put him in touch with Jumbo Elliott who eventually brought Sydney to Villanova.

Because of the boycott over apartheid, South African runners, even black South African runners, were essentially quarantined, and prevented from running internationally. In other words, because the South African regime had discriminated against blacks in their own country, the IAAF's response was to discriminate against them everywhere. This always struck me as wrong-headed, and Jumbo obviously felt the same way.

Even though it became a political issue when Jumbo gave him a scholarship, the IAAF were powerless to ban Maree from competing in American intercollegiate meets. It didn't take Sydney long to establish his credentials as the leading college athlete in America. He went on to break my Villanova records and won the NCAA championships.

Maree had style and grace. The first thing you noticed about him was his smile. He was as black a black man as you're ever apt to see, and those beautiful white teeth served to accentuate the smile. He was quiet, and always impeccably dressed.

I'd always felt badly for him because he wasn't allowed to compete at the international level and was I looking forward to racing against him in Philadelphia. But, once again politics got in the way and Sydney wasn't allowed to participate in the race. The word came down from the IAAF that if Maree ran, everyone who ran against him could be contaminated and would face sanctions.

The world's media were there to cover the meeting but their attention was not on the competitions but, instead focused on the political issue. Most athletes, Walker, Masback, Dixon and myself were prepared to run but being the gentleman he was, Sydney withdrew from the race and saved us any potential fallout from IAAF rulers.

I won in 3:52.88. It was the fastest mile in the world that year, and my best outdoor figure to date.

Although he couldn't run, Maree watched the race from a spot in the stands near the finish line. After I did my lap of honour, I went back over to him, and he reached over the railing with both hands. *Sports Illustrated* ran a double centre page picture of the two of us with our arms locked in a sign of peace and friendship.

The story was as much about Sydney being kept out of the race as it was about my winning. I was also the featured on the cover of SI. This was my third cover picture.

The Golden Miles

In the late 1970s, looking to establish itself as a tourist destination, the oil-rich Emirate of Dubai had proposed hosting a series of track events, but it quickly became apparent that most of the world's top athletes were reluctant to travel to the Persian Gulf.

As an alternative, the Dubai officials arrived at a sponsorship arrangement with the IAAF. In return for a "donation" of nearly half a million dollars from the sheikhs, the IAAF would present eight Dubai Golden events over the next three years.

The first of the so-called Golden Miles had been run in Tokyo in September of 1978, and was won by Britain's Steve Ovett, but when it came time to defend his new title at Oslo's Bislett Stadium the following July, Ovett would be a no-show.

"Why should we have to go to Norway?" he sniffed, "the best milers are British. Let the rest of the world come to us."

Many other athletes were frankly embarrassed by Ovett's churlish attitude.

"He reminds me of the lift operator," said Rod Dixon, "after he's reached the top, he'll have to come down again, and then he'll meet all the people he was rude to on the way up."

In Ovett's absence, Norwegian promoter Arne Haukvik had rounded up a thirteen-man multi-national collection which included virtually every other top miler in the world: Walker, Scott, Wessinghage, Moorcroft, Masback and I were there. So were Steve Lacy and the Australian Ken Hall. Scots Graham Williamson and John Robson were included in the field, as were Takishi Ishii of Japan and the host nation's top miler, Bjorge Rudd.

Rounding out the field was Sebastian Coe, a twenty-two-year-old Briton who just ten days earlier had established a new world record in the 800 metres, posting 1:42.4 on the same track.

Both Coe and myself were somewhat dismissed in the pre-race speculation. Coe had never before raced a mile in such significant company, while my heavy indoor schedule was supposed to have taken its toll on me.

On the day of the race, I went out for a jog around an idyllic fjord near the Panorama Hostel and met Seb Coe. He was venturing into what were for him uncharted waters, and he began asking me what to expect later that evening.

I pointed out that fifty-seven second laps would be fully six seconds slower than his 800 metre pace and that he should be able to handle that with little effort. But, he expected "those stamina men" to exert themselves in the third lap, and wasn't sure what his own response would be facing into the last.

I knew Seb was acting up a bit and probably testing my responses to reinforce a bit of confidence. I'd seen him run magic 800s and I knew he had a 3,000 metre background from schools competitions. I could see the political glee in his eyes and knew well that this guy was bursting to let loose his mile talent.

Coe was smart, calculating and always meticulously well prepared. I knew he wouldn't run in this company if his father Peter didn't think he was up for it.

American Steve Lacy, suffering from a cold and realising that he had little chance himself, offered take the pace out early and stay there as long as he could. That was a wonderful development for the race promoters, because up to that point no one was prepared to be the rabbit.

Lacy's sacrifice had an unsettling effect on me; I was tired and planned to run conservatively in the hope that I'd be in with a kick over the final 200 metres.

There was a real sense of anticipation about the race. Athletics fans who come to the Bislett stadium every year for this meeting are some of the most knowledgeable in the world. More records are broken at this stadium than any other worldwide. There are only six lanes and it is more like an indoor arena because of the proximity of the spectators to the runners who cheer and bang the side advertising hoardings making a thunderous noise.

On that memorable summer's evening in Oslo, Lacy took off at a ferocious pace as if he was running a 100 metre sprint. Immediately, I knew this was different, this was serious business – I'd never experienced anything like it before.

I was dead last around the first lap and expected the pace to ease for the second. But the leaders kept pushing. By the time I hit the back straight, I knew I had to get back into contention, and passed several runners, but made up little ground on those in front. Scott had by now taken over the lead from Lacy.

With 500 metres to run, Coe drew up on Scott's shoulder, and passed the American before the bell. At about the same spot, Walker was in the process of overtaking me when he heard the leader's three-quarter split – 2:52 – and realised that his four-year reign as the world record-holder would end in less than a minute.

As Masback passed me early on the fourth lap he looked at my face and he saw a look of rage.

I was thinking "Of all the people to be passing me now, Craig F***** Masback."

Eamonn Coghlan: **A life in pictures**

"It was the most profound running experience of my life – different to anything that had gone before. It really meant nothing to anyone else in the great scheme of things. But to me it was an emotional and physical triumph beyond my wildest expectations. Nothing compared to the feeling of ecstasy that enveloped me when I crossed that line."
Eamonn Coghlan on becoming the first athlete over forty to run the mile in less than four minutes.

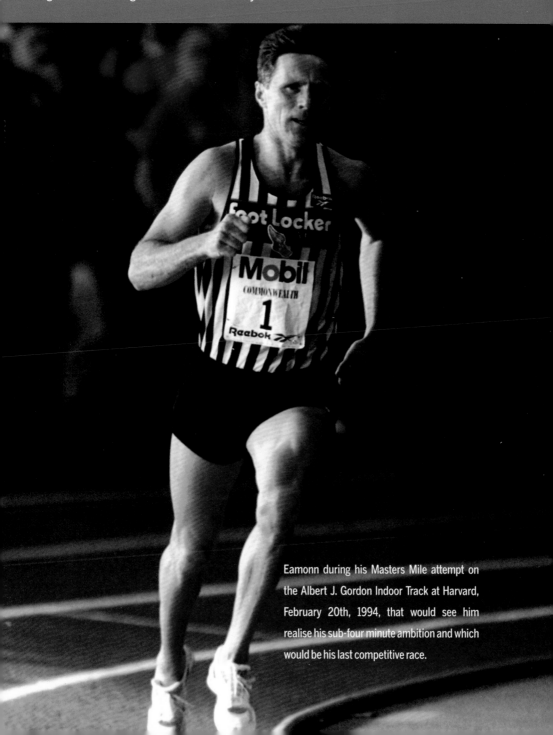

Eamonn during his Masters Mile attempt on the Albert J. Gordon Indoor Track at Harvard, February 20th, 1994, that would see him realise his sub-four minute ambition and which would be his last competitive race.

This page, top left: Eamonn in his pram, summer 1954. Top right: First day on campus, 1971. Right: Out with Yvonne in 1973. Above: Winning his first NCTAA Mile in Cobo Hall, Detroit, 1975. Far page: Eamonn winning the Under-14 Dublin Cross Country Championship in 1967 – his father hid behind a tree (far right) as Eamonn passed. This is the first photograph of Eamonn ever published in a newspaper.

Eamonn's mother, Kathleen, and father Bill at home on Cooley Road, Drimnagh, with Eamonn and some of his haul of trophies and medals in the background.

Eamonn and Yvonne on their wedding day 28th October, 1976. They were married in the Church of Our Lady of Dolours in Glasnevin.

Eamonn, Suzanne, Eamonn Jnr, Yvonne, Michael and John at Eamonn Jnr's graduation from The University of South Alabama with a marketing degree in 2005. Suzanne works with Anglo Irish Bank in corporate lending. Eamonn Jnr is a golf club professional in Azalea Country Club, Mobile, Alabama. Michael is currently involved in promotional work in Dublin and is pursuing a career in the media. John is following in his father's footsteps and has achieved All Ireland Championship success on the track. He is studying engineering at DCU.

At Suzanne's (front right) wedding to Ravesh Lalloo (front left) in 2007, are the Coghlan clan. Back row: Bill, Mary, Eamonn, Ann and Brendan with Mrs Kathleen Coghlan (centre) front row.

Shortly after breaking the World record for the 4 by 1 mile relay at Belfield on August 17th, 1985. From left, John O'Shea, founder and chief executive of GOAL, Frank O'Mara, Marcus O'Sullivan, Ray Flynn and Eamonn.

Bill Coghlan, Tom Gregan, Eamonn, the legendary Jumbo Elliott and John Hartnett at a gathering in Villanova in 1974.

Backstage with Bono and Adam Clayton at a U2 concert in the Meadowlands, May 1987. Yvonne was pregnant at the time but wasn't due for a fortnight. The day after the concert she went into labour and Michael was born that evening.

Eamonn with Ray Lumpp (left) and Jim Rafferty of the New York Athletic Club, who were major influences on Eamonn's career.

That sinking feeling: John Walker celebrates his win in the 1976 Montreal Olympics. Eamonn trailed home in fourth behind Ivo Van Damme (103) who took silver, and Paul-Heinz Wellman who took bronze.

This page, top: Legends on the run in the shape of Eamonn, Thomas Wessinghage, Steve Ovett and John Walker in the 1983 Golden Mile in Oslo. Above: Running in the Mobil Grand Prix Stockholm 1993. Left: Friend and countryman John Treacy, Marathon silver medallist in the 1984 Los Angeles Olympics. Far page: Winning the British AAA's Championship, 5,000 metres, 1979. Mike McLeod (22) finished second ahead of Rod Dixon (not in picture)

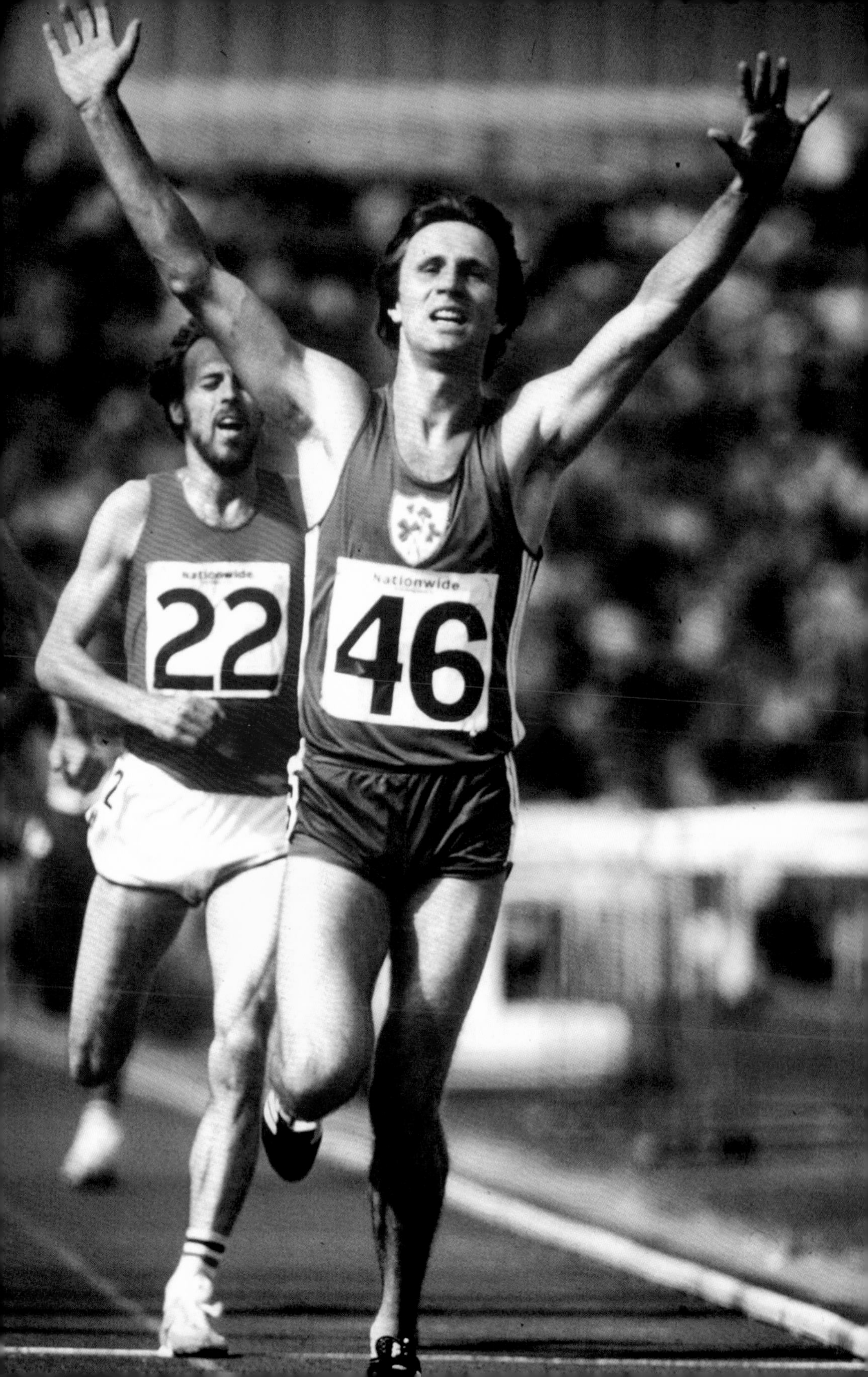
Nationwide
22
Nationwide
46

Worth waiting for: Eamonn crosses the line to win the 5,000 metres final in the World Championships, Helsinki, 1983. Far page: The decisive moment as he passes Dmitri Dmitriyev on the final turn and expresses both joy and relief at the same time.

Past and present: Eamonn with world indoor hurdles champion, Derval O'Rourke, at the 2006 Texaco Sports Awards, during which Eamonn was inducted into the Hall of Fame.

Right: With fellow Villanova graduate and Olympic silver medallist, Sonia O'Sullivan, at the New York marathon in 2002.

Once he got by Scott, Coe ran freely and easily, gliding to the tape and a new world record with me back in fourth in 3:52.5 – a new Irish record and a personal best.

The Golden Mile had been an astonishing and history-making event. Before I'd left for Oslo, Al Franken asked me to persuade Coe to come to the US for the indoor season the following winter. I knew Franken thought that by having Coe v Coghlan, it would guarantee sell-out crowds at his promotions in LA and San Diego.

While the prospect of this match up sounded appealing in principle, I thought "The American indoor circuit is my territory and my turf. Why would I want Sebastian Coe to pitch up?"

I never delivered the message.

To Russia with the runs

When the Soviet Union invaded Afghanistan in December of 1979, it provided the pretext for a United States led boycott that would eventually see dozens of nations withdraw from the 1980 Moscow Games – the second of three consecutive Olympiads whose composition was dramatically affected by politics.

American President Jimmy Carter initially attempted to exert pressure on the International Olympic Committee to cancel or move the games, but, having failed at that, persuaded the USOC to announce its withdrawal the following April.

Many nations, including West Germany and Japan, subscribed to the American position and followed suit. Other US allies, including Great Britain, France and Italy, endorsed the boycott in principle but left the final decision to their respective Olympic Committees, all three of which opted to participate.

The boycott dashed the Olympic hopes of my Villanova team mates Don Paige, Mark Belger as well as my friends Steve Scott, Edwin Moses and Mary Decker.

A group of dissident American athletes who disagreed with the government position filed suit in an attempt to overturn the boycott. The court ruled against them on the grounds that the USOC was a private organisation and therefore not subject to the usual constitutional protection. The court also claimed that since the USOC had made its decision by secret ballot, the argument that it had been pressured by the administration was insufficient to cause it to fall under the realm of "government control."

In the end, eighty nations participated – sixty did not. Some of the latter countries allowed their athletes to participate in an ex-officio capacity. (When those athletes won medals, no flags were raised, and the Olympic hymn was played in lieu of a national anthem.)

Since a boycott was never seriously entertained in neutral Ireland, I would get a second bite of the Olympic cherry.

Months prior to the 1980 Olympics in Moscow I rejoined Metropolitan Harriers. I had felt bad for the previous years that I'd somewhat abandoned Gerry Farnan when I transferred to Donore. With his health in serious decline, I thought it appropriate that if I win the gold medal, I should do it as a Metro man. There were no hard feelings with the Donore lads. They knew exactly where I was coming from and respected my decision. They even made me an honorary life member of their club.

For weeks prior to the 1980 Olympics, I had a pain in my shin. I attended numerous doctors but to no avail. The Irish team left for Moscow in mid-July, but I had decided to stay at home in Ireland until the last moment so as not to get caught up in the hype. My races were only over the last couple of days and I felt that there was no point in sitting around Moscow for two weeks.

Prior to Moscow, I ran seven races in a stretch of nine days. When I look back at it now, I realise it was madness. In my diaries from that summer, I complained non-stop about the drag in my leg, but I continued to train exceptionally hard between races with what only months later would be diagnosed as a stress fracture in my left tibia.

But that was only the start of my problems leading up the Olympics. On Yvonne's birthday – a mere nineteen days prior to my departure – we went out for a bite to eat. Half-way through the meal I began to feel clammy and queasy. By the time I got home I was violently ill and spent most of the night vomiting to the point of pain.

I spent the next week in bed. I was in a pitiful state. One doctor diagnosed me with the flu, while another diagnosed an inflamed gall-bladder. I could barely summon the energy to get to the toilet let alone entertain any thoughts of training.

When I emerged from that frightful experience, I was as weak as a kitten. I traipsed up to the track at Belfield as though I were facing the gallows. I did a 3,000 metre time trial with Jerry Kiernan who didn't like the look of me, or the time I clocked. I might have done better with a Zimmer frame.

Meanwhile the word from Moscow was grim with reports of sickness running through the Irish camp prompting me to take a five-gallon drum of water when I finally departed on July 26th.

Of course the sight of this large drum of liquid aroused all sort of interest when I touched down in Moscow. Hauled into a customs room, I had to spend an hour trying to convince suspicious officials that it was good, clean, healthy Irish water. Or so I hoped.

By the time I checked into the Olympic Village, I was feeling tired, gloomy and not at all impressed.

The Olympics are usually a celebration, but in Moscow there was a pervasively joyless, almost military atmosphere. Everywhere you went you'd have to queue up and show identification; once you reached your destination it would turn out to be another drab depressing place.

Yvonne came to Moscow accompanied by her sister Patricia. My father was there too as President of the Irish Federation. I thought their presence would be a diversion from the competitive pressures of the games.

But the opposite proved to be the case. I wasn't allowed anywhere close to their hotel and even meeting up casually proved to be a major undertaking.

I had arrived into Moscow just in time to see Steve Ovett beat Sebastian Coe in the 800 metre final. The big build up to this duel proved to be somewhat of an anti-climax. Ovett pounced Seb at his usual spot, 230 metres out, and established a gap Coe was unable to make up. It was regarded as the major shock of the games; Coe was the world record holder for the 800 metres and Ovett wasn't rated over the 800.

I ran into Seb in the Village the following morning. He was visibly upset over the result, which had come as a complete surprise to him.

Coe and I arranged to go for a jog together that afternoon, and when we met up along with Ray Flynn, his father Peter was with him. There was a bit of small talk, mostly Peter moaning on and on over the fact that Seb hadn't won the race.

I remember thinking "Gee, he ought to be delighted. He still won a silver medal, and that it was not as bad as finishing fourth," but they had taken it badly – not just because Seb lost the gold, but because of who won.

There was no love lost between Coe and Ovett. Peter said that his son would come out really hungry in the 1,500 metres later in the week. He was right. Coe won the final impressively, leaving Ovett back in third place.

As Seb and I ran, my mind kept straying from the conversation to the pain in my shin. I didn't say anything to him about it. I didn't say anything to anyone in Moscow – I reckoned that if I told anybody, it wouldn't be long before the other competitors would know about it, too, and they'd be like sharks smelling blood in the water.

My plan going into the Moscow Olympics was simple: "Don't win the heats, don't win the semi-final and keep all the aces for the final. Keep the opposition guessing."

This was my mantra during preparation for this redemptive race, the one that would banish the misery of my fourth place in Montreal.

But as I got my mental approach right, the body once again let me down – the stomach bug made an unwelcome return and with it came a non-stop dose of the runs.

I barely got out of the heats to qualify for the semi-final, and I somehow picked up enough energy for the semi-final to miraculously qualify in third. It's relatively easy to hide any weaknesses in the preliminary rounds and I managed to keep my difficulties a secret.

I found myself able to block out the pain in my shin – that wasn't a problem. But the bug had massively depleted my energy reserves, and you can't hide from that.

I had one day of rest before the final and hoped against hope that I might find some energy, something to pull me through the final.

Dr. Moira O'Brien, the Irish team doctor gave me some tablets. "Don't worry," she told me in her best bedside manner, "this will put a plug in the hole."

It did and I was grateful for the respite – but still no energy – just a feeling of emptiness and one of impending doom.

The 5,000 metre final line-up was strong. I knew the main danger would be posed by Mirits Yifter, the ageless Ethiopian known as Yifter the Shifter. He had already won the 10,000 metre gold medal five days earlier and I thought that he might be jaded after his efforts.

Yifter was a legend. He had spent his youth working in factories and hadn't begun to run competitively until he joined the Ethiopian Air Force. He was at least thirty-eight, and possibly as old as forty-three that year in Moscow. No one had a clue how old Yifter actually was. He enjoyed the mystery.

"Men may steal my chickens, men may steal my sheep, but no man can steal my age," he said when pressed on the subject by reporters the day before the race.

He had been an Olympian since 1968, and had won a bronze medal in the 10,000 in Munich in 1972. The African boycott in 1976 had cost him a chance to compete in Montreal, but he came to the 5,000 final having impressively won the 10,000 metres in 27:42.7, with Finland's Kaarlo Maanika second and Yifter's countryman Mohammed Kedir third.

All three would be running as well as Suleiman Nyambui of Tanzania who qualified as the fastest loser, Switzerland's Markus Ryffel and my compatriot, double

World Cross Country Champion, John Treacy. I tried my best to ignore them before the race. I had enough problems to contend with without worrying about them. While this was the Olympic final I tried to trick myself into thinking it was only another race. I believed that if I could muster up a little bit of strength I could handle Yifter's speed on the final straight. I believed he was more worried about me than I was about him.

From the moment the race started, I felt utterly depleted. My legs felt heavy and there was no bounce in my stride. It was like driving on two flat tyres. The pace was average and it allowed me to stay in contention and hide in the pack.

Over the final two laps, we were all bunched up together with no one willing to make a move. It seemed like they were playing right into my hands as we gathered at the bell. I was cruising, still strongly in the hunt in an attacking position safe on the outside. Or so I thought.

I'd kept Yifter in my sights. He was boxed in against the rail and I held him there while the other Ethiopian, Kedir, maintained the lead. As we entered the back straight with 300 metres remaining, I entertained serious thoughts of winning. As if to order Kedir moved out wide creating a gap for Yifter who I tried to keep Yifter boxed in – but he made it through. I took the lead briefly to test him but he responded immediately launching his attack for home 250 metres out.

I was in trouble then and there. I was too all-out trying to stay with him instead of being in a controlled stride pattern. I simply hadn't another gear in me. I kept digging deeper and deeper looking for a kick, but it wasn't there.

Halfway through the final turn Nyambui passed me, but not with such great speed. I thought I could run at him again. Then on the final straight I felt my legs, my arms and my wobbling head betray me. I could feel sweat pouring from me as though I had turned on a tap.

There was nothing in the tank. Déjà vu, Montreal, 1976. A living nightmare.

Yifter heading for first. Nyambui in second, and I'm third, struggling and agonisingly hanging on to my third place. Suddenly, it all slipped away. The Finn, Maaninka caught me over the last few metres.

When he flashed by it was like I was crying for help. I was pleading, trying to summon the energy to stay with him, but it just wasn't there.

All I could think was "F*** it. I've blown it again." Unlike 1976, where my failure had been a shock to the system, this time, because of what I'd endured in the weeks leading up to it, I had all the excuses in the world. I had run a perfect tactical race but simply had no fuel in the tank.

This, I thought, is what the Olympics is all about, getting it right on the day. It's not a case of not having the talent – it's more a case of luck not being on your side.

Finishing fourth in the Olympics is regarded as the worst possible position. To finish fourth on two occasions almost seems absurd.

And like all world-class sports people who have failed to translate their raw talent into victory or a medal, it's a burden that I have had to deal with virtually every day of my life.

Living with failure

U p until the 1980 Olympics, I'd commuted back and forth to the States between racing and training. My performance in the Games was another disappointment and when I finished fourth again Gerry took it even harder than I did. He had retired from the fruit trade and had opened a snack bar called The Snug on Little Mary Street, in the heart of the markets.

He had to listen to all the slagging from his customers. They'd pile in for their feed of greasy bacon, eggs and sausages and declare "Ah, that f***** Coghlan is useless, he couldn't run to catch a f***** bus."

It was typical inner-city Dublin slagging. They were built up once again, only to be let down. Gerry had so much belief in my ability to win Olympic gold, my losses profoundly hurt his pride in front of these know-alls.

I was ready to give up running. I was twenty-seven and was gripped with a profound sense of gloom.

Ever the optimist, Gerry Farnan said "No way, you're still a young man and there is plenty of life left in those legs. Go back to America and live full-time. Go there and make some real money, because you're not going to do it here in this f***** begrudging place."

He was right. Yvonne and I talked of expanding our family and getting on with our lives abroad.

I approached the Irish Tourist Board in Dublin and asked Joe Malone about a transfer to the New York office. Joe obliged, working behind the scenes to broker an arrangement with Donal McSullivan, who was Bord Fáilte's Executive Vice President for North America.

Before taking up my formal position as Youth and Educational representative in Bord Fáilte's New York office, Yvonne, Suzanne and I headed for San Diego for the winter. Yvonne was now pregnant again and we were expecting our second child in June. On the flight to America was Roddy Carr, son of the legendary amateur golfer Joe Carr.

Roddy had played on the winning Walker Cup team in 1971 and had recently begun working for Mark McCormack's International Management Group (IMG) in Cleveland, Ohio and was managing several of their clients – Seve Ballesteros among them.

Four days after our chance encounter, Roddy and another IMG executive, Peter Smith, came knocking on my door. In the early Eighties, track and field was moving from under-the-table payments toward what would become outright profession-alism, with prize money and guaranteed appearance fees. IMG had recognised the potential and were looking to jump on the elevator while it was still at the ground floor.

The two guys told me they had signed up Sebastian Coe and marathon runner Bill Rodgers, and they thought they could increase my income substantially. I agreed to meet with them in New York the following month at the Millrose Games.

When Gerry Farnan urged me to relocate to America, he had suggested four new goals for over the next four years.

To become the first person to run under 3:50 for the indoor mile.

To win the European 5,000 metre title in Athens in 1982.

To win the first IAAF World Championships 5,000 metres in Helsinki in 1983.

To win gold in the Los Angeles Olympics in 1984.

This was typical of Gerry's approach to life.

"Lets forget the past and move positively on to the future," he'd remind his athletes. Four more years of grinding it out to fulfil the dream of becoming an Olympic champion!

From the time I was a young boy he had an unrelenting belief and a faith in my ability to run and to win at the highest level. It was luck he felt was against me. Not talent.

In the twenty-five years since Bannister, four minutes in the mile had become relatively commonplace, at least among the world's elite milers, but a sub-3:50, Gerry reminded me "Would represent a milestone in athletics history."

I had by now been coined "The Chairman of the Boards," because of my unbeaten streak of wins on the boards. Joe Goldstein, a public relations agent in New York gave me this moniker as part of a publicity campaign to promote the Millrose Games.

The nickname stuck. Every event I attended, whether it was a race, a dinner engagement or television appearance, I was always, and still am to this day, intro-duced as "The Chairman of the Boards."

By the start of the 1981 indoor season the thoughts of running under 3:50 for the mile was a fantasy – I had barely overcome both the effects of the illness and the stress fracture which had hampered my performance in Moscow.

For several months, I only managed a little jogging daily and certainly no track speed workouts.

But the indoor season was where my bread was buttered and I had made advance deals with the meet promoters. I was in an average state of fitness, but clearly not at the top of my game when I agreed to run my first mile race, as a favour to friend Ray Flynn in a low-key event he helped to organise at his old college, East Tennessee State University. Ray invited several friends and rivals too – Don Paige, Steve Scott and Ray himself would be among the starters.

When I showed up at track-side, I was ridiculed by my opponents live on television. During my post Moscow convalescence, I had managed to acquire the beginnings of a pot-belly. Assistant meet promoter Flynn, who was wearing a tuxedo, couldn't restrain himself from joking about my middle-age spread.

Scott and Paige joined in and made a complete fool out of me. I held back and smiled and remembered thinking "F*** you guys, I might be out of shape now but I'll get your asses before the season's over."

Paige won the race from Scott and Flynn but under the circumstances I was pleased to clock 3:59.1. I began to think that if I could get a few good weeks of speed work in I might after all be ready to crack a good one. I was quietly confident I could go under 3:50 before the season would end when I left Tennessee and returned to my training base in San Diego.

Training in the warm San Diego weather allowed me to get my speed right back and three weeks later I beat Scott running 3:54.3 in the Los Angeles Sports Arena. One week later I ran 3:53 flat winning my fourth Wanamaker Mile. The time was a Madison Square Garden record, one that would stand another twenty-four years before being broken by two-hundredths of a second by Bernard Lagat the future World Champion at 1,500 and 5,000 metres.

Having run that fast on what was universally regarded a slow track, I was more encouraged about my prospects of running under 3:50 before the season ended.

I met with the IMG at their New York offices in the General Motors Building on Fifth Avenue. Roddy Carr and Peter Smith met me in the lobby and escorted me upstairs, and in short order Mark McCormack himself appeared.

"Come on, we'll go into Arnold's office," suggested McCormack, and the next thing I knew I was sitting in Arnold Palmer's chair in an awe inspiring office filled with all sorts of golf memorabilia.

They spoke of maximising outside income. They said they could get me commercial endorsements – shoe contracts, apparel product endorsements, better appearance fees, speaking engagements and what have you. For this, they would charge their standard 25% commission on everything earned, but their financial services people would look after my credit card bills, my insurance, stock market investment advice and even pay my mortgages.

It all sounded impressive and exciting as I sat in a high pressured situation in Mr. Palmer's office. They were looking at me and waiting for an instant decision. At the end of the meeting I said "I'll tell you what: I'm already making around fifty grand on the indoor circuit, I have a shoe contract with adidas. There's no point in my paying you for what I can get on my own already, but I'll pay you 25% on whatever additional income you can generate beyond that."

They agreed and almost the next words out of Smith's mouth were "Can we have your roll-a-dex?" IMG didn't even know the names of the indoor race directors or for that matter the promoters in Europe.

I stayed with IMG until 1986. They eventually signed up John Walker and Steve Scott as well, but their contract with IMG was even briefer than mine.

Neither the IAAF nor the Athletics Congress in the USA were particularly happy with IMG's appearance on the scene – it was somewhat premature because the meet promoters weren't keen to enter into negotiations with them. Up until then relationships and financial deals were on a personal basis with no agents involved nor even allowed. Breaking this psychological barrier was going to be a long, hard process.

With only a few months to go before the birth to our second child it was difficult leaving Yvonne alone with baby Suzanne as I zig-zagged my way around the USA and Canada.

Media attention in my career was once again building up in Ireland – the ghost of Moscow, just like Montreal had vanished. I would frequently get calls from the *Irish Independent's* Tom O'Riordan, the *Irish Press's* Jimmy Meagan or the *Evening Press's* John O'Shea looking for a scoop or advising me how I should run.

Every Saturday morning, RTE Radio's Jimmy Magee from would call for an exclusive live interview. RTE television didn't cover the races but ITV in Great Britain did have exclusive coverage on Dickie Davis's Saturday afternoon sports programme. Dickie spoke fondly about my exploits in America, but as though I were a British rather than an Irish runner.

Before I'd make my record attempt in San Diego, I returned to Canada for two more successful outings where I clocked back-to-back meet record runs in Toronto and Ottawa. The Ottawa track was a tiny, shallow banked, thirteen laps-to-the-mile set-up. My 3:57.9 time was acknowledged as a world record for an "undersized track." However, an incident in that race would cast a shadow over the following week's showdown with Scott and the world record attempt

During the final lap, I made a split second decision to cut-off Scott. You never want to pass somebody on the turn indoors, especially on an extremely tight thirteen-lap track, so I figured it was now or never, and as we went into the final turn. I cut right in front of him and knocked him completely off stride. It was like roller-derby. He gave me an elbow and I gave him an elbow back, but I got into the lead, took off with 40 metres to go and won. He was not pleased.

Steve didn't lodge a formal protest, but he did complain to anyone who would listen, including the Canadian press. He declared "I'll get him back in San Diego next week and I'll break his world record!"

I flew back and trained on the San Diego ocean-front for the next week. With the racing I had done to date, I thought it more important to rest rather than trying to train hard. I didn't want to leave it all behind me on the training track.

There was a huge amount of hype leading up to the Jack-in-the-Box Invitational but I did my best to avoid wasting any mental energy talking about the race to the media. The less I thought about it the better.

Walker and Scott had predicted that there would be a world record and I knew Scott believed it would be he who'd get it. My only comment was that he might break the world record – but that he would finish second.

He was running well and he was hungry for revenge.

But, I felt confident and believed the pressure was on Scott. I didn't want a world record, I wanted to run under 3:50 and I wanted the action to be stronger than pre race words and predictions.

I needed help with my task and recruited my former Villanova team-mate Tiny Kane to do the rabbit job for me. Having Tiny take the pace would even make a statement and I knew I could trust him to deliver for me.

On the night of the race, I was watching the six o'clock news when I heard the announcer saying "We're live from the Sports Arena. Coming up tonight we have American Steve Scott and New Zealander John Walker running against Eamonn Coghlan, and they're going to go for the world record for the mile. Beside me here now I have Steve Scott to talk about what we should expect tonight…"

Scott was doing a live interview, and I thought "Here it is only 6.30pm. The race isn't for another four hours or so. I'm sitting home in my living room relaxing, and he's already at the arena!"

Great," I thought, "he'll be mentally drained hanging around that place all night."

In the course of the interview, Scott made reference to the fact that I'd cut him off the previous week up in Ottawa, said he was going to make Coghlan eat the track later that evening. I just laughed – I was going to be burning it up.

There was always a bit of distance between Steve and I. We communicated, we talked, but it wasn't with the sort of camaraderie I shared with most of the other top runners. Ours was a rivalry, and it was a strained relationship – especially when we were competing in California, which he regarded as his home turf.

Later that night, I took out a Metro racing vest with the big capital M emblazoned on the front which I'd borrowed from Tommy Swift when I'd rejoined the club and decided to wear it rather than my Discover Ireland one. Since returning to the club, I had won a few local races in Ireland and believed that wearing it here in San Diego would be a good omen. I then took my superstitious look in the mirror, smiled and shook my fists at myself.

"Go for it," I said. I felt terrific.

I arrived at the arena an hour-and-a-half before race time. I checked out the scene inside and could see all my fans in their "Flamin Eamonn" green t-shirts in the best seats close to the finish line. A great cheer erupted as I did a test run out on the track, looking for any potential loose spots and then got away from the action and went outside to take my warm up jog around the car park.

It was now just half-an-hour before the race and there were all these people carrying Irish flags emerging from their cars and drinking beer. It was like a tailgate party you'd see at an American College football game.

I knew that Scott believed that I'd go with either half a lap or a full lap to go, but on this night I decided to surprise him and go into gear with two full laps to go – making one move and one move only.

Tiny tore off from the sound of the gun and went through the first quarter in 56.3 seconds. Scott followed with Walker taking up third position and me in fourth.

It was critical that I imposed myself mentally on the guys while at the same time maintaining a really smooth running pattern.

Tiny kept the pace through half way in 1:55.6 and three quarters of the way through Scott, who I thought would try and box me in, had taken over in 2:55.4.

But I now had Scott where I wanted him, and with exactly two laps I seized control of the race and surged past him to thundering noise – stunning Scott who never responded to my move.

I wound up running 3:50.6, a new world record. It was the sixth fastest ever, indoors or out and the fastest on American soil.

While I jumped and danced around the track with Tiny, the media were surprised to find me disappointed in my post race interviews. It wasn't the world record I wanted, I explained, it was the first sub-3:50 barrier I had come to do and I had failed by just over half a second.

These were the new demands I was putting on myself and reflected my growing sense of belief. What was once regarded as impossible – running faster indoors than out – was now a reality.

I desperately wanted to be the first to run under 3:50 but realised I had time on my side – or so I hoped.

Unstrapped for success

We returned home to base ourselves in Ireland for the summer European outdoor season. Yvonne gave birth to our second child Eamonn Jr. A fine lad he weighed in at eight-and-a-half pounds.

While my profile soared in the United States with my indoor wins, my stock remained questionable at home: My Olympic performances continued to plague me, and I was more or less written off by the Irish media as a has-been.

Not one athletics correspondent from Ireland made the trip to Rome for the IAAF World Cup where I was selected to represent the Rest of Europe team in the 5,000 metres, even though I had won a few meetings on the Grand Prix circuit.

One writer described my career as "An old athlete whistling by the grave ready to fall in."

Adidas had the contract to provide gear for the European team and their latest line of running shorts had built-in briefs – in other words built in jock straps.

Theoretically, this was a vast improvement over the system we'd used back at Villanova. There, you just grabbed a jock off the rack, wore it, and then threw it back into the laundry. You always got a clean one, but in a sense they were community jock straps.

Since I knew we'd be wearing adidas in Rome I hadn't packed a jock, but when the gear was handed out it turned out the shorts didn't have built-in jocks after all.

I had to point out this embarrassing oversight to Kay Guy. Kay was the wife of Al Guy, BLE's international secretary. Years later, both Kay and Al would be responsible for catching three time Olympic swimming gold medallist, Michelle de Bruin, with the botched urine sample now renowned as the Whiskey in the Jar episode.

Kay had been assigned the Rome duty as a perk, and when I mentioned the jock problem to her, she said "Don't worry, I'll get you one."

I thought no more about it.

When she came back to me on the morning of the race, I was momentarily flattered and then alarmed; she had considerably over-estimated that which needed to be supported. Not only was the cup too large, but the waist size was 34 inches, instead of the 28 size I was wearing then.

There was no time to look for a replacement, so I had to improvise using a large safety pin, similar to one you'd use to tie a baby's nappy, before I headed off on the team bus to the Olympic Stadium.

It was a hot and humid day. Somehow, between my warm-ups and my pre-race stretching, the safety pin came loose and disappeared and my jock was hanging down through my shorts.

I completely lost my racing focus as I struggled for a remedy. I didn't know whether to withdraw from the race or just take it off and run sans jock. I was just positioning myself on the starting line when suddenly I heard a voice from the stands "Hey, Steamin' E-min!"

It could have been only one person – Jack Nash, my one-time Villanova roommate, dressed in his full naval officer's uniform and looking as though he wanted to chat while here I was, less than thirty seconds away from the start of the World Cup with something of a problem dangling from my shorts.

"See you later," I shouted as I struggled to maintain some degree of dignity.

For the first couple of laps I held onto my jock strap. Every time I let go of the damn thing it would fall down and I soon found myself falling completely out of touch with the leaders even though the pace was a pedestrian 74 seconds per lap.

With four laps to go I told myself "This is bullshit," and determined to make a move. I could just hear the television commentators at home, saying "He lost in '76, he lost in '80, and now in another world championship event, Eamonn Coghlan can't do it when it counts."

I put the jock strap out of my mind, took off, and eventually caught up with the front runners and, with a lap to go, hooked up in a race with Hansjorg Kunze of East Germany, the two of us racing the final 400 metres in 52 seconds.

I held him off and put the win down to a combination of determination and fear. I was frankly worried about the criticism I was bound to get back home, and I knew that if I didn't win, nobody was going to want to hear about a jock strap.

The following day's Italian papers had a photograph of me crossing the line, arms outstretched and an oversized jock strap dangling from my shorts between my legs.

I returned to New York shortly after to run in the inaugural Fifth Avenue Mile – the brainchild of promoter Fred Lebow who was determined to put on a spectacular show.

Fred's powers of persuasion were such that he got every top miler in the world, save Ovett and Coe, to run in New York that September. John Walker, Steve Scott, Steve Cram, Ray Flynn, Mike Boit, Thomas Wessinghage, and Sydney Maree and myself all committed to run in it and I got tied up promoting the race, which would finish on Central Park.

But by the time September rolled around, a controversy was brewing. IMG had brought BBC on board to televise the race back to the United Kingdom. When the Beeb heard that I intended to compete wearing my Discover Ireland vest, the Beeb threatened to pull the plug on the grounds that the slogan represented overt commercialism.

They sent word that they wanted me to wear something else. I said "No way. It's my country. What's commercial about that?"

I wasn't sure whether it was the word "discover" or the word "Ireland" they objected to, and stood my ground.

I also knew Fred wanted me to run more than any other athlete he had recruited: Fred was smart and knew the value of the Irish support I had amassed in America and my presence in the Fifth Avenue would support ABC's television ratings.

The race sponsors tended to side with me, noting that I had officially registered the Discover Ireland logo with the Irish Federation and that it had been approved for competition.

The pro-Coghlan faction decided to turn the tables and seize the initiative. Press agent Joey Goldstein arranged for a photo-op of me posing on the steps of St. Patrick's Cathedral, wearing a business suit opened in the front to reveal the purportedly offensive Discover Ireland t-shirt.

The resultant coverage was huge – the story ran in the New York papers and television stations, and produced a backlash against the Brits, with the Beeb eventually backing down in the face of the outcry.

Hundreds of thousands of New Yorkers lined Fifth Avenue to watch the race, which Maree won in 3:47 with me finishing a tired ninth. It was late September and the long season had taken its toll and I couldn't find the reserves to deliver a decent performance in front of my new "home" fans.

They were now very much home fans: we had taken the decision to relocate to Rye, New York, where we rented a large, four-storey "mother and daughter" mansion, otherwise described as a semi-detached.

Rye was known at the time as the capital of the Irish Mafia. When he worked in America, Joe Malone had been one of the first of the Irish to live in the Westchester town.

Living in Rye, with its close-knit Irish-born community, gave us a tremendous sense of stability. While they knew of, and were very proud of, my accomplishments on the track, to our Irish neighbours we were just Eamonn and Yvonne from Dublin. We regularly socialised and entertained in one another's houses, and the big Irish hangout was a pub called Kelly's on Midland Avenue.

From the time I was a boy, Gerry Farnan had always insisted on my incorporating one day a week of complete rest into my training regimen, and over the years Friday had traditionally been my rest day.

For the first three years we were in Rye, I was working for Bord Fáilte, commuting to the city each day on the New Haven Railroad to the office on Fifth Avenue. Fridays developed into something of a ritual.

I'd wait for the later train, which had a bar-car, because I knew I'd run into the other Irish fellows. We'd have beers on the train, and once we reached Rye we'd go to a pub near the station called the Mug & Ale for a few pints. It was almost like home.

Donal McSullivan was suave and debonair, and was known as Mister Irish Tourism in America. He looked after me exceptionally well and gave me the necessary time to train.

While McSullivan was courtly, Joe Kennedy, who was in charge of the New York office, was a tough military man who'd been up in Canada before being transferred to the States. He was going to make sure the board got its money's worth out of me.

My main job at the time was to go around to the different universities in the USA promoting Irish Tourism.

When I was to visit a campus, my arrival would be announced by a promotional campaign that said "Eamonn Coghlan Knows Ireland – He Runs It!"

It was a hands-on job. I recall travelling on a private plane out of New York and landing in a field up at Oneonta College, where I was to speak to the students. We landed in a blizzard, and reindeer came right up to the plane when we taxied to a stop. I was picked up in a four-wheel jeep and taken to the college – only to discover that not a single student had showed up.

From the late 1970s onwards, it seemed as though whenever anything controversial happened back home I was sought out for a response. If there was a bombing in the North, I was unofficially expected to be a voice for Ireland.

I used to have *The Irish Times* and the *Indo* mailed to me so I could keep up with the home news and tried to stay reasonably well-informed, but – particularly once I was working for the Tourist Board – I was careful to steer clear of political and sectarian matters.

Over Thanksgiving of 1981, I was invited to run for the first time in the Manchester Road Race up in Connecticut. Historically there had been a strong Irish presence in this event. It had been founded by the Tall Cedars of Lebanon, which was an offshoot of the Orange Order, and several years earlier a fellow named Pat Tierney had brought Danny McDaid over from Ireland to compete. His motive was to bring in Republic of Ireland athletes as a counterweight to the more visible presence of athletes from a different tradition.

I wore my green Discover Ireland running vest and I won the race in record time. A few days after I returned to New York I was called into McSullivan's office.

He produced a photograph of me winning the race from a newspaper and said 'What's this?"

I was wearing my green vest and my number – 26.

Donal said that word had come back that I'd intentionally worn the number to represent the 26 counties of the Republic, and that the people up in Manchester were making a political issue of it.

When they'd issued me the number I'd never given it a thought. Looking back on it, somebody probably did give me that number intentionally, but it had meant nothing to me at the time.

"You're right," I told McSullivan. "They probably should have given me No. 1."

On my 29th birthday – November 21, 1981 – I was matched against the great Kenyan Henry Rono in an International cross-country race at Belmont Park, the race course on Long Island.

I respected Henry enormously; he was tough as nails and an absolutely incredible runner. Three years earlier, in the space of just eighty-one days, he'd broken four world records – at 10,000 metres, 5,000 metres, 3,000 metres, and the 3,000 metre steeplechase.

The boycott had cost him a chance to run in the 1976 Olympics, but later in the summer of '78 he won gold medals in both the 5,000 and the steeplechase at the Commonwealth Games.

I managed to beat Rono every time I ran against him, whether it was cross-country, indoors, or outdoors. Years later, Henry became a high school coach in New

Mexico. I beat him that day at Belmont Park. It was right after that I began to notice an unremitting pain in my left leg.

A good race – but one I would remember for all the wrong reasons – it was the harbinger of one of the worst years of my life that would be dominated by one feeling and one word. Pain.

Pain – total pain

The pain really started in January 1982. I thought I was suffering from shin splints, and sought advice from one of my new running partners, Dr David Thomashow. X-rays revealed that I had a stress fracture of the left tibia. This diagnosis belatedly confirmed that the injury was the same one that had hampered my training leading up to the Moscow Games the previous year.

I was ordered to stop running for six weeks wiping out my indoor season and my second attempt to run under 3:50.

It also hit me hard in the pocket being a case of "No dash, no cash."

It was my first taste of serious injury and it was to effectively keep me from running for an entire year.

I grew impatient, frustrated and depressed. I was hired by NBC to do some television commentary and while I valued the experience I would get incredibly frustrated when I saw Steve Scott winning races in relatively slow times.

I never realised how much running meant to me. I was okay when I was in control and able to run, but I became a crank and a moody son of a bitch when I couldn't. Yvonne was far from happy with my attitude, which cast a pall of gloom and unhappiness in the household. It was a trying time for her as she tried to bring up a young family as well as cope with grumpy Eamonn.

In the solitary confinement of the basement in our home in Rye, I attempted to maintain fitness with workouts on a stationary bike in the hope of getting back for the outdoor season and, in particular, for the European Championships which would take place in Athens later that summer.

For four hours a day, I'd pedal away with an altitude simulator back pack, which looked like an oxygen tank with a face mask strapped around my head. This would help increase the amount of stress on my heart and lungs and by the end of the rehabilitation period I'd be cardiovascular fit and ready to get straight back into running training immediately. At least, so I thought!

Six weeks later, Dr Thomashow gave the all clear to resume training. I brought my running gear along and we agreed that if he said it was okay, we'd go on a slow jog from his office.

I was so excited to get the all clear and anxiously headed out for my first run in weeks. But after just a few hundred yards I had to pull up with a ferocious pain in my Achilles tendon.

"Doc, I'm f*****," I said.

"Come on Cogs, you're only joking," he responded.

I thought the pain in my shin was bad, but this was different. This pain was concentrated in an area no bigger than the size of a pinhead, right on the back of the calcaneus – the heel bone. If I applied pressure a millimetre from the epicentre I felt nothing, but to gently touch the spot would cause an excruciating amount pain. It was like someone jamming a nail right into the bone.

I saw my whole world ending there and then in front of my doctor.

Over the following months, there was no sign of the injury clearing up. I'd get out of bed in the morning and it would take half-an-hour before I could so much as stand on it, let alone walk. I used crutches just to get across the room to go to the bathroom.

I had cortisone injections to see if they'd help. They didn't.

It was put into a cast for a few weeks in order to immobilise the foot. That didn't work – in fact the pain was worse – it was frightful.

It was a living hell for me. I thought "This is it – my career is over." I had heard stories about Ronnie Delany's career ending as a result of an Achilles injury and I feared this was my turn. I was scared by the thoughts of "What will I do if I cannot run again?"

The longer the injury dragged on the worse I became. I started drinking a lot more beer than I was used and began to pile on weight. Drinking became something of a refuge.

I felt that, in the absence of running, life had no real meaning.

Even playing with the children, Suzanne and Eamonn Jr. became a chore – I was simply going through the motions without any real commitment.

As if that wasn't enough, I got a phone call from my father to tell me that Gerry Farnan had dropped dead in his living room and had been found there by his eight-year-old son, Robert on his return from school. While Gerry struggled with his health for years, the news of his death was a shock. I no longer had his shoulder to lean on.

I flew back to Ireland for the funeral deeply upset – it was though I had been injected with a chemical such was my despondency.

It was a funeral similar to Jumbo's a year earlier; but while Jumbo's bond with his former runners was powerful, Gerry's was even more so. Jumbo made time for the best athletes, but Gerry made time for everybody.

Over the years he'd taken kids from the streets of Ballyfermot and Drimnagh and fostered them, building up their self-esteem, irrespective of whether they became great runners. And if a kid was short a few quid, Gerry would give it to him.

All of those people showed up for the funeral. Tears flowed that day and I was no different to the hundreds who mourned a much-loved man.

Gerry's death forced me into action and I made a huge effort to pull myself out of the slump – but first I needed to get fit. While I knew I wouldn't be ready for the European championships, I had to hope for some sort of a cure from the pain.

A chance encounter with my old rival, Thomas Wessinghage, who was studying to become a doctor back in Germany, paved the way to my rehabilitation.

Wessinghage had always seemed more like a doctor than a miler. His calves always seemed to be bigger than a runner's should have been, and he was invariably serious, almost profound, and gave the simplest question deep thought before answering. At the end of the day he probably over-analysed everything – including his running. He was invariably friendly and courteous, though, and he was particularly helpful on this occasion.

Thomas couldn't believe that I was still out with the same injury, and recommended I see a Professor Klumper in West Germany. Professor Klumper specialised in Achilles injuries, and Thomas was sure he'd be able to help.

Our journey to Klumper, who was attached to the University of Freiburg, bore all the hallmarks of a trip to Lourdes so desperate did I feel.

Our spirits sank when we pitched up at his office to find that he was away on holidays and that his assistant, a Dr Dietmann, would see us. I didn't want to see him, I wanted the main man. I was close to tears.

But we had come too far to turn back and I took some solace when he announced "I vill be able to solve your problem for you."

I was taken into an operating theatre, where I was given an injection of some vitamin substance and then told to lie face-down on the table. Then he brought down this machine, stepped out of the room, pressed a button, and zapped me with a dose of radiation right at the spot of the injury.

"Okay, you can go now," he told me. "I vill see you again in two days. In ze meantime, I vant you to jog for ten minutes zis evening."

"Jog?" I thought, "you must be joking." I hadn't jogged a step since that day in

February. I could barely stand on it.

"No," insisted Dr. Dietmann. "You vill jog."

That evening we drove to nearby Zurich where the Weltclasse athletics meeting was taking place.

I put on my gear and went for a light run with John Walker and Ray Flynn who was at the time emerging from my shadow. Ray, from Longford, would be the first Irish person to run under 3:50 for the outdoor mile – a record which stands to this day at 3:49.77.

There was still considerable discomfort, but I was able to make my way around for the prescribed ten minutes, only half listening to Walker's conversation while at the same time wondering was I going to be all right.

Two days later we drove back to Freiburg for two more blasts of radiation treatment over the next two days and two more runs of ten minutes each day. By the end of the treatment we flew home to Ireland with just the hint of an ache, and by Sunday one week since we'd left for Germany, the pain was gone.

"It was," Yvonne recalls to this day, "a miracle." I not only had Dr Dietmann to thank, but also one of my most competitive opponents in Thomas Wessinghage who went on to win the European Championships in Athens. I was delighted for him.

When the pain completely disappeared, I vowed myself off the beer and dedicated myself to return to complete the mission which Gerry and I had set out on. To run under 3:50 for the indoor mile, to win the World Championships 5,000m in Helsinki and the Olympic Games in Los Angeles.

I had learned from my mistakes and I planned on not doing anything stupid again, like over training. I'd been out for nine months, so I was going to be cautious.

Odd injuries, aches and pains have a habit of disrupting your preparation and my goal was to stay clear of anything that might cause one.

Every day, twice a day I met Marty Ludwikowski in the Rockefeller Estates to train.

Marty was my great pal who was a high school superstar but struggled somewhat at the collegiate level.

He had graduated from Manhattan College and worked in the athletics facility. Marty devoted himself to me. It was as if he sacrificed himself to help me achieve my goals because he felt he had gone as far as he could. He was always the one to pull me up and push me along.

He understood my moods.

Hail, rain snow and even ice-storms we battled every day towards getting ready for the indoor races in 1983. At times it was tortuous. Three evenings a week, on top of the twice daily running workout, I'd go to the magnificent indoor corporate gym in Pepsi Cola's world headquarters in Purchase, New York.

This multi-million dollar facility was the first state of the art gym built for corporate fitness for employees. I had become friends of some of the executives since they'd sponsored the Fifth Avenue Mile and I was invited to use their facility as often as I needed too.

While sweating it out here doing my weight training and stretching exercises I'd blast out U2 songs – their success and their sound was inspirational as I battled my way out of the doldrums towards what I hoped would be a hugely successful 1983. I was focused more than ever before to prove to myself and to the world that I could deliver where it counted. At world class level. Nothing was going to stop me this time. And I was happy.

My father's final race

Prior to the start of the season, the meet promoters doubted that I could return to top form after a year's absence. "Is Eamonn still Eamonn," one declared. Satisfied in my own mind that the comeback was on track, I proposed he pay for my performance only. "But it'll cost you more if I win."

"The Chairman of the Boards is back," declared an article in the *LA Times* following back to back wins against the man who helped my recovery – Thomas Wessinghage – in the opening two races of the 1983 season.

Delighted with the results, I rang my father in Dublin and invited him to the States. I was scheduled to run in the Millrose Games in the Garden, in Toronto, in Dallas the following night, and then back in the Meadowlands in New Jersey to run in the Vitalis Olympic Invitational.

I thought he'd love the idea of travelling around to the meets being treated like royalty, because I knew he was a bit down following my injury strewn season the previous year.

Getting off the plane at Kennedy Airport I thought he looked awful. His face was as white as a sheet. I asked him if he was all right and he said "I'm grand. It was just a long flight, that's all."

At the Millrose Games that Friday night, I easily won my fifth Wanamaker Mile, clocking 3:54.4, with Wessinghage again a distant second, 40 yards up the track in

3:57.95. Afterwards, Dad and I crossed the street to the Pennsylvania Hotel to attend a Villanova reunion that was in full swing. Later, as the party wound down, the throng moved en masse over to the Old Stand pub to the "Eamonn Coghlan Room" for the usual post race piss-up and sing-song.

Gregarious by nature, Bill usually loved meeting up with my friends and former team-mates at these gatherings, but on this night he sat quietly on his own away from the excitement.

I thought I had said or done something to annoy him because he was in dreadful humour. I was almost making excuses for his rudeness and put it down to jet lag and tiredness.

By Monday he seemed to be feeling better, and accompanied me to Manhattan College for a track workout at their indoor facility.

I was running three by three-quarter mile repeats, and he was timing me. He was announcing my times as I came through, and they'd all be 62, 61½, 60 as I'd pass each quarter mile split. I couldn't figure out what was going on. He was giving me times a second or two slower than I was actually running them. I ended up doing them all in 2:58 each.

"I wanted to push you a little bit harder," he told me when he confessed to the subterfuge.

Before we left the gym that evening, he insisted on challenging me to a race over sixty metres.

"Oh, come on," I implored, "let's get to hell out of here." But he insisted, as he still fancied himself as a bit of a sprinter at sixty-three. So we had a bit of a race.

He was staying in our third-storey guest-room. As he climbed the stairs that night, Yvonne later recalled, he mentioned that he'd felt the pain in his arm again and that he felt indigestion as a result of eating Mexican food.

I was up early with the children for breakfast the next morning.

"Where's Granddad?" I asked Suzanne.

"He's still in the bed... will you go see what he's doing chicken?" I suggested.

Suzanne returned with the news that Granddad was still asleep.

I thought it odd that he was asleep in light of the five hour time change, but decided to let him have his rest. Once the children had been fed I went out for a six-mile run. When I returned he still hadn't come downstairs, so I went up to check on him.

As I climbed the stairs I felt that something was terribly wrong. When I opened the door, there he was, seemingly asleep with a smile on his face. Behind him on the wallpaper an ocean-side scene, with the sun setting behind the sea, formed a backdrop to his still form.

"Dad, are you getting up?" I asked once, then again more anxiously, "come on, get up, you lazy git!"

When I reached out to touch him I realised that he was dead. He was freezing cold, and rigor mortis had set in. When I lifted his head I saw that all the blood had drained to one side of his head.

I didn't cry – the tears would come later.

I simply didn't believe it. I went to the door and screamed for Yvonne.

"Yvonne, Yvonne. He's dead."

Somehow I suspected it when I went into the room.

My friend Dr Tomashow came immediately and told us that he had probably died from a massive heart attack. He explained that he could order a post-mortem, but that if he did we might be dealing with it for a matter of some weeks. The other alternative was that he could sign the death certificate, in which case we'd be able to get the body back to Ireland straight away.

"Whatever you think is appropriate," I said quietly.

The New York Times, February 2, 1983

RYE, N.Y., Feb. 1 (UPI) —*William Coghlan, father of the distance runner Eamonn Coghlan, died during his visit today at his son's home here while on a visit from Ireland. The sudden death of his father, who had come to the United States in hopes of watching his son set a world best indoor time in the mile, forced Coghlan to withdraw from Friday night's race in Toronto, where he was to oppose Alberto Salazar, and Saturday night's indoor meet in Los Angeles. Coghlan will go back to his native Dublin and return in time to compete in the US Olympic Invitational at East Rutherford, N.J., on Feb. 12, a spokesman for the meet said.*

Dave did a fuller examination and filled out the death certificate. I was still in total disbelief as we went down to funeral home to select a coffin. We chose a very large lead lined one suitable for air transport.

I kept saying to myself "Why in God's name did this have to happen here and why now, just as I was getting ready to run the best times in my life." I dearly wanted him to see me at my best and that would now never happen.

My boss in the Tourist Board, Donal McSullivan, did everything he could to make arrangements for us to fly his body to Ireland and we managed to get him home the next night.

There was a huge attendance at his funeral at the church on Clarendon Street, where he'd attended mass since he was a boy. The police escort from the church to

Deansgrange Cemetery would have made him proud.

Then when they went to lower him into the grave, the coffin wouldn't fit. The big casket we'd brought from America was too wide for the grave, so we had to wait there while they dug it out further. He would have got a laugh out of the fuss created.

I stayed in Ireland for another week and before I went back to the States my mother pulled me aside and said "Eamonn, don't be blaming yourself for what happened to your father. He was where he wanted to be and he got to watch you run in Madison Square Garden. All you can do now is go back to America and break that world record. That's what would make him happy."

With those words ringing in my ears, I returned to New York feeling older, sadder and conscious that I had lost the three most important men in my life in a short space of time – my Dad, Jumbo and Gerry Farnan. Death can be a wake-up call and I vowed to make the most of what remained of my career and to honour the effort and time those three men had put into my life.

Record breaker

A couple of years earlier, when the New Jersey Sports Authority initially had gone to build the track at the new Brendan Byrne Arena, I was asked by Ray Lumpp to consult in its design.

Ray was meet Director for the Olympic Invitational and agreed to move the meeting from Madison Square Garden to the New Jersey venue. Ray valued my opinion on how the banks and turns should be shaped and got me a contract with the Authority. They went for a ten lap to the mile track, instead of the traditional eleven, made the banks steeper than in San Diego and placed fibreglass underneath the two inside lanes to give it more stability.

The previous year I had pointed out a serious flaw with the bends on each of the turns – about a metre of straightaway appearing in the middle of the arc, which would break a runner's stride and possibly result in a fall. The New Jersey people wanted to have the fastest indoor track in the world, even faster than San Diego's, and a world record in the mile – preferably one set by Eamonn Coghlan – would achieve that distinction for them.

They took my advice and re-shaped the turns.

I'd arrived at the Meadowlands two days before the US Olympic Invitational to test the track. It was perfect. Then, as I was driving back to Rye I found myself in a massive snowstorm – the Blizzard of '83.

The storm tied up the entire East Coast of the United States. I-95, the New Jersey Turnpike, the George Washington Bridge, they were all closed down. It took me five hours go get from the Meadowlands back to Rye, a distance of just over thirty miles, and by the time I arrived home word came through that the meet had been cancelled.

Ray had had little alternative to pulling the plug. Not only could spectators not get to and from the arena, but most of the athletes had yet to arrive, and since the airports all along the east coast of the US were closed, they had no way of getting in.

The chances of breaking the 3:50 barrier in the Meadowlands appeared to have completely disintegrated with the blizzard. Then Ray came up with an idea.

The US National Indoor Championships at the Garden were traditionally scheduled to be the final indoor meet of the year, but Ray Lumpp approached me and asked point-blank "If I can get the Olympic meet re-scheduled in the Meadowlands on the Sunday after the Nationals, do you think you can break the indoor record?"

In a word I responded "Yes."

Exercising remarkable diplomatic skills, Lumpp managed to get the meet rescheduled – the world record attempt was on. Head of US Track and Field Ollan Cassell wasn't happy with the move. He thought I'd pull out of his meet to favour the Meadowlands. I didn't however, and won in 3:57 two days before the re-scheduled Olympic Invitational.

Two of Yvonne's aunts from Ireland were visiting on Long Island, and unbeknownst to me, Yvonne invited them to the house in Rye on Saturday.

I was far from pleased and fearful that having to play host might disrupt my concentration. I got into a huff and decided to spend the night in seclusion. I didn't need to pretend to be nice. I was in my pre-race bad mood and did not want anyone around.

I drove off to New Jersey and checked into the headquarter's hotel, the Meadowlands Hilton, a day early, arranging for two limousines, one to collect Yvonne and the children the other for the aunts the following day to take them to the meet.

I felt bad about being rude but decided I wouldn't call Yvonne to apologise. I knew we'd probably argue and I didn't need any hassle to upset me or the positive energy required to attack the record.

After the race would be good enough, I surmised. Besides, I always remembered Gerry telling me that a true champion athlete had to have the mentality of a "Mean selfish bastard going into battle."

Lumpp, the meet promoter, had arranged with ESPN television network to show the mile live, at halftime of that afternoon's Los Angeles Lakers versus Boston Celtics basketball game. That meant that the starting time was pegged to the progress of the NBA game and we wouldn't know until just a few minutes beforehand exactly when we would be called to the start, but it was projected to be at 5.00pm.

After a light morning run and breakfast, I opted to stay penned up in my room away from all the pre-meet activity in the hotel lobby. Around three o'clock the phone rang. It was Ray Flynn calling.

"Oh sorry, I hope I didn't wake you. Am I interrupting anything? Sounds like you're a bit groggy. Just wondering what time you are heading over to the meet?" he asked.

"No, just relaxing," I responded.

The only thing he had interrupted was my mental and mathematical preparation. I had just written four figures down on a piece of paper: 58, 1:56, 2:54, 3:49.

"I'll meet you at 3:30 in the lobby and we'll take a lift over to the arena together."

With that, I stuck the paper into my diary. A short time later when I changed into my running gear, I rewrote the final time 3:49 on the insoles of my racing shoes and took my usual good-luck, superstitious look in the mirror, smiled and shook my fists at myself and said "You big bollox, this is it, kick ass, this is what you've sacrificed your life for."

I then left the room on a mission I knew I could achieve.

The Brendan Byrne Arena was hopping with energy. I could sense the expectation from the knowledgeable crowd most of whom had turned up for the mile.

At exactly 5:00pm, the half-time buzzer sounded between the Lakers and Celtic basketball game. My pre-race warm up was spot on and I was in a mental zone the like of which I had never before experienced.

I felt the tension but ignored the slightest hint of distraction as fans roared to me from their seats. I could see Yvonne and the kids by the start line and knew by the nervous smile on her face that my rude behaviour of the previous night had been forgiven.

ESPN television came over live to the Arena. Ray Lumpp did his job and had given me my chance to create athletics history. I had no choice but to go for it with all my might and energy.

I had recruited Ross Donoghue my New York Athletic Club team-mate and former Villanova runner, to be my unofficial rabbit. I didn't sit down with him to discuss the plan. Marty Ludwikowski did that. Ross knew what I needed done up front and didn't want it officially mentioned that he was a rabbit. He was a very talented runner in his own right, and would have thought that an insult.

The draw had Ross Donoghue on the inside lane, me next, with Flynn, Scott, Jose Abascal of Spain, Todd Harbour from Santa Monica and Jay Wood from Brigham Young on the outside. It was perfect. I feared no-one. Scott might be the danger man but he hadn't won a race for some time.

Ross went straight into the lead, and Abascal made a move as if he intended to jump right in behind him. At that moment I made a split-second decision – "No Way!" – and instead I cut right in front of Abascal and into second place.

I got myself into position right behind Donoghue, who took us through the first quarter in 56 seconds. Right on time.

"Relax, just sit behind him," I said as if talking to myself. We followed Ross in Indian file reaching the half way mark in 1:56.

"Great, I feel easy," I thought and then nudged Ross on the hip, more or less telling him to push on, push on, go faster. But, to my astonishment, he had enough and dropped out of the race.

I was on my own and forced to take up the lead. I was now the rabbit for the runners behind with just less than half the race remaining. I didn't panic. I was flowing I just decided to keep going as hard as I could. The slightest lapse in pace could be the difference of hundreds of a second – and the record lost. I didn't even hear the time at the three-quarter mark, but with two laps to go I could hear from the excitement generated by the audience that someone was coming up on my right shoulder.

I assumed it was Scott and that spurred me on. I didn't look back. That would be a sign of weakness to my pursuer. I didn't hear the three-quarter mile split, but I knew I was on target. All the lessons I had learned since my days in Villanova and on the circuit over the years came in to play.

I ran close to the inside curb. I leaned very low on the turns, catapulted off the steep banks into the straights and simply flowed painlessly along. I kept going and going putting on more pressure, running as though I was a runaway train. The crowd of 12,000 packed into the arena were on their feet, clapping and shouting – encouraging me all the way. Even the athletes competing in field events took time-out and stood in the infield to cheer me along the way.

Sprinting my way through that last lap was the most exhilarating rush of speed I ever experienced – on any track – any time. I felt like I was running on a cushion of air. There was no pain, no distress, nothing holding me back. I could put my foot on the gas and go at will. There was just a positive flow of energy pushing me effortlessly all the way beyond the finish line.

When I broke through the finish tape I threw up my hands up high in celebration and looked up at the clock. I knew I'd done it.

"That," I sighed to myself, "that was for you, Da."

The overhead clock had unofficially timed me in 3:49.6. Almost immediately an ESPN commentator came running over to me and said "Eamonn, it's not official yet, but it looks like you may have gone under the 3:50 mark..."

I turned and said with a grin "No, I know I've gone under the 3:50 mark!" I knew I had never run that fast before and I knew the feeling was totally different than any of the hundreds of races I had competed in all my life. I was sure I'd done it as I danced the Irish jig around the track on my lap of honour.

A few minutes later, the official time was announced:

"Ladies and gentlemen. In first place in a new world record, the fastest time ever run on American soil and the first person in history to run a mile indoors under 3:50 in a time of three minutes and forrr...." The announcer was drowned out by the cheers and couldn't be heard. But I saw the official time going up on the board 3:49.78 and jumped for joy. "And second, Ray Flynn, in…"

"Ray Flynn? Holy Shit!" Until that moment I'd thought it had been Scott challenging me. I was thrilled to learn that it had been Ray, who ran 3:51.2.

Scott was third, setting a new American record of 3:52.28 and Abascal wasn't far behind, in 3:52.56 in a new Spanish record.

My projected splits had been eerily prophetic. The final time was exactly that which I'd written into my shoe.

Yvonne and the children had made their way onto the track and my first words to her were "I'm sorry for last night."

"Don't be stupid," she said, "I knew exactly what you were going through. Congratulations and well done."

For my world record performance, I didn't get a financial bonus. Ray gave Yvonne a fabulous $3,000 fur coat. "You get everything," he said, "it's her turn to be rewarded for helping you."

Becoming the first person in history to break the 3:50 barrier was only part one of the plan set out by Gerry and me after the disappointment of Moscow. I had no time to sit back on my laurels.

After a short period of rest it was back to the grindstone in preparation for part two; the first IAAF World Championships to be staged in Helsinki, Finland the following August.

I had now moved from the sports pages to the front pages of newspapers all over

America. The Discover Ireland slogan on my racing vest gained enormous publicity for Irish tourism. IMG had negotiated a better deal with adidas for shoes and clothing and with Pepsi Cola. Pan Am provided us with first class fights wherever and whenever we needed them. Guinness contracted me to launch and promote their new non-alcoholic beverage, Kaliber, flying me to and from the USA on Concorde to record television commercials.

Life could not have been better for us as we settled into the community in Rye. I was invited to Radio City Music Hall in New York to take part in and television special call *The Night Of One Hundred Stars*. It was an awe-inspiring evening. Here was I, the kid from Drimnagh, on stage with some of the greatest sports legends in the world.

One of my heroes was Muhammed Ali. I used be allowed up in the middle of the night to listen to his world heavyweight title fights on radio. Here in Radio City, I got to meet the Man himself in person.

Before the show went on air, I went into the bathroom to freshen up. Right beside me washing his hands and looking in the mirror was Ali. Just the two of us – all alone.

"How's it going?" he asked. I couldn't believe he was talking to me.

"Oh great," I said.

Then I boldly proclaimed looking at myself in the mirror, "Hey Ali, you know what man?"

"What's that?" he replied.

"I can't wait 'til tomorrow."

"Why's that?" he responded.

"Cause I'm getting better looking every day."

Well he cracked up with laughter and turned to me and said "I like that man, give me a high five."

"Wow," I thought to myself. Here am I in the loo in Radio City Music Hall "high fiving" it with Muhammed Ali.

Meanwhile back in Ireland on a short promotional visit, I had a most bizarre encounter when *The Runner* magazine decided to do a cover story on me. I had taken renowned athletics photographer Steve Sutton on a journey around the Dublin and Wicklow mountains. He also took shots of me in doorways of Georgian Dublin and then up to where I started my running career, the Phoenix Park.

I was always proud to tell visitors about the Park and loved returning home to train there. Steve wanted to capture the cover shot for the magazine there at a specific time when the early evening light would be at its best. We went to an area near the flower gardens and I posed at the base of a hill with the green grass acting as the backdrop.

He was all excited with this spot, when we were confronted by a park warden. "You cannot take commercial photographs here with out permission," he said.

I kept quiet while Steve explained that we weren't taking commercial shots and that he was with Eamonn Coghlan.

"I don't care who you are taking photos of, you cannot take photos here without written permission from the OPW," he went on to say.

I then explained that the photos were not commercial but for a sports magazine and that I'd had my photo taken here hundreds of times in the past.

He got really pissed off and said he'd call the Gardaí if we didn't move off. "Listen sir," I said, "this is a sports story giving a positive image of Ireland in America and besides I work for Bord Fáilte, if that well help. We only have a few minutes of light left, please let us finish."

"No stop now," he said and moved off.

Five minutes later a Garda arrived and told us that we had to obey the park warden.

I called Tom O'Riordan in the *Irish Independent* and relayed the story.

Next day the OPW issued a statement to say that I'd face six months in jail for breaching park rules. As it turned out we got the photograph from one of the first pictures taken before the warden had arrived and it appeared on the cover a month later – as well as photos of the warden arguing with me.

From April – feeling distracted by all the attention – I decided to stay at home in Rye and go back to my twice and sometimes three times a day training.

I put Jumbo's philosophy back into action "Live like a clock, get up at the same time, eat at the same time, train at the same time, and Goddam it shit at the same time every day."

There would only be family distractions: Taking Suzanne to infant school in the morning, playing with baby Eamonn, walking the dog and doing the odd bit of DIY. It was a rather simple life wrapped around the training routine.

Sometimes athletes get carried away with success. You can sit back, become complacent and take your talent for granted or, you can over do it, constantly looking for better performances out of your body. It's a fine line trying to establish the perfect balance.

In my view, doing too much is more dangerous and I didn't want to fall into that trap. I'd approach the World Championships with the same tenacity as preparing for the sub 3:50, but I had to be patient and very careful.

New Zealander Rod Dixon, a bronze medal winner in the Munich Olympics at 1,500 metres and a runner who I greatly respected, moved in to the Rye area to prepare for his forthcoming marathon début in the New York City Marathon and I had him to train with on long runs through the Rockefeller Estates.

Rod was also a relaxed person and loved to party off the track. He didn't get all caught up in training, training, training. He was great at motivating me and I believe I was a big help to him. All in all the balance between my personal life and my athletics career was perfect – it needed to be as I prepared for the next and possibly one of the most significant races of my life – the first running of a 5,000 metre World Championship race at Helsinki.

The early 1980s, athletics was undergoing a dramatic transformation. The tradition of 'shamateurism' and under-the-table payments had given way to a more realistic means of compensation. The IAAF had not only accepted the commercialisation of athletics, but had made a bold move to cash in on the trend by establishing a quadrennial World Championship that would bring together the sport's best athletes in an international carnival.

The first of these had been announced just before the Moscow Games, and although he wouldn't live to see Helsinki himself, Gerry Farnan had been quick to grasp the impending significance of the event.

Heretofore the International Olympic Committee had dominated in promoting athletics as the centrepiece of sport's greatest festival. While this had been beneficial for the Olympics, the IAAF had remained in an ancillary role.

From the athletes' standpoint, the World Championships figured to be even bigger than the Olympics. Not only would Helsinki be the first such meet, but it would be one conducted in an absence of the turmoil and politics that had characterised the Olympics over the years.

In the months prior to the World Championships my training was going great. I was injury-free and I felt stronger than ever. I was psyched.

I had a series of outdoor meets starting in San Jose losing to Scott in 3:56. Then I won a thrilling 5,000m in Eugene, Oregon in 13.23.3 running the last 400m in 52 seconds before getting revenge on Scott over the mile in Berkeley, California in 3:52.5. I raced myself into great shape and won a mile in Vancouver Canada all alone in 3:54 to break their All Comers record before departing home for the European season.

I was on a high coming to race in Europe especially Oslo where I was brought down to earth finishing fifth in the mile, even though I'd run a personal outdoor best in 3:51.5

Coming home to Ireland during the summer was always difficult. Training in Santry or Belfield was unlike New York for two reasons. Firstly the weather. Trying to battle the wind and rain was distracting and frustrating and then listening to people. Here it was always "How do ye think you'll do. Do you think you can beat those Africans?"

In New York you were guaranteed good warm dry weather and people would tell you "Hey man, you'll win!" It was always positive, positive, positive. It was this atmosphere and attitude I liked most of all.

I was invited to London to compete in the British AAA Invitational Mile at Crystal Palace. I hadn't been feeling well. I was suffering from a bit of a cold.

The race was being televised back to the United States, and NBC had built it up as a collision of the outdoor world record-holder Coe, the indoor world record-holder me, and the American indoor and outdoor record-holder Scott.

The race turned out to be a disaster for me. I had no bounce or no rhythm in my stride. I felt awful.

Scott surprisingly went on to win, Coe was second, and Graham Williamson was third. I struggled home fourth, in 3:57.61. I was really pissed off. I knew I could have run this time in training and here I was returning to Dublin, a melancholy figure, feeling sorry for myself.

With the World Championships just weeks away I was left thinking "Here we go again." Was I getting sick? Had I peaked too soon?

The questions filled my mind. It had been a year since Gerry's death and here at home in Dublin I was all alone, I hadn't got him to talk to. I needed his advice and shoulder to lean on.

On a whim, I visited Gerry Farnan's grave, the first time I had been to it since his death and the first time I saw the epitaph on his tombstone.

"Don't quit when you are beaten.

Fight back to an even more glorious victory

Not only in competition, but in life."

I thought "That's exactly what Gerry was teaching us kids when we were growing up. Don't quit, fight, fight, fight. It was an emotional moment. I bent down on my knees, said a prayer, as if I was talking directly to him and then plucked up a handful of grass from the grave and stuck it in my wallet.

"You'll be with me all the way," I whispered.

As I was about to leave I heard a voice.

"Mister, are you Eamonn Coghlan?"

It was to voice of a small boy.

"Yes, I am."

"Can I have your autograph please?"

I signed a piece of paper and headed off.

"Good luck in the World Championships, I think you'll win it."

Two moments of inspiration – in a graveyard.

For the following two weeks, I chose not to train hard, but rather allow the lost energy return to my body. No track workout, just jogging easy on the grass on the Polo Grounds of the Phoenix Park.

This is what Gerry would have suggested.

Redemption in Helsinki

I'd been reading the book *The Winner's Edge* by Dr Denis Waitley, when I arrived in Helsinki and it armed me with positive thoughts. Unlike Montreal and Moscow, I decided to walk in the opening ceremonies and take it all in and enjoy every minute of the World Championships.

Helsinki was ideal setting for the first World Championships. There would be no boycotts and there'd be more athletes competing than in the Olympics. Track & Field was almost a national sport in Finland, which had a tradition going back to the days of Paavo Nurmi.

The stadium itself was impressive. Unlike most venues in Europe, which had been built for soccer, this one had been constructed specifically for athletics. The crowd was nearly on top of you creating an intimate theatre similar to an indoor arena. I proudly carried the Irish flag around the stadium in the opening ceremony and felt that I was going to enjoy every bit of the championships.

I spent the first few days watching my friends and peers perform in their respective events. Grete Waitz won the very first gold medal, in the Women's Marathon. Mary Decker won the Women's 3,000. Carl Lewis won the 100 metres and the long jump. Greg Foster won the high hurdles, and Edwin Moses won the 400 hurdles.

When I'd see the Stars & Stripes go up the flagpole at the medal ceremonies, I visualised the Irish tricolour in its place. I wanted nothing to stop me from winning. When I officially registered and received my race number it was 442. I couldn't help think shit "Is this an omen? I got fourth in Montreal, I got fourth in Moscow. Does this mean second here."

I eliminated the thought immediately.

There was some controversy as to whether heats should be run. There would only be nine runners eliminated from the three heats and some countries wanted to by-pass them and go into a semi-final. But the organisers decided they didn't want to disrupt the programme and opted for the heats. It didn't bother me at all. There would be three races in the space of five days.

As a matter of fact, I felt that there would be some 10,000 metre runners doubling up and by having the heats and semis, they'd be tired by the time the 5,000 final would take place.

I'd already decided that I wasn't going to take the lead from anyone in the opening heats which were run in horrendous wet and windy conditions. I wanted to run as easily as I could to qualify and to conserve as much as I could both mentally and physically, even though I knew back in Ireland they'd already be speculating "Is Coghlan all right, or isn't he?"

But I had already learned the hard way – you do not look into or judge anyone on the strength or weakness they show in preliminary rounds.

Between the heats and semi-final, I relaxed. I'd read my *Winners Edge* take gentle swims, get massages and have the odd beer in the athletes recreation area come evening time. Anything to keep my mind away from running.

In the semi-final, I came second to the Russian, Dmitriy Dmitriyev, although I closed over the last 100 metres and caught him at the wire I knew I could have passed him but again, I was thinking "Winning the semi-final means nothing."

The Irish media were in a state of hyper awareness. I could sense the excitement from home. The scribes were more nervous about my prospects in the final than I was. I could understand – they had been down this road with me so many times before it must have seemed like an emotional roller-coaster mission to them. They wanted me to win this one as much as I did.

Yvonne had stayed back in Dublin so as I could focus on my job without having to worry about her "holidaying in Helsinki." She purposely withheld how much of a build up there was at home.

U2 were playing in the Phoenix Park, the All-Ireland football quarter-finals were on in Croke Park, Seve Ballesteros was leading the Irish Open at Royal Dublin, but the focus of attention from the public was Coghlan in Helsinki.

Doc Thomashow had come to Finland as a spectator and took me on a sightseeing tour on my day off between the semis and the final. During the course of our trip, we never once talked about running.

On our return, we went to the evening track session. I was sitting in the stadium with a bunch of friends and Irish team-mates, along with Jim Kilty, the Irish team coach, and Bobby Begley, who was there as the team manager, along with my agent Brad Hunt from IMG.

It was a lovely, sunny evening, and as we watched the track events play out, Brad asked me what I thought of the 5,000 field and where did I plan on making my move.

"Right there," I said, as I pointed down on the track to a spot 120 metres from the finish line.

"Don't you think you might be leaving it a bit late?" asked Brad.

"No," I replied, "right there and I'll make one move, and one move only."

Later that night I went to a social gathering at the athletes' village with Bobby Begley and some of the boys and had a couple of bottles of Heineken, which drew a few comments..

On the morning of the final, I woke refreshed and ready mentally to go into battle. I remembered *Winners Edge,* and all the positive advice offered by author Denis Waitley, so I made sure that I got out on the right side of the bed – where there wasn't a lot of room – and my room mate Louis Kenny who would run in the marathon later that day asked what I was up to.

"I'm getting out on the right side of the bed, got to start the day on the right foot." He thought I was touched.

Throughout the day I did my best to relax I tried to keep my mind off the race. I needed all the mental energy I could muster: Any thoughts that did creep in were to simply to remind myself not to run under pressure and to avoid trying to control the race from the front.

In sizing up the field I had pegged Thomas Wessinghage as the man to beat. The German doctor had been running well was the most experienced one in the race. Doug Padilla figured to be tough. The American had had a great indoor season, and had a history of winning 5,000 metre races at Madison Square Garden that matched my consistency in the Wanamaker Mile. Wodaj Bulti, another Ethiopian, had performed well in qualifying.

One wild card was Dmitriyev. Until I'd run against him in the semis two days earlier, but I knew nothing about him other than the Russians had a habit of producing surprises.

Another was Martti Vainio, who would be running before his hometown crowd and who had already picked up a medal in the 10,000 metres that week. I figured a fast pace might tire him out. Rumour had it that he was on drugs – he tested positive years later.

The East German, Werner Schildhauer, would also bear some watching. All in all, it was a strong field, but there was no one stick-out performer you could point to and say "He's the one to beat today."

I wanted to be left alone for the afternoon and told team coach Jim Kilty to go ahead of me to the stadium. As I changed into my running gear that afternoon, I could feel the tension run right through my body.

"This is it. This is what you've come here for, to be the World Champion."

As I did my checklist, I placed the vest, number, spikes, dry gear, water, towel, walkman and credentials into my bag when all of a sudden I thought about Gerry Farnan. I retrieved the blades of grass I'd plucked from his grave from my wallet, and tucked them into the key-pocket inside my running shorts.

"You might beat Coghlan once or twice, but by Jesus you won't beat him a third time." – Gerry Farnan.

From the time I was a kid, he used drill this into me, always reminding me to be positive. This time, I said to myself "You'll be with me in this race," as I took a look in the mirror, smiled and raised my fist directing the punch at my chin. "When you come back to this room, you'll be the champion."

I left the room happy and confident. On my way out the door, I noticed a bunch of telegrams and letters from well-wishers on a table. I didn't want to start reading them there and then but decided to open the one on top.

"Remember all the hard work you've done in the Rockies. You are well prepared and you will be the Champion of the World. Best of luck today in the final." – Rod Dixon

I'd already decided I wasn't going to look at the other runners in the warm up area the way I had in Montreal. By now I knew the procedure, knew the calling system, and knew how much time I had.

Rather than get ready on the warm up track, I went down into a tunnel to get away from everyone and stay in my own little world. I had already identified this sanctuary in the days before and planned on being there. All alone focusing in on the job at hand, I put on my walkman headphones and listened to John Cougar Mellencamp's song *It hurts so good*. I played it over and over.

It was dark and dimly-lit, but on this scorching afternoon it offered a cool respite from the heat. It occurred to me that I was getting that "indoor" feeling, which I considered a good omen. The only distraction came when a troop of foot soldiers came marching by me in military precision as I did my stretching. At first I thought I was in trouble for being here, but they didn't even notice me.

The calling room was quite small, and we sat around eye-balling one another at close quarters. Everyone was nervous.

They might not admit it, but before a big race like this, everybody is scared. I tried to avoid all eye contact, but knew I was being analysed by the others. This was the final day of the championships and my race would be the last individual track event.

I sat in the calling room looking at Mary Decker win the 1,500 metres on the monitor. She achieved the double. At the same time, Sergei Bubka won his first world title and Steve Cram beat Steve Scott to claim the 1,500 title. I was determined that I was going to be amongst the winners that day too.

When we came out onto the track, I noticed Irish flags interspersed throughout the crowd. Some of them were borne by guys from our team, but I noticed that a couple of our most enthusiastic supporters who'd been pals of my father, Sean Callan and Harry Gorman, were in the stands with a large tricolour. I thought I'd seek that one after I'd won.

I'd broken the race down into three stages. Stage one would consist of the first seven laps. Stage two would be getting from six laps to go to just four laps left.

And when stage three arrived, I was going to be a miler again and no one in this field could beat me over a mile.

"This is it. I'm ready," I told myself as we were called to the start.

I reminded myself of my key thoughts one more time:

Watch Wessinghage, he's smart, he can lead me to the gold.

Don't panic.

One move, and one move only.

Over the first half of the race I remained in the back third of the pack, establishing a position in the second lane and out of any potential trouble. It was a reasonably comfortable pace, but as I trailed most of the field I could almost hear the Irish commentators saying "Coghlan is looking to be in a dangerous position. He might want to start thinking about moving up."

I was determined to stay right where I was. Dmitriyev had moved into the lead, but I wasn't watching anyone but Wessinghage.

With six laps to go, it was into stage two. I began to move up carefully making sure not to waste too much energy and tucked in right behind Wessinghage.

Dmitriyev was in the lead pushing the pace followed by Padilla. I was happy. Most of the field began to fall back which relieved some of the pressure.

With three and a half laps to go, Dmitriyev began to sprint away from the field. I was now in my miler's mode. I knew it was fast but felt in complete control. Padilla had fallen back and Wessinghage wasn't going after the Russian.

"Thomas must be tired," I thought.

With 800 metres to run, the Russian had opened up a significant lead, and there was still no response from Wessinghage. Calculating by now that this wasn't going to be the German's day, I decided to pass him and gradually haul back the Russian.

"Don't panic, relax, relax," I reminded myself.

With 400 metres to go, I knew it was only Dmitriyev and me that were in contention, and while he had a twenty metre lead, I had plenty left in the tank. As I headed down the back straight, I caught up with Dmitriyev. I was feeling so good there and then that I could have gone right by. I was on a high.

Feeling no pain or discomfort with the four minute mile pace we were on. I purposely chose not to pass him. I waited and waited as if I was hunting him down, wearing him out mentally. I knew his legs were shot and I knew he was under fierce mental pressure almost as if to say "When are you going to pass me?"

I took a quick glance over my shoulder and saw the rest of the field were a long way back. There was no danger at all from behind.

I was dying to go by him. It was a real temptation, but I forced myself to wait until we were coming off the final turn, at the exact spot I'd pointed out the night before.

Then, reaching the spot, I drew abreast of Dimitriyev, turned, glanced at him, and when I saw the look on his face I knew I was about to be the World Champion.

I clenched my fists, smiled and said "I got it. I got it. I got it for you guys," meaning Gerry, Jumbo and my Dad. They had all my life been there to support and inspire and now on the greatest stage in the athletics world they wouldn't get to witness what they'd told me I could one day do.

The combination of emotions I felt at that moment was incredibly powerful. It was as if my entire career flashed before me at that moment – leaving Villanova and then going back, Jumbo and Gerry and my Dad, the disappointments of the Olympics, it all just bubbled up in my head as I surged into the lead.

In that brief instant, I could feel tears welling up inside me as I pulled away from Dmitriyev. I almost immediately opened up a ten-metre lead over the next fifty and then, down the straight, I embarrassingly half spread my arms saying to myself "I don't believe it!"

It was the greatest thrill I had experienced in my career to date. I crossed the finish line and immediately gave the sign of the Cross and said a prayer of Thanksgiving. I took the grass from my pocket and remember saying "Thank you. You were here Gerry, all the way."

I got a lot of stick later for making that gesture coming off the last turn, but it wasn't meant to be cocky or arrogant. Some said I was being disrespectful to Dmitri Dmitriyev, but it wasn't that either. Those who criticised me hadn't a clue what I had to overcome to get that point.

To this very day, people ask me "What did you say to the Russian?"

One newspaper columnist joked "What did Eamonn Coghlan say when he passed the Russian? Answer: Drink Kaliber, 'cause Smirnoff leaves you breathless."

It was a joyous day to be Irish. Ireland hadn't had a major win in international sport for a long time. The country came to a stop. Bono announced my victory to his audience at the Phoenix Park. Golf punters left the golf course to watch the race in the tented village and the roar of the crowd in Royal Dublin reverberated down the course.

Back in Dublin, my mother hadn't been able to bring herself to watch the race and had gone to the Good Counsel Church on the Mourne Road in Drimnagh to pray for me. She arrived there only to find it locked and had to retrace her steps, praying for me all the way home.

She got as far as the Cooley Road when she heard one of her neighbours shouting a familiar name "Coghlan. Go on you can do it. Go, go, go Coghlan," the roar coming from an open window.

When the noise subsided she asked the neighbour, Mr. Johnson, what had happened.

"Jesus, Mrs. Coghlan, Eamonn has just won the World Championships," he replied.

My winning time was 13:28.5, nearly two seconds ahead of the runner-up. I actually didn't know what had happened behind me until I looked back after I crossed the finish line and saw someone lying on the track. That turned out to be Vainio. Schildhauer and Dmitriyev were also there, but they were on their feet.

As it turned out, Shildhauer had passed them both and gone into second. Then, just a couple of metres from the finish line, Vainio had half-thrown himself, half-stumbled, and his momentum had somehow carried him across the line dead level with Dmitriyev. The two of them were clocked in the same time – 13:30.3, and it took a photo finish to determine which had been third.

When the photo came out, poor old Dmitri Dmitriyev got fourth. I felt sorry for him, because he'd done all the work and had nothing to show for it. He'd set himself up as the sacrificial rabbit, and I'd taken advantage of it just the way Walker had taken advantage of me in 1976.

I knew exactly how he felt. I'd been there.

I jogged around the track taking my lap of honour, stopping to shake hands with people eventually getting to Sean Callan and Harry Gorman whereupon I collected the Irish flag and continued my victory lap.

"I'm a World Champion."

"I'm a World Champion."

"I'm a World Champion."

I kept repeating this over and over in a state of suspended disbelief as I stood on the rostrum listening to the National Anthem. In the end it seemed so easy. Yet the last mile was covered in 4:03 and the last 800 metres in 1:55 – all the work and sacrifice had finally paid off.

When I'd first broken the indoor record back in 1979, Kenny Moore had told me "Eamonn, your life is going to change from here," and I knew that my life was going to change from this moment on as well. I'd given the people of Ireland something to cheer about for the first time in a long time.

Having finished fourth in two straight Olympics, I'd disappointed them and disappointed myself, but this went some way to make up for it.

This time I'd shown that I could do it when it counted.

I knew from talking to Yvonne that the country was at fever pitch over my win – but I had no idea what to expect when I got home.

As the plane taxied across the runway in Dublin airport, I could see throngs of people, and when we stopped on the tarmac John Treacy urged me to be the first off the plane and insisted that I wear the medal around my neck.

When I stepped outside, I realised what I had achieved for Ireland. There were hundreds of people waiting to share this historic moment – press, dignitaries, friends, family – all there to acknowledge my return and my achievement

In years to come, wild and joyous spectacles like this would become more familiar – I'm thinking of the return of Stephen Roche after his Tour de France win, Barry McGuigan when he won the World Featherweight Title, the Irish soccer team after Rome in 1990, and Philip Walton walking off the plane with the Ryder Cup in 2001 – but in 1983 it was still quite unique. Ireland hadn't had a sporting moment like this to rejoice about since Delany in 1956 – and when Ronnie won the Olympic gold, the whole country hadn't watched the race on live television.

We made our way through the throngs to a VIP lounge, where I did a quick Q&A with the press. Then we were given a police escort to Yvonne's mother's house in Glasnevin.

Two nights later there would be another police escort, this time from Glasnevin down O'Connell Street to the city centre, where I was feted at a civic reception at the Mansion House, hosted by the Lord Mayor, Michael Keating.

I was pleasantly surprised by the turnout. People lined the streets and applauded as the car passed by, and a huge crowd had gathered on Dawson Street awaiting my arrival.

I couldn't help but think "What would it have been like if I won the Olympics, not once but, twice."

Though I savoured the moment, I still hadn't found what I was looking for.

At the time, there was absolutely no financial support for sports people in Ireland. I was making good money and I was passionate about drumming up a debate on the issue.

I decided to seize the moment and suggested that the country might prepare for the upcoming Los Angeles Games by initiating a grass-roots "Operation Olympics" to support and develop future Irish Olympians.

Later that evening, I was collared by a member of the Olympic Council of Ireland, who chastised me for my remarks.

"If there's any fund-raising to be done we'll look after it ourselves," the IOC man warned me, "we don't need you to be passing the hat for us."

I was stunned. I'd spoken off the cuff, but with the best of intentions. It had never occurred to me that I might be stepping on what someone else might have considered their personal turf.

The following day, myself, Yvonne and the children Suzanne and Eamonn were invited to Áras an Uachtaráin to meet President Patrick Hillery and his wife Maeve for afternoon tea.

I was truly honoured by the invitation. All my life I had run past 'his house' in the Phoenix Park and often wondered what it was like.

President Hillery and Maeve were most gracious and formally offered his congratulations to me on behalf of the people of Ireland. During the course of the formalities, both Suzanne and Eamonn went missing. Mrs. Hillary panicked a little when I began to wonder where they'd got to.

Suddenly, I heard Mrs. Hillery scream "Jesus Mary and Joseph, look at them out at the fountain, Paddy." Both children had slipped out the door into the rose garden and were about to climb into the water. I smiled as the President of Ireland went running out through the door to stop them from falling in. Yvonne and I laughed for days at the thought of the President chasing after our kids.

It was a warm memory from a wonderful time – a time when I felt I had realised not just mine, but everyone's expectations.

Coghlan – the fellow who finished fourth – was now the fellow who finished first.

And it felt very, very good.

The emotion in the Garden was something I'll never forget. Tears flowed and Marcus came over to congratulate me. He had a big smile on his face as he shook my hand and said "Well done Chairman." I was thrilled, relieved and quite frankly astonished that I had done the business. In my wildest dreams, I could not have imagined coming back from such a series of injuries and setbacks to claim my seventh Wanamaker title.

Gerry Farnan was right – never give up.

Part

THE BOARDS

HE MILE

With Suzanne on the streets of his beloved Manhattan, wearing the Discover Ireland T-Shirt that would land him in all sort of bother with the BBC.

IV

Countdown to Los Angeles

After my World Championship exploits, I returned to New York to prepare for the next part of the four-year plan Gerry Farnan and I had sketched out, the Los Angeles Olympics. I was ranked Number 1 in the world at 5,000 metres and made enough money to buy a small three bedroom raised ranch style house in Rye.

Through 1983 I continued to work for Bord Fáilte, but pressure was starting to build within the office. I was lucky that Donal McSullivan had more or less allowed me to come and go as I pleased, but the value of my promotional work hadn't been universally recognised.

There was pressure on McSullivan from some of the subordinates who wanted to know "How can Coghlan get all this free time off to run?" At that point I was earning close to $500,000 a year from running, so I decided to leave the board. Rather than getting IMG involved, I was able to negotiate a pretty good deal, one that suited all concerned and one that got McSullivan off the hook.

I would leave my job as a full-time employee, but they would pay me the equivalent of my salary and a bit more to officially wear Discover Ireland on my running vest. I had told them somebody else had offered me $35,000 a year to wear their logo and the response was "Oh, no, we'll pay it!"

We shook hands and I departed with no rancour whatsoever. Some of those people I worked with at Bord Fáilte are among my best friends to this very day.

But I was now a free man and a full-time professional athlete.

If only I could stay healthy.

In pursuit of an Olympic gold medal, I failed dismally to follow my own advice. I began to train far too hard clocking over one hundred miles per week. I got carried away with being a full-time athlete thinking that if I did a little bit more I could run faster, be stronger than ever before.

I was now 31-years-old. I didn't realise it at the time, but it was probably more rest I needed than more training. Out of running meant out of work. In January of 1984, I discovered I had another stress fracture of my right tibia and was forced to abandon the indoor season and another golden jackpot. For the second time in as many years, I spent the winter training in the basement of my house, riding a stationary bike and trying to maintain my cardiovascular system through indoor exercise. The longer it went on, the more frustrated and depressed I became. This time I didn't have an office to go to and had all the time in the world to think of nothing but injury and the ever-dwindling amount of time to the Games.

I tried to stay fit by running in the swimming pool at the Rye YMCA each morning for hours on end.

Besides working out in the pool, on the indoor bike, and at the Pepsi Gym, I tried to aid my recovery by grinding up eggshells into a fine powder and mixing it with milk. That was supposed to be to give me an infusion of calcium – but it didn't work.

To maintain muscle strength I even took to electric shock treatment. I'd hook electric pads to my calves, quadriceps and hamstrings and send bolts of electricity to the muscles causing them to contract.

At night, I'd sleep with an electronic-bio-unit that would send electric waves to the bones to speed the healing process. That didn't work

The best training for running is running. Try as I might, nothing could replace that vital ingredient. By summer time, I hadn't put in the miles and it looked increasingly obvious that my Olympic dream was over.

I returned to Ireland early that summer. I knew I was kidding myself when I entered the Cork City Sports in the hope that I might race myself to fitness. I ran a disappointing 5,000 metres but still I wasn't quite ready to give up.

Up to now, I hadn't divulged that I was injured and was still hoping against hope that I could whip myself into shape for the Irish Championships in a fortnight's time.

After Cork, I drove down to Goleen in West Cork, where Jimmy and Margaret Rafferty had rented a holiday house. I thought I'd avoid scrutiny from the Irish media, who were by then up to their eyeballs in speculation about the world champion's prospects for the upcoming Olympics.

When I arrived at Santry for the National Championships in July, I was still experiencing excruciating pain. Now both shins felt like they were broken – but I didn't want to give up – I didn't want to let go.

John Treacy, who had already qualified for the Olympics at 10,000 metres and who was also controversially entered in the marathon, opted to run in the 5,000 metres for a speed workout.

My duel with John was the highlight of the meeting. John was in great shape and had already put in some spectacular times that year.

I knew he was more prepared for the marathon than for a 5,000 metre race and under the right circumstances I should have been able to beat him. But, here in our Nationals he was hammering me right into the ground.

I couldn't stay near him. Halfway through the race, the pain became so unbearable that I had no option but to stop and drop out, publicly conceding that the

Olympic dream was over once again. There was almost a pall of sadness over the track as I hastily left the stadium that afternoon.

Neither the media nor fans wanted to believe what they had witnessed. Attempts were made to try to convince me to change my mind. Noel Carroll telephoned and asked me to hold off making the decision for another week. But it was too late. I had suffered for too long and the well-wishers had only become aware of my condition in the course of a few days.

I was dealing with physical and mental torture for months. It was more a relief to finally let the anxiety go.

Later that week, I received a phone call from the Olympic Council of Ireland. Noel Carroll had evidently relayed word that my decision was final. The OCI wanted me to return my Olympic blazer.

"You what?" I asked.

A year earlier I'd been asked to consult with the fashion designer Paul Costello about the make up of the team gear. Now they wanted to confiscate the blazer. "But," I was told, "you can keep the sunglasses."

I told the OCI man that if he wanted the jacket he could come get it himself. He never did. I still have it hanging in a wardrobe at home.

In the end, I did get to the 1984 Los Angeles Olympics, but as a commentator for RTE, not as a participant. I'll have to admit it was very hard looking at the games and feeling sorry for myself. I spent most time in between work, partying and wondering "What did I do to deserve this?"

Said Aouta went on to win "my event" the 5,000 metres in an Olympic record of 13:07. My only consolation was that I doubted very much after witnessing his scintillating performance that I'd have been able to match him, but felt confident that I could have been among the medals.

A couple of nights before the Olympic Marathon, I ran into John Treacy at an Olympic Council reception at UCLA. John had once again crashed out in the 10,000, but now he was going to run in the marathon.

Treacy hadn't officially qualified for the marathon, and in fact he'd never run one before. Jerry Kiernan and Dick Hooper had qualified, and since there was a spot open, Al Guy somehow used his influence with the IAAF to get him in as the third man on the Irish team.

John was always cunning, and he'd never tell you exactly what he was thinking. He kept his cards close to the vest, but that night I could sense that he was deadly serious about his marathon début. I somehow got the feeling that he might sneak in and get an Olympic medal.

John was well prepared and his pedigree as a double World Cross-Country winner and his ferocious determination were good indicators that he would succeed. Like myself, he had suffered a serious back injury the previous year and I believed the enforced rest might not have done him any harm.

I was working with Jimmy Magee in my pundit's role on the final day, doing the colour commentary for RTE. From our press position in the stadium, we watched the progress of the marathon through the streets on the TV monitor. Two hours into the race, Carlos Lopes of Portugal was leading comfortably, but Treacy was hanging right in there.

As they entered the stadium Lopes had a lead of almost 400 yards on Britain's Charlie Spedding, while John was in third place.

They went around for the second time, and as Lopes headed toward the tape Jimmy was saying "And here comes Carlos Lopes, thirty-seven years of age, a double world cross-country champion…"

Right in the middle of all this I was watching the back straight, where Treacy not only overtook Spedding, but started to run away from him.

"And John Treacy is sprinting away from Charlie Spedding! He's going to win the silver medal!" I shouted excitedly.

With that Jimmy Magee turned around and gave me a whack in the chest.

"Coghlan," he whispered, "you don't comment off-camera!"

Jimmy had wanted to be the one to tell the Irish people that John was going to win the silver – and I had stolen his thunder with my breach of decorum.

Watching John win silver was a terrific moment and I suppose it provided some momentary consolation: But I couldn't keep away the thought that I would never have the opportunity again to claim my own piece of Olympic metal. My Olympic days were well and truly over.

And I had nothing to show for them.

The pain of victory

The 1980s represented the highlight of my athletic career: During this era I ran over seventy sub four-minute miles, broke my own world indoor record twice (in 1981 and '83), won the World Cup and World Championships at 5,000 metres, and etched my name in the books forever as I bounced back from injury to win my sixth and seventh Wanamaker Miles.

Looking back on that decade, it was also the most difficult period of my running career. I was almost perpetually injured and struggled to just get on the track, much less compete.

In retrospect, I reckon that my effort to come back from injury in 1983 probably took its toll the following year, costing me a chance to participate in the Los Angeles Games. Indeed, 1984 was for all intents and purposes, a lost year.

From 1984 onward, it was just one injury after another. I tried to rest my weary bones by training on the bike and in the swimming pool, but when I first tried to run in January of 1985, it seemed as if all the work had gone to waste. At the end of the first week I tried my first sustained run, a ten-mile jog up in The Rockies, and discovered that I had no energy whatsoever. I was totally exhausted.

I was also bothered by a groin strain accompanied by lower abdominal pain; and then I came down with a dreadful case of diarrhoea. By now, I was approaching the onset of the indoor season and my body seemed to be breaking down right in front of me.

Dr. Dave Thomashow suggested that I begin eating as many peanuts as I could in an effort to raise my protein levels. I stuffed myself with bananas, and tried to revive my energy level by drinking copious amounts of a new sports drink, ERG.

The circuit began up in Canada, and while I won the mile in Ottawa I felt awful both during and after the race. The groin had bothered me and I had grave doubts about what way the season was going to go.

The following week I went up to Los Angeles for the Sunkist Invitational Mile. I won, in a time of 3:56.34, but the groin injury hampered my ability to lift my legs the way I needed, and I had to dig deeper than ever to hold Steve Scott off.

On the recommendation of John Treacy, I flew to Boston, where a doctor at Children's Hospital administered shots of cortisone and butazolidin, a substance used to treat sore race horses.

Whether it was from the injections or from Dave's more homeopathic approach, the pain did begin to ease off somewhat, but then at Madison Square Garden the next week I was experiencing some pain both in warming up and doing my strides, so I decided to curtail the pre-race preparation. I'd try to do it all in the race and hold back for as long as I could before making any move.

I waited until three laps to go and then passed both Masback and Wessinghage to take the lead. I was amazed that I was able to pull away and win as easily as I did, in a time of 3:53.82. It was my sixth Wanamaker Mile title and tied Glenn Cunningham's record.

The next day I flew to Chicago, and on Sunday afternoon I won despite another struggle with the groin. I had a ferocious battle with Scott in that race. With half a lap to go, where I'd normally have turned on the jets and left him, I discovered that I struggled even to get by him.

Still concerned about my precarious condition, I returned to Rye and consulted yet again with Marc Chesnov, my newly appointed physical therapist. I couldn't even do a proper stride because of the groin strain.

Enter Mr. Tool.

The contrivance was a device of Chesnov's own creation. Because the location of my deep groin strain was otherwise inaccessible, the physical therapist had invented Mr. Tool, which, basically, consisted of a screwdriver with a large ball bearing welded onto the point. Its application was at once gruesome, painful – and effective.

Marc jammed Mr. Tool right into my crotch and into the highest point of my groin to hammer the hell out of the scar tissue. It hurt like hell, but it seemed to help.

The following weekend I returned to Toronto, where I won the Maple Leaf Mile in 3:59.05, and then flew to Dallas, where I won a two-mile race in 8:20. I arrived back in New York in the midst of a February snowstorm, and found myself thinking "To hell with this; I really ought to go back to California to train," but managed to banish the thought.

The next weekend I was scheduled to compete against Sydney Maree in the US Olympic Invitational Meet. The centrepiece event had by now been rechristened the Ford Meadowlands Mile.

With all the injuries, I didn't expect to perform well, but I won the race, literally on the wire. I just beat Sydney by a few scant hundredths of a second when I out-leaned him at the line running 3:53.8.

The entry in my diary that day consists of one sentence: "I don't know how I ran that fast."

Once I'd done my lap of honour, they were waiting to interview me on television. Because Ford had sponsored the race, someone tried to put a blue baseball cap with the Ford logo on my head.

"Hold on," I said. "What's this?"

They explained that I'd just won a Ford Taurus and that they were going to present me with the keys on television as soon as they finished the commercial break.

"A Taurus?" I said. "Come on, I'm not going to drive a Taurus. That's a women's car. You've got to do better than that."

They'd be coming back live in less than half a minute.

"What do you want?" asked the slightly agitated Ford rep.

"How about a Thunderbird?"

By now we were inside ten seconds from going back on the air. He thought quickly "Okay. I'll organise it for you." So they slapped the hat back on me and went straight into the television interview.

A few days later I went up Rye Ford, where I picked out the new Thunderbird.

I kept it for a few months and then traded it in for a red Alfa Romeo Spider Veloce. I still have that car in my garage in Dublin.

A couple of weeks later, my injury woes got worse when I stepped on a rock while training in New York and sprained my ankle.

It was the final straw: I declared that my indoor season was over and that I wasn't going to compete again for the rest of the spring. I fled to the Bahamas for a holiday with Yvonne and the kids and wondered whether I was ever going to be pain free again.

The groin was still bothering me, my ankle was weak and my Achilles tendon was sore. Then I began to feel a dull ache in my left shinbone that turned out to be another stress fracture.

I was a mess.

I stopped running altogether, but continued to train on the bike and in the swimming pool. My rationale was that if I'd been able to perform as well as I had during the indoor season despite all those injuries – and without an awful lot of training – with six weeks rest I might still manage to get myself into running shape for the outdoor season. But, I was only fooling myself.

In August of 1985, John O'Shea flew from Dublin to Zurich, where a trio of Irishmen – Marcus O'Sullivan, Ray Flynn, and Frank O'Mara – were performing in the Weltklasse Meet. O'Shea, the Director of Third World Charity GOAL wanted them to come back to Ireland to run on a relay team that would, he promised, shatter the world 4 x 1 mile record. The event would take place not in an Olympic setting or a World Championship meet, but as part of a Charity Day on the UCD campus at Belfield.

O'Shea and me went way back. In his earlier career he had been an enterprising, if opinionated, journalist for the Irish Press, and I had become accustomed to his ringing up at all hours of the night and morning in his quest for another scoop.

He had brought the same determination to GOAL, the charity he had established in 1977. Having gathered the support of sports stars, he had known in his previous incarnation, O'Shea had put together an organisation that would raise millions for the starving in Third-World nations.

It had occurred to O'Shea that a country which could boast so many of the world's top milers had a great chance to best the standard if they could only be persuaded to unite in that common goal.

Although he knew Marcus O' Sullivan, Frank O' Mara, and Ray Flynn would each have to give up at least one paid race at the top of their games, he had thrown down a challenge which each, in the end, found irresistible

The question came as to who was going to be on the relay. At that time we had seven or eight sub four-minute milers in Ireland, so it was questionable as to who was going to be on it.

It was definitely going to be Marcus, it was definitely going to be Ray, and there was going to be Frank, but I wasn't in shape at the time, and there was a bit of controversy over whether or not I should be included.

I knew I most definitely shouldn't run. I could hardly jog with the injuries I was dealing with.

Noel Carroll was asked to use his powers of persuasion to convince me to participate.

I told Noel "absolutely not," but when he told John O'Shea that, John decided to ring me himself.

O'Shea was more aware than anyone that the attendant publicity would be even greater if "Coghlan" was a part of the relay team.

"You're running," he told me, "if you don't show up, you can f*** off, and I'll put John Treacy in your place. He can run better than you anyhow, but I'm telling you right now that if Frank O'Mara, Ray Flynn, Marcus O'Sullivan, and John Treacy do break the world record and you're not part of it, you'll regret it till your dying day."

"But John, I'm injured, I can't run fast. I'll let the team down," I responded. "Injured my arse. You just get yourself to Belfield tomorrow night," he said, hanging up the phone.

I had no choice but to run and I feared that I'd be the one to screw up the record attempt.

When I arrived at Belfield at 6:30 that evening, the stadium was nearly empty and it looked like it was going to be a total waste of an evening. In one sense I was delighted and hoped the event wouldn't go ahead. On the other, I felt bad for O'Shea after all the work he'd done to put the meet on. He was told by the BLE that he had no permit and could not put on an athletics event in Dublin without their permission. He basically told them to f*** off.

About an hour to go before the event was supposed to start, I headed off with the boys for a warm up run. When we came back 45 minutes later the place was absolutely packed! People just came out of the woodwork to witness this world record attempt.

I was selected to take the first leg and run against John Treacy who'd been "demoted" to the B team.

There was a two-pronged motive behind this. One was because if I did screw up my time, the others might be able to make it up. The other was by having Treacy race against me, they knew that pride alone would force me to stay ahead of John, especially over a mile.

That's exactly how it turned out. John pushed me all the way around the four laps and I managed to hold him off to hand the baton over to Marcus in the lead.

As it turned out we broke the World record in a time of 15:49.08 – a record that stands to this day. I was the only one on the team who failed to break the sub four barrier.

The real winner on the night was O'Shea's charity, which managed to raise £20,000.

The bite is worse than the bark

After I had matriculated in Villanova, Marcus O'Sullivan had continued the transcontinental tradition when he enrolled there in the autumn of 1980. Marcus was the last of Jumbo Elliott's Irish recruits. A quarter-century later, O'Sullivan now oversees the athletics programme at Villanova, where he has been Head Track & Field Coach since 1998.

I never actually met Marcus until after he had received his scholarship to Villanova. Donie Walsh had recruited him back in Cork and had brought him to Jumbo's attention. O'Sullivan hadn't won any championships or broken any records as a schoolboy in Ireland, but Donie told Jumbo that he had both speed and stamina, and that with a few years of the proper training he had the potential to become a good one.

Walsh didn't often talk a kid up like that, so Jumbo knew that if Donie said Marcus was good, he probably was good.

I met him in his freshman year. He came up to visit us in Rye, and baby-sat our children. Almost from the start he exceeded expectations. I think once he got to Villanova and saw the opportunities ahead of him, he grasped the nettle right away and went with it. Once he began to win collegiate championships and broke the Irish 800 metre record, he began to recognise his own talent, and he focused his energies on becoming a great runner.

Marcus reminded me of myself in many ways: In his running style, in his belief in himself, and in his approach to training. I knew I was the one he'd looked up to, and that one of his big running goals was to beat me. That first win came in the Sunkist Invitational in Los Angeles in 1986.

I had in my ageing years as a runner, tried to look at a new means of improving my performance in my attempt to win the Wanamaker mile for a record seventh time.

I opted to go on a special diet Eat to Win by Robert Haas, which was being bantered about by tennis great Martina Navratilova and golf legend Jack Nicklaus.

It required me to completely reduce my fat and protein intake and increase my carbohydrate intake. I had Yvonne cook special meals, weighing everything and when we'd have guests over for dinner, she'd have to prepare a special meal for me. I became obsessed with the diet.

The end result was that I lost about fourteen pounds in weight from an already fit weight of about one hundred and forty. I was gaunt and sick and looked wretched. I lost all my power and strength and couldn't muster the speed required for the final kick in a race. Nicklaus subsequently ditched the diet and went on to win the Masters in 1986, becoming the oldest man to do so at forty-six.

After Marcus beat me in Los Angeles, I feared the worst as I headed to New York for the Wanamaker Mile. In New York it came down to an Irishman who might prevent me from getting the record seventh win – a record that was unlikely to be broken. But I knew that I was edging inexorably towards middle-age and that time might be running out. But I didn't want to give up. I couldn't let running go.

But my feeling of impending doom was on the money. Marcus ran an outstanding race to claim the first of his five Wanamaker's, while I slid out of Madison Square Garden determined to return one more time.

I desperately wanted to beat Glen Cunningham's record.

And the first thing I needed to do was get off that damned diet.

In December 1986, we all returned to Dublin to spend Christmas with Yvonne's family in Glasnevin. On St Stephen's Day, I went for a fifteen mile run and with just a mile-and-a-half left to go, was running down the North Circular Road towards Phibsboro.

Thirty yards in front of me a car had halted at a pedestrian crossing and a group of boys, accompanied by a black-and-white sheepdog, were crossing in front of the car, pushing their bicycles along. A mother holding the hand of her child was walking along the sidewalk.

When the youths appeared to be dawdling in the middle of the street, the driver gave a beep of his horn to hurry them on their way. The youngsters instead stopped where they were and began to curse.

When I heard one of them shout "F*** off, you stupid f***** c***," I slowed down and told the kids "Cut out the bad language, it's Christmas. Have some respect!"

With that, one of them turned around, pointed at me, and told me to "f*** off." Then he set the dog on me.

The dog went straight for my feet and legs. He bit me, taking a chunk out of my thigh and then another out of my calf before the kids took off.

The woman and child by then had disappeared – as had the car. Like a total idiot, I decided to chase after the kids. I guess I wanted to see where they lived.

When I caught up with them, they set the dog on me again and he took another small bite out of me. By this stage they must have panicked and felt that the dog was going to kill me, because one of them threw his bicycle in an attempt to separate the two of us.

When I looked down at my leg, I could see the calf muscle protruding through my running tights. Covered in blood, I went back out on the road, put up my hands, and stopped the first car that came along and told the driver who I was and what had happened.

He took one look at me, said "Oh, Jesus!" and drove me straight down to the Mater Hospital, less than a mile away. En route he turned to me and said "You're the very man. Will ya give me some advice as to how I should lose a bit of weight for the New Year?"

"Just get me to the hospital," I pleaded, "we'll worry about how you'll lose the weight another time."

In the Emergency Room, they managed to peel off my tights and clean up the wounds. They couldn't stitch them, but had to let them heal open, so they just packed them with surgical wool.

It was three hours since I'd left the house on my post-Christmas jog and I knew Yvonne would be worried. Eventually I managed to contact her and fill her in on what had happened.

As I was about to leave the hospital, I mentioned to an attending doctor that I had a pain in my arm. After an X-ray, it turned out I'd broken the third metatarsal bone in my hand. It must have happened when the kids threw the bicycle at the end of the melee.

The medical team suggested putting my hand in a cast for three or four weeks, but I wasn't having any of that. The indoor season was fast approaching and I was determined to go for my seventh Wanamaker win.

The doctor told me the only alternative was to perform surgery and put a couple of screws in my hand. Since that procedure would only keep me in hospital for a few days, I elected to go that route. I was admitted and scheduled surgery for the following day.

As I was brought to my overnight ward one of the nurses turned to me and said "Oh, by the way, there's a friend of yours in this ward."

When I asked who it was, she winked "Oh, you'll see."

They rolled me off the trolley and onto the bed. I looked up and directly opposite, there was a guy grinning at me from across the room. At first I didn't even recognise him.

"Fanahan?" I finally asked, "is that you?"

"Ah, by Jesus, it is, boy," he said in that chirpy Cork accent of his.

He'd weighed nearly fourteen stone when last I'd seen him, and now he'd shrunk down to less than eight. In lieu of a bed, he was strapped to a Thompson table. He was literally on his back twenty-four hours a day and couldn't move. Every two hours they'd invert him – basically flip him over on the bed so he wouldn't get bedsores.

I shuffled across the room to talk to him and asked what had happened. The last I'd heard, after all, he'd been on the mend from surgery back in August.

It turned out that during the surgery to repair the injury to his vertebrae they had discovered a tumour in his back. The diagnosis was multiple myeloma.

The doctors were hopeful that they'd been able to remove the cancer. Now they were going to implant a six-inch steel rod where they'd removed the vertebrae so his back would support him. His surgery was scheduled for Tuesday – a day after mine.

The doctors were obliged to report the dog attack to the police and the following day all hell broke loose. There were headlines all over the place and the press were trying to get into the hospital to interview me.

There was speculation that the injuries might cost me the upcoming indoor season, and there was even a public outcry demanding the implementation of leash laws in Ireland.

Even in the midst of his pain, Fanahan managed to motivate me over those few days we spent in hospital together. This was typical of him. He could only see the positive side of anything, no matter what it was. His outlook was infectious.

He wanted me to get back into shape, head back to the States, regain the Wanamaker Mile title and then go for the world record for the 2,000 metres, which had been my objective for 1987.

By the time I returned to the States a few weeks later, the pain had subsided and within a couple of weeks I felt able to start racing.

History in the making

It was only as the years went by and I began to accumulate Wanamaker wins that I began to realise that I was going to be very much part of the history of the Wanamaker Mile. The Madison Square Garden ambience is unlike that of any other arena. Beyond the history and tradition of the place, the Garden is imbued with a unique atmosphere all its own.

You could lead me in there blindfolded and I'd know where I was – the unmistakable odour is a mixture of stale beer, cigar smoke, and elephant dung. The circus only comes to New York for one week a year, but for the other fifty-one weeks that smell never leaves it.

Smoking has been banned inside Madison Square Garden for years now, but the residue of those old stogies from bygone years never leaves either. It must be ingrained into the seats.

I know Ali fought Frazier there, the Knicks have won NBA Championships there and the Rangers a Stanley Cup there, but the electricity generated by a track crowd at the Garden was in my view unmatched. The fans know their track and field, and the vibrations from the fans and the vibrations of the old wooden track produced a chemistry you wouldn't find anywhere else in the world.

By 1987, I had met Glenn Cunningham, and I'd met a lot of the great milers who'd won that race before me – Freddy Dwyer, Jimmy Rafferty, Kip Keino, Marty Liquori, and Filbert Bayi. And as I won four, five, and six of them and now had a chance to surpass Cunningham, I realised that it was likely to be recognised as one of the greatest achievements in indoor running. I think that's why, in coming back after being beaten by Marcus O'Sullivan in 1986, I put such a huge effort into getting my body right to try and win it for the seventh time.

I wanted to really etch in stone what people had told me all along – that I was the greatest indoor miler of all time. But I wasn't, really, until I went past six and into my seventh Wanamaker Mile, able to confirm it in my own mind.

But believe it or not, going into that race I was as confident as I'd ever been in my life. I knew it was very important for me to run a perfect tactical race. I not only had Marcus to contend with, but Steve Ovett had come over to run in the Wanamaker for the first time.

The day before the race we appeared together at a press conference, and Steve was asked his thoughts about running on the boards. It was his first time – and he wasn't really sure what to expect; he said he thought it would be "Kind of like being in the circus."

He said that he preferred outdoor running. Then he was asked about the eleven-laps-to-the-mile track, and said "It's a bit of a joke, actually. It's like running around a bathtub with no faucets."

I didn't say anything at the time but I took it quite personally. I felt as if he was trying to make fools of us – not just me, but Marcus and Jose Abascal – with his snobbish attitude.

The following night we were on the starting line for the race. There were two staggers, with four runners on the inside couple of lanes, and then ten yards up, four on the outside lanes. I'd actually requested that I be placed up on the outside stagger, because I didn't want the people on the outside coming in on top of me on those tight indoor turns when they'd merge together on the back straight.

Ovett was also in the front stagger, and as we were standing on the line he seemed confused.

"What are we supposed to do?" he asked me.

I explained to him that we had to stay in the outside lanes until we could break, and pointed out to him the spot where we'd be allowed to move inside.

"But, Steve," I added, "be very careful going around this first turn, because there are faucets on this bathtub."

Ovett ran well off the pace and was never a factor in the race finishing up in ninth position.

Mark Fricker, the rabbit, set the pace over the first half-mile before giving way to Abascal, and then Ray Flynn took the lead with two laps remaining.

I bided my time, and was warily charting Marcus. Then, entering the final back straight, I went into overdrive and blew past Marcus, Abascal and Flynn in one giant sweep to open a decisive gap before Marcus realised what was happening.

I won in 3:55.91, with Marcus second and Abascal third.

The emotion in the Garden was something I'll never forget. Tears flowed and Marcus came over to congratulate me. He had a big smile on his face as he shook my hand and said "Well done Chairman."

I was thrilled, relieved and quite frankly astonished that I had done the business. In my wildest dreams, I could not have imagined coming back from such a series of injuries and setbacks to claim my seventh Wanamaker title. Gerry Farnan was right – never give up.

"Forget the shinbones that kept getting fractured, and forget the dog that bit him five times and helped break his left hand, and forget the diet that almost ruined him," wrote Frank Litsky in the *New York Times* the next morning.

"Forget all the bad things that sidelined him so often. Eamonn Coghlan is back. Last night, the thirty-four-year-old Irishman won the most glamorous race of indoor track, the Wanamaker Mile, in the most glamorous of indoor meets, the 80th annual Wanamaker Millrose Games in Madison Square Garden. He won the way he had won so often in the past, with a driving, blasting finish that had the screaming capacity crowd of 18,122 on its feet. Coghlan's time of 3:55.91 was nothing special for him, but a victory by the most popular miler of this era is always special. This was the seventh time Coghlan had won the Wanamaker Mile, starting in 1977. That bettered the record of six he shared with Glenn Cunningham, the hero of the galleries at another Madison Square Garden a half-century ago, and it earned him the award as the meet's Outstanding Athlete."

After winning my seventh Wanamaker, I headed out to Los Angeles to run in the LA Times Invitational, where Will Kern had put on a 2,000 metre race. The 2,000 metres is an unusual distance, indoors or out, and the sole reason it was being included on the programme was to provide me with an opportunity to break the world record. I did just that, running 4:54.07, smashing the previous record by nearly two seconds. When I got back to the hotel around midnight in California, I rang the Mater Hospital so I could share the news with Fanahan and to see how he was getting on.

"Sorry," said a nurse, "Mr McSweeney has been discharged."

I was elated to hear that, of course. I asked if she had his phone number, but of course they couldn't share that information. I dialled directory assistance in Ireland, asked for a Fanahan McSweeney in Silverspring, County Cork, and actually got the number.

The phone rang and rang. I realised it was around 8 am.

"Fanahan?"

"It is, boy. Good morning to you."

He apologised for having taken so long to answer the phone, explaining that he had to get around the house in a Zimmer Frame – a walker.

When I told him I'd broken the record, he didn't even seem surprised.

"Sure I knew you could do it," he said.

Six thousand miles away and the tears were streaming down my face. Tears of delight, not because of the record, but because Fanahan was out of hospital, on the mend, and free of his cancer.

Or so I thought.

Coming off the phone Fanahan's last words of encouragement were "All you have to do now boy, is win the World Indoor Championships."

The first World Indoor Championship was scheduled to take place in Indianapolis a couple of weeks later.

I was favourite to win the 1,500 in the inaugural meet, but in a qualifying heat I was tripped from behind by German runner Dieter Bauman on the second lap and tumbled heavily to the deck.

I bounced back on my feet and threw in a 53-second quarter to catch the leaders. I appeared to be in a position to qualify, but then coming off the final turn I misjudged the finish line. There were two almost identical posts just a yard or two apart, and I eased up at the first, allowing Canada's Dave Campbell to slip past me and take the qualifying spot by one-hundredth of a second.

Through team manager Ronnie Long, the Irish federation lodged a protest, on the grounds that the tripping incident had cost me a place in the final.

As it turned out, there were ten qualifiers for the women's final and only nine for the men's, so it wouldn't have been hard to find an extra spot. But the protest seemed to fall on deaf ears. Most nations, including the United States, supported me, but the Spanish and Italian delegations didn't.

The boardroom debate continued for several hours. NBC, which was televising the event, wanted me in the final. They'd paid a tidy sum for the rights to the first World Championship and were now faced with the prospect of showing a race from which the "Chairman of the Boards" had been excluded.

The panel hearing the appeal suggested that my one ray of hope might come if Baumann came forth and confirmed in writing that he had in fact accidentally tripped me. The television footage didn't conclusively demonstrate that there had been actual physical contact, but I rolled up the leg of my trousers to show the spike marks on my leg.

As it turned out, Yvonne who was sitting in the stands with team coach Sean Naughton, had divulged to him while I raced that she had a dream the night before and in it I got tripped up! Seconds later I was down.

I spent much of the afternoon and early evening vainly searching for Baumann, even touring the nearby restaurants. It was late that night that the German returned to his hotel. When I explained the situation, Baumann refused to accept responsibility for the tripping incident.

"No way," he told me.

He had a very good reason to keep me out. He thought he'd have a better chance of winning.

I was out of the World Championships and went off and got royally drunk that night in an attempt to brush off the disappointment, only to find out the next morning when I woke up with a terrible hangover, that there was a possibility that I would be reinstated.

Frank O' Mara came knocking on my room door "Hey, Coghlan, get up, you are back in." I jumped into a hot bath and tried to sweat out the alcohol. Then I got back into the bed with two track suits on, hoping this might help. I had a few hours to get ready. Eventually, O'Mara came back and announced "False alarm, it was overruled again."

Yvonne was with me during the Championships and was heavily pregnant at the time. That took my mind off the disappointment as we counted down the days to the birth of our third child, Michael Gerry (after Gerry Farnan), who was born on the 13th of May.

Missing out on the Championships had been a major disappointment to Fanahan McSweeney – and the ailing McSweeney saw himself as a vicarious participant in my career. Winning that prestigious event had been a goal for 1987.

On the European circuit that summer, I travelled to London for a mile race at Crystal Palace, when I'd unexpectedly run into Fanahan. The confirmed bachelor had his new girlfriend in tow, and introduced me to Jean Dorgan.

As we chatted away, Fanahan asked "Did you ever do anything with that ould site you bought in Porterstown?"

I told him that hoped to build soon – it was a site I had purchased some years before – and planned to hire a builder when I returned to Dublin.

"I told you I'd be happy to do it," said Fanahan.

Fanahan was returning to Cork via Dublin, and arranged to meet me at the Dublin Airport on the way back. I brought along the plans for the house, but when I showed them to him it was obvious that they didn't meet with his approval.

"This looks like no more than a couple of bungalows slapped together," said Fanahan. "Eamonn Coghlan should build a house for himself where the likes of Sebastian Coe and Steve Ovett and Edwin Moses will come to visit and say, 'By Jesus, didn't Coghlan do well for himself?'"

I then produced an American set of plans I'd brought along as an alternative. He liked them much better.

"That's the sort of house you should build for yourself," he said.

Fanahan agreed to personally oversee the construction of the new house as project manager. "By Jesus, if you're 3,000 miles away in America them builders will rob you," he said. "You'd never know what kind of shite they're putting into it."

Further into the mire

Eamonn Coghlan of Ireland, the world indoor record-holder in the mile, said yesterday that he would miss the coming indoor season because of an injured back. Coghlan, who lives in Rye, N.Y., missed a step at his home three weeks ago and tore a ligament in the sacroiliac. He has been unable to train since.

— **Wire Service Dispatch, December 31, 1987**

From a running perspective, this was devastating news. It became apparent that it was going to cost me the upcoming 1988 indoor season – and at this stage of the game I knew I didn't have many indoor seasons left.

Throughout January and half of February, it was a struggle just to cross the street. If there was a car coming toward me, no matter how far away, I was like an old person trying to hobble across the road. It seemed as if every time I tried to come back from an injury something else would happen: And I found myself wondering if this time it might have signalled the end of my career.

It was mid-February before I was fit enough to begin jogging again – and I found then that the groin strain was still lingering.

The '88 indoor season was a complete washout, but I did pick up some work doing television commentary for NBC and ESPN.

In my absence Marcus O'Sullivan won his second Wanamaker Mile, and a few weeks later there was widespread speculation that he'd be going after my indoor record in the Vitalis meet at the Meadowlands. Sean O'Neill had come over from Ireland to serve as the rabbit. Two other Irishmen, Frank O'Mara and Gerry O'Reilly who was mentored by Gerry Farnan, would also compete and help with the pace. I was longing to be in it myself.

The day before the meet I was asked to come out to the Meadowlands to test the boards and make sure all was in order for the record attempt. Coe was also sched- uled to run in the 3,000 metres and appear at a press conference that day, but when his flight was delayed they asked me fill in.

"I'll be rooting for Marcus to break my record," I told the press, "it's his turn."

I had been appointed the honorary starter for the race. I remember lining up the field, saying "On your marks," and then firing the gun.

Then I said to myself "What the f*** did you just do? You've just sent him off to break your record."

I expected O'Sullivan to eclipse my world record in the Meadowlands in that race, but Marcus fell short, winning in 3:50.94, however, Marcus could take some solace in the knowledge that his time made him the second-fastest indoor miler in history.

Over that winter, I also threw myself headlong into what I hoped might pave the way for a post-running career through my involvement with a Connecticut based firm called Execom.

I came away from Villanova with a degree in marketing and a minor in communications, as my early experience with Equity Bank aptly demonstrated, I was hardly an expert in either.

Over the next decade, beginning with my job at Bord Fáilte and the negotiations I found myself involved with in dealing with the commercial aspects of sport, I acquired, sometimes by osmosis, a fairly substantial background in the subject.

Although I was sometimes flying by the seat of my pants, somewhere in the back of my mind I knew I was gaining a foundation I might be able to put to use.

As I struggled through my injuries in the late 1980s, I figured that the game might be coming to an end. While I still wasn't prepared to give up on running, I now had three children, Suzanne, Eamonn and Michael while Yvonne was, once again, pregnant.

While I had several ancillary jobs going, such as my involvement with the Manufacturer's Hanover Corporate Challenge programme and Heochst Celanese, I was realistic enough to know that those had come my way because of my visibility on the track. If I was no longer performing, they could end as quickly as my shoe deal had done – a pretty sobering experience for an athlete. I was wondering whether I ought to think about getting a full-time job, or at least establishing a fall-back position.

Kieran O'Reilly, a recreational runner who was prominent in New York Irish circles, suggested that I get involved in the communications field. Kieran was a former Aer Lingus executive who'd left to found his own company, EXECOM – Executive Communications, Inc.

Execom was based up in Connecticut, not far from where I lived in Rye, and specialised in setting up programmes to enhance the communication skills of business executives through coaching and workshops – both in spoken and written presentations, interviews, and public appearances.

Under Kieran's guidance, I went into training to become a communications coach. I was excited about the programme – it was an opportunity to expand into a new career doing what I thought came naturally. Over that winter, I sat in on seminars he conducted for the likes of Perrier, Norden, and Aetna. After six months of that I attended a seminar for Cadbury's and, and afterwards I told Kieran "I'm ready to go and do it now."

So off I went on the road. I led my first programme. It was something I actually enjoyed doing, and since I knew I could do as many as I wished a year, there was a sense of security. It was comforting to know that I could do something besides run.

As my new career blossomed, my running went downhill. I continually questioned myself, wondering if it was worth all the trouble. I seemed to be focusing on how hard it all was rather than thinking about the positive side of things.

I went back to Ireland for Fanahan and Jean's wedding in Cork, and while I was in Dublin I stopped by to check out the house, which was under construction. When I got to Porterstown I couldn't believe the size of it. One of my friends said it looked like a hotel, which I took to be a compliment.

At the same time I found myself wondering "Do I really want to come back here?"

In America one would see the first signs of spring; but Ireland was still windy, wet and miserable. To make matters worse, Dublin itself seemed unkempt and untidy, and there was a pervasive depression.

People I'd speak to seemed to have no interest or motivation. The whole attitude struck me as bad. You'd hardly have known there was a Celtic Tiger lurking around the corner, and I found myself seriously questioning whether I wanted to return home the way we'd always planned.

Fanahan and Jean had come over on their honeymoon, and stopped off to visit us in Rye. It was wonderful seeing him, because we hadn't had much one-on-one time at the wedding. He was able to rekindle my lagging spirits somewhat. I'd achieved a couple of the goals he'd laid out for me in the hospital a year and a half earlier, and getting to the Seoul Olympics was another part of that equation that would bring my career to a "grand finale."

In reality, I was kidding myself trying to hold on to the athletics career. I was feeling a bit more in control of my running and I tried to be patient. I kept reminding myself that the Olympics were still several months away.

Fanahan's visit inspired me – in reality I continued to struggle. I was fighting a losing battle. It was a fight that deep down inside I probably knew I couldn't win in the end – but I kept reminding myself of Jumbo's adage – "You've always got one good race in you." I hoped that maybe it might come at the right time. Every day was a new struggle, but I wanted to see this thing through to the bitter end, rather than quitting.

As summer approached, I knew in my heart I wasn't going to win an Olympic medal. I knew I'd have to be terribly lucky to even make it to the final. But I just wanted to go. I wanted to share in the Olympic experience one last time.

Olympic ignominy

D uring the course of my career, I had a number of disagreements with the Olympic Council of Ireland on the question of Olympic qualification. In the past it had been a philosophical issue, but as the 1988 Games approached it had been put to the test.

It was clear by then that my career was winding down. Now aged thirty-five and with a long history of shin, back and thigh injuries and assorted aches and pains, I wanted to finish up with a flourish by making it to one more Olympics.

Fanahan McSweeney had urged me to give it one more chance – and somewhere in the back of my mind was Jumbo's reminder.

Perhaps, if I could somehow manage to qualify, that "one race" might be an Olympic final.

I struggled through the summer of 1988, turning up all over the USA in pursuit of the 5,000 metre qualifying standard and failed. I finally achieved it in August at the Ivo Van Damme Memorial meet in Belgium, beating the mark by a mere two-tenths of a second.

Back at the hotel in Brussels, I was elated to have made the time, but concerned because I knew that I was getting near the end of the line. I was sharing a room with John Treacy who'd run really well that evening.

John was sitting on the edge of the bed, counting out the $5,000 cash he'd received as an appearance fee.

"Jesus, Coghlan, think about it, all this money, isn't it great?" said Treacy. And with that he threw the whole stack of bills up into the air.

It was like a shower of confetti coming down on top of us in the room.

What he didn't know was that while he got paid, I had received no appearance money for that race in Belgium. My pay-days on the European circuit had come to an end and I didn't even recognise then that I was no longer a viable commodity.

I suppose the meet promoter thought he was doing me a favour by giving me a chance to qualify for the Olympics.

My name was included on the panel nominated by the BLE for Seoul, but the Olympic Council of Ireland had other ideas. I returned home to New York to find my telephone answering machine flashing with what seemed to be an inordinate number of messages. Almost all of them came from journalists, looking for my reaction to what the *Sunday Press* described as "the OCI's appalling decision" not to send me to Seoul. The word was that the Olympic Council didn't think I was good enough to go.

My reaction was to the point "I didn't cause a controversy," I said, "all I did was qualify for the Olympic Games. The Olympic Council of Ireland caused the problem."

Once word leaked out, a public outcry quickly developed. Under immense pressure from the Irish media over such shabby treatment of a sporting icon, the Olympic Council eventually reversed its decision and put me back on the team.

No sooner had I been nominated than I got a phone call from Brendan Foreman, an official of the Federation who was also the treasurer of the Olympic Council, reminding me that I had to pay my trust fund money if I wanted to go to the Olympics.

"You must not have been paying attention," I told him. "I haven't been racing. I haven't earned any money this year."

I then composed a letter to Primo Nebiolo, the president of the IAAF, explaining this, and sent a copy to BLE. Of course, I never actually sent the letter to Nebiolo, but BLE believed that I had, and backed off.

Having been selected to the Irish team, I continued to train in the stifling heat and humidity of New York for the last few weeks. I was working out mostly alone, finding it difficult to concentrate positively on the Olympics. In reality, I knew my swansong in Seoul was something I was not particularly looking forward to.

Right before I was scheduled to leave for Seoul, Yvonne gave birth to our fourth child John, two weeks ahead of schedule, on September 6th. I questioned whether I should bother going or not. It was as if I was looking for an excuse to miss the inevitable. Staying in New York looking after the four children while she recovered meant more to me than the Olympics.

But, Yvonne would not have any of it. She'd already arranged for a child-minder to come out from Ireland to assist her.

I flew to the Far East via Alaska. I'd never been to either place before, making the entire trip another journey into uncharted territory. It reminded me of the day I'd left Shannon for the United States seventeen years earlier. I was flying to the other side of the world and into the great unknown. I was scared, scared of the outcome I felt in my bones before I landed in Korea.

Despite their original reluctance to have me at Seoul, Pat Hickey of the Olympic Council of Ireland greeted me warmly on my arrival. He was genuinely delighted to see me and I appreciated his encouragement given the massive misgivings and doubts I was experiencing, which at times threatened to overwhelm me.

On a more realistic level, I harboured no real illusions about winning a medal, or, probably, even reaching the final in Seoul. I'd just wanted one more chance to share the Olympic experience, and I knew this would be my last. I was cheating myself and afraid to let go.

While I got out of my heat, I did not feel in control of my running. I pretended I was all right and that it would be easier in the semi-final. But in the 5,000 semi-final I got bumped on the sixth lap, and lost concentration completely. I was like a novice runner while the young legs of my competitors took off and left me standing almost still.

My legs got heavier and heavier and I could feel myself being sucked to the back of the pack as if I was taken in with a vacuum cleaner. It was humiliating and lonely running alone. The temptation was to just say "forget it" and walk off the track, but Daley Thompson had stationed himself in the infield, near the edge of the track and was shouting "Come on, Eamonn!"

Daley was a two-time Olympic decathlon gold medallist. In Seoul, he was struggling too, but he took the time to stay there and cheer me on. Lap after lap, each time I'd pass by Thompson would be there encouraging me to keep it going and not to quit.

I did keep going, but I trailed the entire field over the final mile and finished fifteenth out of sixteen runners.

Now, I had to admit at thirty-six-years-of-age that I never would. But I had to give it one more try. I had seen Fanahan lying on his deathbed and whatever belief he had in me to succeed I just had to go with in the hope I could do something.

It was as if Fanahan had replaced Gerry and Jumbo after they'd passed away. I needed that crutch, that figurehead to inspire me to keep on going. I think it was a case that they had so much belief in my natural ability and in the end it was luck that wasn't on my side.

There is always one more chance an athlete looks for and deep in the back of my mind I still could not let it go. I had nothing else to do but "Run, Run, Run!"

Dopers

On the night of the 100 metre final at the Seoul Olympics, I was seated in the stands with John Treacy and Ray Flynn, along with the Irish cyclist John McQuaid.

When the gun went off, Canada's Ben Johnson absolutely exploded out of the blocks and in an almost preternatural display of speed, left Carl Lewis in his wake to win in a world record time of 9.79 seconds.

It was a stunning performance, one that caused most of the 100,000 in attendance at Jamsil Stadium that night to wildly cheer in unison.

The Irish contingent was not among the celebrants. Neither were most of the other world-class athletes who witnessed the feat.

The reaction was more like "Oh, Jesus. He's got away with it." I didn't just suspect that Johnson had cheated, I knew it, and the widespread reaction among all of us was one of profound disgust.

I had seen Johnson's development from the time he had first emerged on the scene as a Toronto schoolboy. A few years earlier one of my Canadian friends Mike McIntosh, a Jamaican by birth and who coached in Scarborough, Ontario, had first alerted me to his suspicions as Johnson's times suddenly began to improve beyond any reasonable expectation.

To anyone who was running on the indoor circuit in those years it was perfectly obvious that something was going on. Ben's body was literally changing before our eyes. You might not have seen it from meet to meet, but it was apparent from year to year. It wasn't just that his muscles and veins looked ready to burst out of his skin: His eyes looked like they were going to bulge out of their sockets, and the whites of his eyes appeared to have become discoloured with jaundice.

Two days later the suspicions were confirmed when Johnson tested positive for the steroid nandrolone. He was stripped of his gold medal and, ultimately, banned for life. His world record was also stricken from the books.

The scandal emanating from the Johnson episode may have been the first time the public at large was even aware that drug use might benefit sprinters. For years steroids had been considered the special province of weight men: shot-putters, hammer and discus throwers had been exposed with an almost monotonous regularity, and while no one had ever accused them of taking steroids, there had been reports that the Finns were availing themselves of a practice called "blood doping" as far back as the 1972 Games in Munich.

What happened in Seoul in 1988 set off the alarm that there was a serious problem with drug usage in sport, but around the Olympic Village the reaction was a combination of shock and relief that what we all knew had been confirmed. Most of us were thinking "Well, good. He finally got caught."

At the same time, I was aware that Ben Johnson was merely the tip of the iceberg. For several days, rumours swirled that the other shoe was about to drop, this time on Florence Joyner-Kersee.

Flo-Jo won three gold medals in Seoul – and then inexplicably retired from the sport. Officially, she never failed a drug test, but a few years later she would be dead, at 38, ostensibly the victim of a heart attack.

I had watched Flo-Jo's development over the years too, and it seemed that the evolution of her physical characteristics had been even more dramatic than Ben Johnson's.

Her body had undergone a startling transformation. You could see the bone growth in her jaw, in her cheeks, in her forehead, and she had gone from being a pretty good sprinter to absolutely supernatural. The suspicions about her weren't just about steroids. The talk among athletes was that she was using HGH – human growth hormone.

Joyner-Kersee was a flamboyant figure who, at the time, reigned as the face of women's track and field. With her self-designed outfits and her elaborately painted long fingernails, she had captivated the imagination of the public.

Suffice it to say that had she followed Johnson into the Hall of Shame that summer it might have dealt a blow from which the Olympic movement might never have recovered.

I don't know this for a fact, because as far as I know she never failed a drugs test, but the word among athletes was that she'd allegedly tested positive for something, but was supposedly let off on condition that she walk away quietly from the sport.

Put it this way: She'd just captured three gold medals. She was the hottest property in track and field. She could have made a fortune in appearance money right after Seoul. Why else would she retire at the prime of her career?

From the time I first arrived in America seventeen years earlier, I had heard rumours and innuendos about different athletes, but you wouldn't know what to believe. I always dismissed the rumours and simply got on with the job and tried not to think of who might or might not be on drugs as I lined up for my races.

My only experience with performance enhancing drugs was at Villanova when we'd make periodic visit to Dr. Boyle, the team's physician, for a Vitamin B-12 shot in the arse. It was almost a joke amongst us. I'd run into Schappert or Hartnett and they'd say "Eamonn, you didn't get your B-12 shot today?"

The use of drugs never fitted into the equation. If you weren't interested in looking for them, you didn't pay much attention to what was going on around you. It was partially my background in coming from Catholic Ireland. You just don't cheat, period.

But from the time of my first Olympics in 1976, I'd heard rumours about the Finnish runners and blood doping, and there were always suspicions about the Eastern Bloc. In later years you'd hear plenty of stories about Italians, Spaniards and North Africans too. At the Los Angeles Games in 1984, there was a lot of talk about American athletes, particularly sprinters. The use of drugs "Who's doing what?" became the dominant topic of conversion.

Prior to the 1980 Olympics, I was inquisitive and needed to know more about drugs and blood doping and what real benefit I could get out of their use. I consulted with Dr. Terry McGuire, an Irish physician, who competed in athletics for the Civil Service AC and who had in previous conversations voiced his suspicions about many athletes in the sport using drugs.

Terry explained how performance-enhancing substances worked, while warning of their dangers. His description of shrinking testicles, damage to the liver and other organs, and widespread acne, painted a grim and unappealing portrait.

"Besides," he pointed out, "there's no point in taking them and then getting caught and blowing everything you've achieved."

McGuire also mentioned that he'd read the study that Tony Brien, who was my team-mate in Donore Harriers and a former National Cross-Country Champion, had recently completed his thesis on the subject of blood doping.

He'd gone to Marymount College in Kansas, where he'd taken a PhD in sports physiology. He gave me a copy of the thesis and I went about studying it with keen interest because, bottom line – blood doping couldn't be detected.

In his study, he explained how he'd take two pints of blood from the athletes and after a period of time and training, he'd injected it back into the athletes to maximise performance. The theory was that by increasing the athletes red blood cells, the body's ability to absorb oxygen would improve dramatically and therefore increase the level of the athletes overall endurance. In other words, the athlete could run faster for longer periods without going into oxygen depth. Some people were dubious about its benefits, but Tony Brien pretty conclusively demonstrated that blood doping did work.

He did random testing with the athletes he chose for his study group, so while he'd blood-dope some, he didn't others. He measured the training regime over a period of time and established that blood doping was indeed effective.

I'd never even considered that. The whole thought of taking blood and injecting it back into one's body seemed rather repulsive to me.

And by then there'd been refinements. Instead of preserving the whole pint of blood, they could put it through a centrifuge, spin off the red blood cells, and inject those back into you. That was effective, but it was also dangerous.

They'd also learned that you didn't even necessarily have to do it with your own blood. In many cases, blood donated by a family member would work just as well.

After I read about that, I was having a few pints with my brothers Bill and Brendan one night and told them about it.

"Hey," they said, "if you ever want some of our blood, no problem."

I never did.

Following the collapse of the Berlin Wall and the reunification of Germany, Stasi documents were unearthed exposing that the East German government had for years overseen a programme of systematic doping. The principal culprits (or, perhaps, victims, since in many cases the guinea pigs didn't even realise they were the subject of clinical experiments) were the swimmers, but the East German files also implicated several sprinters, along with Waldemar Cierpinski, who had won the Marathon gold medal at Montreal in 1976.

The Germans were undone primarily because they were pretty stupid crooks, leaving a trail of evidence by maintaining extensive records of their activities.

A few years later the Finns were exposed, almost by accident.

At one World Cross-Country Championship, six Finnish skiers were caught in a blood-doping scandal after they tested positive for Hydroxylethyl starch, a plasma volume expander and masking agent against Erythropoietin, the red blood-cell stimulant familiarly known as EPO. Neither the Finns nor the doctors and coaches who treated them had been aware that the World Anti-Doping Agency had developed a urine test that could detect HES.

After more than a decade of dominance that began in 1972, Finnish runners abruptly vanished from the landscape. Although they were never directly implicated in blood doping, at least one of them implicated himself.

Kaarlo Maakina, the Finn who had taken the bronze medal ahead of me in Moscow in 1980, subsequently underwent a religious conversion and became a born-again Christian. As an affirmation of his new found faith, he owned up to having cheated his way to his Olympic medals by blood-doping, and purged his conscience by throwing both his 5,000 bronze and 10,000 silver medals into a lake.

Frank Shorter, the 1972 marathon winner who had finished second to Cierpinski four years later, threatened to bring a lawsuit to force the IOC to award him the '76 gold medal as well.

"Athletes deserve a level playing field," said Shorter, "a deterrent has to be created by letting people know that there is no statute of limitations on what I view as a fraud perpetrated on sport."

In view of Maanika's admissions, it was suggested that I might have a similar case. The Finn had by his own admission cheated his way to a bronze medal that should rightfully have been mine.

While there was an opportunity for me to do that, I never ever considered pursuing it. It was gold I wanted, not silver, not a bronze. Besides, when the Olympic Council were asked if they'd consider pursuing "my case," word came back that blood doping was not officially banned nor could it be detected back in 1980.

For most of my competitive career, I had the attitude that since I'd been breaking my balls everybody else could have been, too. I was regularly tested, and always believed that if you got caught, you were guilty. It was a black-and-white situation as far as I was concerned, and I never allowed myself to go down that road.

I did always find myself wondering "Where do they get these steroids?" I wouldn't have even known where to start looking. At the same time, as the drug issue became more pervasive, I was forced to educate myself about it.

The common misconception is that taking steroids makes you run fast. That doesn't happen. The athlete is required to go on a programme and develop over a period of time, and he or she is not necessarily improving his performance as such, what he's improving is his ability to train longer and harder because his body is able to recover much quicker.

The other benefit is that steroids hasten the recovery time from injuries, and if ever there was a candidate for that, it was myself once my body started falling apart.

During the period of my physical decline as I was approaching the Seoul Olympics in 1988, I was seeing a sports doctor in New York for treatment on my ailing back.

During the course of one of my visits the subject of the use of steroids in track and field came up in conversation. At this stage of my career the injuries were mounting up. I was so frustrated because I knew I was at the end. My mind knew how to run but my body wouldn't allow me. For the first time in my life I was tempted to cross over to the dark side.

The doctor didn't exactly suggest steroid-aided recovery, but he did say that they'd certainly help me at my age to increase my strength and speed.

"It's your call. If you want to try it, I'm prepared to write you a prescription."

He did me a prescription, but under a fictitious name. I walked out of his office and found a nearby pharmacy. I knew they wouldn't ask me for identification, and I was literally standing there on a street corner in New York City, looking at the prescription, looking at the chemist shop.

"Will I, won't I?" I kept nervously asking myself. I was really scared, yet I wanted something to help me get the body I needed to run fast again. Finally, I said "F*** it – no. I can't," and tore it up and threw it into the waste bin on the corner.

I don't know to this very day whether that doctor knows that I never used the prescription he wrote. All I know is that at that moment I was on the verge, but I couldn't bring myself to do it.

My finishing pace in Seoul reflected that I didn't cheat.

When Johnson was stripped of his gold medal in Seoul, it was awarded instead to Lewis, who had finished second in the tainted race. I had competed in meets all over the world with the American sprinter and considered him a personal friend. Over the years Lewis would win nine Olympic gold medals, but was himself dogged by intimations that his performances might have been chemically aided.

I'd known Carl since 1978, when Jumbo Elliott had tried to recruit him. Jumbo had even personally visited him, the way he later would John Treacy, but like John, Carl turned him down. I remember how shocked and disappointed we all were when Carl chose Houston over Villanova.

There had been suspicions and rumours about Carl Lewis going back to 1983, that I could recall, but I was always willing to give him the benefit of the doubt. To me he seemed to come across as the clean-cut, natural-born athlete. He wasn't "just" a sprinter: He embodied athleticism and grace.

Besides, you never saw the physical changes in Carl that you did in Ben Johnson. The only thing that changed about Carl was his nose, which he got fixed.

And he was a genuinely nice guy. I travelled the circuit with him for many years, and we shared the headlines at countless indoor meets. I had the utmost respect for him.

Johnson wasn't the only sprinter to get caught in Seoul. Britain's Linford Christie also tested positive, but he got away with it by blaming it on some ginseng tea he'd taken. A few years later he tested positive at a meet in Germany and got banned for life, confirming what many of us had suspected all along. But Carl Lewis passed every test he was given at that same Olympics.

I'd always defended Carl, perhaps because I genuinely liked the guy. He was a fellow member of the fraternity in a way Ben Johnson never was.

Only years later did it emerge that he had indeed been using performance-enhancing substances. Documents revealed that Lewis' drug test at the 1988 Olympic Trials had confirmed the presence of three different types of stimulants. He had initially been suspended, but that was reversed on appeal. He was quietly let off with a warning and allowed to compete, but that revelation, in my view, left everything that he had accomplished open to question.

"Well, f*** you, Carl," I thought to myself. I was extremely disappointed. I had made an emotional investment by siding with him, and in the end I felt betrayed.

Whenever I stepped on the track, I believed I could win, so I never thought about what the other guy might be using. I know some of my opponents relied on altitude training, but I never bothered with that, either, and the same went for steroids. Somehow I would have thought less of myself if I had used them, even though they would almost certainly have helped me recover from the injuries I battled from the 1980s onward.

It was sometimes tempting, but the way I looked at it, if I'd started dabbling late in my career it would have detracted from everything I'd accomplished before, so I never did.

My anxiety seemed to increase with each committee meeting: as a meeting approached I'd find myself almost petrified with apprehension as I was heading straight into an unrecognisable state of depression. Not long after I returned from Seville, I was driving to one of these meetings and found myself fighting off an impulse to grab the steering wheel and drive the car right into the Liffey. I was astonished by the power of the thought, how very logical such a course of action could be and how much I simply wanted to end my life there and then.

Part

THE BOARDS
HE MILE

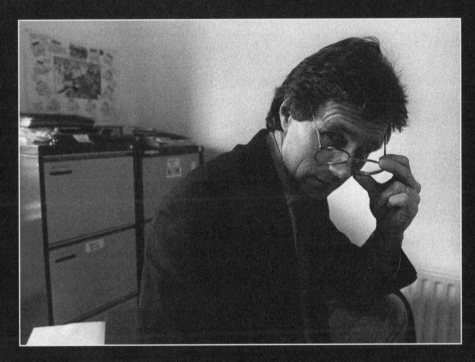

V

Eamonn photographed in the offices of the BLE shortly after he became its Chief Executive Officer in 1991. The politics and in-fighting would exact a huge toll on Eamonn — physically and mentally.

Into the lions' den

My decision to return to the track wars in early 1990 was greeted with some scepticism, even in Ireland. "Without being too cynical, you could easily suggest that Coghlan's bank balance will flourish more than his athletic balance," opined the *Evening Herald*. "Coghlan's comeback may just turn into a sad and embarrassing fiasco."

What seemed a mean-spirited observation proved to be more accurate than not. While I had been recently voted the male Track and Field Athlete of the Decade by the US Athletics Congress, it became apparent in short order that time was catching up with me.

I was struggling badly with aches and pains in my back and hips. All the strength and power I once possessed had deserted my body and spirit. The mere act of getting out of the bed in the morning was even proving to be difficult. I just could not let go and it was a matter of hoping to hang on in there as long as I possibly could

The comeback began auspiciously enough in January when I deliberately sought out a meet promising mid-level competition and won a 3,000 metre race in Hamilton, Ontario. It was my first real race since the last-place finish in Seoul nearly a year and a half earlier, but it was nothing to write home about.

In fact, I won two of my first three 1990 races, but rapidly hit the skids: I finished an inglorious fifth in the Wanamaker Mile behind the winner Marcus O'Sullivan and the following week, running on the Meadowlands track I helped design and where I'd previously broken the world record, I finished seventh in a 3,000 metre race, eighteen seconds behind winner Doug Padilla. Seven nights later my tale of woe continued at the Forum in Inglewood, California when I trailed Padilla home in twenty-two seconds. A week later I dropped out of the US National Championships indoor three-mile after just five laps in Madison Square Garden.

The writing was all over the wall and I didn't want to see it.

Before the season had begun, I had lost my shoe contract with Avia. If that wasn't a good enough indication of what people in the industry thought of my prospects, well nothing was.

My friend, Pete Squires, the adidas promotions representative whose shoe company I was contracted to in the past, had told me point blank "Eamonn, you've got too much class, don't run indoors, you don't need it. You don't need to go out of the sport on a low and you don't need the pity of the fans."

He was right. They obviously recognised something that I wasn't prepared to recognise myself. That I was hanging on by a thread.

But, I knew nothing else, all I wanted to do was run. Running was my bread and butter and I was getting paid not necessarily to win races, but to put bums on seats. That was my justification.

"For Coghlan, this season has been mostly an embarrassment," wrote one commentator in the *Evening Herald*. He was right. I was highly embarrassed and I didn't want to end my career in this fashion.

Asked by the *New York Times'* Frank Litsky, whether I'd be back for another indoor season in '91, I replied "Why would I hang around another year to finish fifth or sixth?"

In the past, I had always been able to rationalise poor performances, writing them off to injury or improper conditioning, but I recognised that my biggest enemy lay within.

My legs were weary, I was nearly thirty-eight years of age – and I felt it. I was frankly ashamed over the way I'd ended my indoor career, but I was realistic enough to know that my time was up. I retired from international competition in Madison Square Gardens, the venue where I had previously run eighteen races, lost two and dropped out of my last.

From the time I'd arrived as a college freshman I had now spent nineteen years in America – literally half of my lifetime. Back in 1980, on the day I returned from Moscow, I'd purchased property in Dublin, and now Fanahan McSweeney, his cancer in apparent remission, had been building a house for us there. The project was nearing completion and that kept me busy shuttling back and forth between New York and Dublin on a regular basis.

For years, Yvonne and I had talked about eventually moving back to Ireland, but I'd always been the apprehensive one and thought of a reason to put it off. Not only did I have unfinished business on the track, but as long as I was running well there were all sorts of business opportunities. Everyone kept running after me. I'd been living the life of a celebrity, and frankly, I'd enjoyed it, so I kept deferring the decision.

That spring I came back to consult with Fanahan about putting the finishing touches on the house. When I returned to New York on May 4th, the anniversary of Gerry's death, I walked through the door of our home in Rye , kissed Yvonne and the children and said "We're going home Yvonne."

"What do you mean we're going home?" she answered back. "We're departing for Ireland on July 31st, I've made up my mind," I said as she stood looking at me in total disbelief.

Yvonne was delighted. The kids, who now ranged in age from two to eleven, would have a chance to be around with their grandparents, aunts, uncles and cousins. We had less than three months to pack up everything and move home to a new life in Ireland.

Exactly what I was going to *do* once I moved back to Ireland was another matter entirely. But then, by chance, on my next house inspection trip to Dublin I ran into Noel Carroll who told me that BLE had been looking for a Chief Executive for two years. The Minister for Sport, Frank Fahey, had become very annoyed with the foot-dragging and wanted to go forward in a "professional" manner by bringing in a responsible executive to head up the federation.

Like many long-established organisations, BLE had traditionally been operated as a veritable fiefdom by an entrenched bureaucracy. Fahey's plan was to stream-line things by bringing in a CEO, which he felt was within his powers, since the organisation was in part funded by the Irish Government. In fact, funds had been approved for the position nearly two years earlier, but nothing had come of it.

Noel asked me if I'd be interested in the job.

"Jesus, I don't know," I replied, "but yeah, it sounds great. I suppose I might be."

I had no idea what I was getting myself into.

Noel Carroll had himself been a former Villanova athlete and Olympian. He'd represented Ireland in the 800 metres both in Tokyo in 1964 and in Mexico City four years later. Carroll was now the public relations officer for the Dublin Corporation, and while he had no official position with either the Irish Government or the Athletics Federation, he was well connected and moved easily between the worlds of politics, sport, and journalism.

Carroll knew better than most where all the bodies were buried, and it wasn't altogether surprising that he would seize the initiative in conveying the "feeler."

He had also been an outspoken critic of the BLE old guard. In a 1989 guest column in the *Independent,* Carroll had blistered the federation for stubbornly clinging to the past:

"All enthusiastic promoters of top class athletics in this country are harassed by BLE," wrote Carroll. "If it's not over permits, it's over money paid to athletes or over the selection of teams or over 'control' and 'authority.'

"Put simply, BLE won't do the job themselves and they won't let anybody else do it. Instead of fighting with runners over money they claim is owed they should be paying runners to involve themselves in their own promotions."

When we spoke over tea that day, Noel and I talked in very abstract terms about the need to bring modern-day management methods to the organisation. One of my ideas was that I could utilise my contacts and bring some world-class athletes to Dublin. I also outlined my thoughts about bringing athletics to schools, reinforcing the club system and removing the stigma of incompetence associated with the BLE.

I also expressed my misgivings. I said I thought the perpetual infighting within the bureaucracy made matters difficult for athletes. In the US, the attitude seemed to be "What can we do to help?" but in Ireland the very opposite appeared to be the case.

A day after that discussion with Noel, I travelled back to New York to complete the family's preparation to move back to Ireland. The next day, the phone rang at the house in Rye. It was the Minister himself.

"Eamonn, Frank Fahey here," said the cheery voice on the other end of the line. "I was just speaking to Noel Carroll, who informed me of your interest. I just wanted to hear it from the horse's mouth."

I told him I was honoured to get the call and that "Yes Minister," since I planned to return to Ireland I *would* be interested in the BLE job.

The next day back in Dublin the *Evening Herald* had a headline reading
"COGHLAN LANDS JOB"
and an accompanying story about the £100,000 salary I'd be getting for a position I hadn't even taken.

There was an almost immediate, and predictable, outcry from the green blazers of the BLE. Describing the appointment as "an impingement on the democratic process," they claimed that Fahey had no right to install a Chief Executive without going through the proper process. It was precisely this "process," the Minister pointed out, which had produced a stalemate that had left the position unfilled for two years already.

When it developed that the Minister had privately secured approval from a three-man board BLE delegation consisting of president Bobby Begley, honorary secretary Liam Hennessy, and Michael Quinlan, the treasurer, it only got the other green blazers' backs up further. Their contention was that any such decision could only be undertaken with the approval of the twenty-four person Management Committee – a committee already notorious for its inability to agree on *anything.*

Those in the BLE who felt they'd been bypassed and bullied, dug in to oppose my nomination. When Minister Fahey appeared at a meeting in the BLE headquarters on Prospect Road to explain his position, he was forced to remain outside the door for over an hour while they decided they'd even deign to receive him.

The next three or four months were total chaos. One day I was in the job, the next day I was out of the job, the day after that I was back in again.

As this political farrago played out, the family moved home to live in Porterstown in Dublin.

When I left Ireland to live in America I had one suitcase in hand. Nineteen years later I was returning with two forty-foot containers, a wife and four young children.

To make matters worse, two hours before we got on the Aer Lingus flight to Dublin the moving company threatened to keep all our belongings in Rotterdam Port and "we would never see them again," if I did not pay up an extra $3,000 for what they considered, excess baggage.

I paid up alright and eventually the containers arrived three weeks after we got home. Later, I sued the company for breach of contract and was refunded not just the $3,000, but the entire cost of the shipping for what the judge considered was extortion.

There was considerable support for my appointment from the grass-roots athletes and, for the most part, the Irish media were highly supportive. In the *Independent*, Tom O'Riordan essentially endorsed my candidacy when he outlined the reasons an infusion of fresh blood was in order:

"Athletics in Ireland have slipped alarmingly over the last six years. There was a fantastic sense of optimism in the mid-1970s, and this reached an all-time high from '78 to '84 when Eamonn's late father Bill was BLE President during most of those years, but it has been very much on a slippery slope ever since," wrote O'Riordan.

"Coghlan himself caused much of this excitement with three world indoor mile records in 79, 81, and 83, an unforgettable 5,000m gold medal strike at the Helsinki World Championships in 1983, and his two valiant, if unsuccessful, attempts to win medals at the 76 and 80 Olympics."

On October 10th, the *Independent* carried a report that "Eamonn Coghlan is almost certain to be appointed Chief Executive of BLE when the Athletics Association's Management Committee meets in emergency session Monday night... An official announcement of his appointment will be made on Tuesday."

That prediction proved overly optimistic. A week later the *Evening Herald* further speculated on the imminent decision or "whether or not BLE will accept Eamonn Coghlan as the Association's new Chief Executive."

Revealing for the first time that the Government, through Fahey, had agreed to make funds available to make up any shortfall between its initial £20,000 grant and the proposed £35,000 salary, Tom O'Riordan informed his readers that:

"Coghlan has had discussions with the BLE President, Bobby Begley, and I understand that these have been very fruitful. In fact, it would appear that the vast majority of members in the Management Committee have now come around to supporting the officers who accepted Coghlan's proposal from Frank Fahey, the Minister with responsibility for sport, in the first place."

But a month later nothing had happened and with the appointment still twisting in the wind, Frank Fahey angrily threatened to withdraw the Government funding already allocated to BLE.

Noel Caroll, who had initially played the matchmaker's role, had heretofore distanced himself from the fray, but in the November 11th *Irish Independent*, Carroll wrote:

"The proposal to appoint Eamonn Coghlan as Chief Executive of BLE has no stated opposition. Unanimous support is guaranteed. The funds are forthcoming. The key figure is ready, willing, and able. The case for the defence is wearing thin, yet the saga continues…. The tail of BLE has been wagging the dog, Irish Athletics, for too long. There is an opportunity now to push forward and bring Irish athletics into the 1990s. If this is not done, the sport will regress further. Eamonn Coghlan's appointment to head BLE at this time is critical. It would be a gross injustice to athletics in Ireland if this matter were allowed to drag on for one day more."

"One day more" may have been optimistic. A week after Carroll's editorial, the *Evening Herald* confidently predicted that "Eamonn Coghlan will almost certainly become the most powerful man in Irish athletics tonight after BLE's management Committee meeting… his appointment is the only item on the agenda, and president Bobby Begley hopes the meeting will be resolved at tonight's meeting."

Needless to say – it didn't happen..

For public consumption, I did my best to stay above the fray, but after three months I'd be less than honest if I said it wasn't getting to me. I was already weary of the infighting, and I hadn't even started in the job.

It was difficult for us all and with Suzanne and Eamonn Jr. just starting their new schools, the general atmosphere in the house was – to put it mildly – strained.

In late November, I accepted an invitation to return to New York for my installation in the New York Athletic Club's Hall of Fame. It was a refreshing visit. I was made feel welcome and appreciated. I began to think that perhaps I made a mistake returning to live in Ireland.

While in New York, Ray Lumpp, the Athletic Director of the NYAC asked me if I'd reconsider his offer which he had made numerous times before – to become director of athletics at the club after his retirement. While I often thought about it, I again said "Ray, thanks but, I am committed to Ireland at this stage of my life."

In light of the carry on at the BLE, I have to confess that I wasn't entirely convinced I was making the right decision.

I flew back to Dublin after the induction and drove straight to Waterford, where the BLE Congress was meeting at the Grand Hotel in Tramore.

I don't know what made me go. In retrospect I didn't know how to play the game, the political game. Perhaps I was set up when asked to attend the meeting and address the delegates. Being innocent and raw politically, I felt that I should continue on fighting for the job and not let the Minister down.

I was initially refused permission to address the group, but pressure from some of the grass-roots organisations forced a change of mind.

I did my best to outline my plan. I told them it was important that BLE move along, that I would be delighted to do the job, and that I couldn't understand why the powers-that-be were still trying to throw up roadblocks to progress.

I opened my address by noting that "When I came here and was told that I could not speak, my immediate feeling was that, for the third time, I did not want the job."

I also recalled an occasion a quarter-century earlier when, as an entrant in a BLE-sponsored junior race, I had been forced to change my clothes behind the trees in the Phoenix Park.

"And nothing has changed in those 25 years," I reminded them.

"We have a goldmine of talent in this country and we don't even realise it. We give out about athletic scholarships to America, but we cannot afford to give them the education, the competition, and the coaching which they get over there. Yet the Irish athletes in America feel alienated and left in limbo. In all my years coming back from America to compete in Ireland, I've never felt athletes were welcomed with open arms."

Then came what Tom O'Riordan reported in the *Irish Independent* described as "the moment of truth."

"Coghlan cast aside his notes and asked for a show of hands. "Would all those in favour of me please raise their hands?" a preponderance of the room did so. When he then asked those who were opposed to his appointment do the same thing, not a single delegate did. With that he walked briskly back to his seat," recorded O'Riordan, "it was a powerful performance."

I was approved as Chief Executive for a two-year term, effective from January 1st. Bobby Begley, the president, welcomed me aboard, noting that "Eamonn's worldwide marketing experience, his leadership qualities, his understanding of athletes, his undisputed knowledge of the international athletics network, makes him the ideal person for the job."

But in what would prove an ominous footnote to his speech, Begley also conceded that despite that night's apparent display of unanimity "I know that there are still people who have reservations about his appointment and simply don't want him around."

Getting on with the job

I was very naïve to think that everything had been settled. As Christmas approached, I'd run into old friends and total strangers, fellow athletes and government officials. They'd congratulate me, wish me well, and inevitably leave me with a warning to watch out for the daggers.

My friend John Maurtiz and his wife Cathy had come over from New York on a visit just after Christmas. He'd heard me talk about the Oman Cup which was held on New Year's day and he wanted to race in it.

It was a bitter cold and windy start to the New Year. The rain and sleet were teeming down when we got to the Phoenix Park. A Dublin City Harriers/BLE official was ensconced in his car, accepting entries through the window.

When Johnny approached to pay his fee he was told "No, No, this window is for the *ladies'* section. You have to go around and stand in a queue on the *other* side of the car."

"But there are no ladies here," Johnny said. "Sorry, you must go to the other side of the car," the official groaned.

Eventually, after paying his entry fee he got to run in the two mile race through the Park, a race he dreamed of running in for years. After it, Johnny looked at me and said "Coach, what have you gotten yourself in for?"

"What do you mean," I said.

"Look," as he held his hand out, "the f***** BLE people gave me a medal for a 10k race, not a two miler."

There was nothing to say really.

Later that day we went over to the BLE offices on Prospect Road in Glasnevin. I had been looking forward to my first visit there, because it was a house my father had helped buy when he was President of BLE. He'd used the money BLE had earned from the world Cross-country Championships at Limerick back in 1979, when John Treacy had won, to fund its purchase.

When we walked back to my office a shock awaited. Everywhere we looked we saw only filth and clutter – dusty boxes haphazardly stacked and grime-covered furnishings. We looked out the back window and saw more piles of trash in the garden.

"Coach," Johnny shook his head, "I don't envy you."

When I returned the following morning for my first official day on the job, the only person there was Ita Barry, the office secretary. She was plainly embarrassed and apologised for the state of the place. She said that no one in the organisation had been willing to come in to clean up before I started and they wouldn't hire professional cleaners.

"I'm going home to put on my blue jeans, and I'm coming back to clean it," she told me.

"Ita, I'll tell you what," I replied. "I'm going home, too. Then I'll put on *my* blue jeans and I'll come back to clean it with you."

That's how the Chief Executive spent his first few days on the job: Clearing trash and making his office habitable.

The paint in the reception area had begun to peel and was badly in need of refur-bishment, but when I suggested that we make it look a little better, I was told it could wait until summer.

"Well," I suggested, "why don't we at least paint the front door for now?" Again this suggestion was rejected.

A few weeks later, Liam Collins came by the office to do a story for the *Sunday Independent*. I hadn't realised the depth of mistrust the green blazers seemed to have for the press until the piece appeared the following weekend.

Even though Collins' story was overwhelmingly positive, both towards me and the BLE, the hierarchy took great offence at his description of what he called "the uninspiring offices of BLE," accompanied by a photograph of me standing outside.

"Sandwiched between a Chinese takeaway and a doctor's surgery, there is no indication that the red-bricked suburban house in Phibsboro, Dublin, is the headquarters of the country's main athletics organisation," wrote Collins. "You know by the run-down appearance of the place that this is an organisation with a major image problem, badly in need of dragging into the 1990s."

I was dragged into a board meeting to explain why I'd allowed a journalist to intrude into the sacred premises, and held up a copy of the offending newspaper story to prove their point.

"That," I replied with a shrug, "is why I wanted this place painted."

It was already becoming clear that many of them shared a motive, and it wasn't to welcome me in. It was to get me out. I'd underestimated the political minefield

I'd stepped into.

My contract with the BLE was for two years, but in February when I laid out my long-range vision for the federation, and included a short list of priorities that needed to be addressed sooner rather than later, I might as well have provided my enemies with a blueprint on how best to thwart me.

In a plea for unity, I suggested that in all the athletics organisations in Ireland there are good people, but we'd got to stop tripping each other up.

I stressed the need for co-operation between BLE, the BHAA, the NACA, the Northern Ireland AAA, the Ulster Sports Council, the Community Games and the clubs and stressed the need to recognise that while each entity was different and separate, we were unified in one common goal.

My objective was to improve the image of the organisation. To that end I thought that it would take at least £250,000 to promote a good international track and field meeting run to the best international standards and featuring world and home-grown stars. And we had quite a few of them including Marcus O'Sullivan, John Treacy, Frank O'Mara, John Doherty and an up and coming Sonia O'Sullivan.

It all might have sounded reasonable, but to the old guard I might as well have drawn a line in the sand.

Even my attempts to design new BLE stationery was taken as a personal affront by many of the green blazers, and led to yet another confrontation.

I'd always considered the Irish name of the organisation something of a stigma. Bord Lúthcleas na hÉireann was a time-honoured name, but most people in other countries and even in Ireland, had no idea what it meant.

I had a commercial artist come up with a design heading that said The Irish Athletics Association, with the Irish translation for the BLE below it in smaller lettering.

The response to the proposal was seismic, ending with one member of the executive pounding his fist on the table as he roared into my face "Bord Lúthcleas na hÉireann was good enough for your father and good enough for generations of Irishmen before you. You should be proud of that name."

The proposed redesign ended in the bin.

In the face of this steadfast refusal to adopt any one of my ideas, my patience was wearing thin and my confidence was being tested. I began to have sleepless nights worrying about what I had gotten myself into. I didn't feel I had the necessary mental toughness to ignore the attitude. I was too sensitive and it was getting to me. I knew they were playing games and I didn't have any powerful allies to advise or support me. In short, *I didn't know how to play the game.*

A death impulse

A
lan Pascoe was a former 400 metre hurdles champion from Great Britain who had become a very successful businessman in sports marketing. His company, Alan Pascoe & Associates (APA), was highly regarded for bringing vast amounts of sponsorship money into British athletics and also to the IAAF.

He established a partnership in Ireland with Padraig Slattery who had a public relations company in Dublin. Their company SPA was building up business and was very interested in taking up the roll to develop sponsorship for athletics in Ireland.

During discussions with them, I had negotiated their monthly fee from about £1,000 to zero and reduced commissions for sponsors they'd bring to the table from 20% to 10%.

As Chief Executive, I was happy enough that SPA had the expertise to deliver the right mix of sponsorship and I arranged a meeting between Padraig Slattery and the BLE Executive.

Bizarrely, I was not allowed to attend.

I discovered the next day that he too, just like Minister Fahey before him, Padraig was left outside to wait for an hour beyond the scheduled time of the meeting.

Needless to say he was pissed off, but said "Eamonn, I understand, they are not used to outsiders, if this goes through it will take some time."

It didn't take any amount of time. I was subsequently called into a meeting and told "It's your job to get sponsors, not an outside agency, that's what you're paid to do."

There seemed to be no end in sight. I didn't know how much longer I'd be able to deal with the "big men" in BLE.

I wasn't allowed to sit in on committee meetings. I could attend by invitation only. Decisions were being made and in many cases I'd be the last to learn of them.

I'd had a number of meetings with RTE's head of sport, Tim O'Connor, in Donnybrook. When I submitted an expense report that included several trips over the East Link toll bridge, I was queried as to why I hadn't driven over the O'Connell Bridge instead – that would have saved them 40 pence each way.

Just as I thought things couldn't get worse – they did.

In March, I travelled to Seville for the World Indoor Championships, but when I arrived I discovered that while there were credentials waiting for the rest of the Irish delegation, there was none for the Chief Executive. My name had been left off the list.

Fortunately I knew the meet officials, so I was able to personally arrange for my accreditation, but that did nothing to alleviate the growing sense of anxiety that was now threatening to overwhelm me.

In Seville, I shared a hotel room with Marcus O'Sullivan who was going for his third straight win there.

Instead of attending any of the events surrounding the championships, I stayed in bed for four straight days and hardly left the room.

Marcus would leave the room at 8.30am and would return mid-afternoon to find me curled up in the bed with the sheets pulled over my head.

"Eamonn, what's wrong? This isn't like you at all."

I wished I could have told him the truth. "I feel real sick Marcus, I must have a bad flu bug," was how I responded.

These were the World Championships. This was my territory – and I should have been on a high both personally and professionally.

I was so used to being around my international athletics friends, all positive people and should have enjoyed their company. I should have been thrilled as Chief Executive of BLE, the Irish Athletics Board, to witness Marcus win his third gold medal for Ireland, but I simply couldn't care.

Deep down I knew the begrudgers had got to me.

In Seville, I was totally swamped with depression. It was a horrible, black feeling that induced an almost chemical-like low and despondency. It was like nothing I had ever previously experienced.

My anxiety seemed to increase with each committee meeting: As a meeting approached I'd find myself almost petrified with apprehension as I was heading straight into an unrecognisable state of depression.

Not long after I returned from Seville, I was driving to one of these meetings and found myself fighting off an impulse to grab the steering wheel and drive the car right into the Liffey. I was astonished by the power of the thought, how very logical such a course of action could be and how much I simply wanted to end my life there and then.

I fought the impulse and then pulled the car over to the side of the road and felt myself hyperventilating with the shock of what I had just thought.

I saw no way out. I used to be the happy-go-lucky full of energy guy, but I was now feeling weak and miserable and felt a pathetic sight in a car in Dublin's Docklands resisting an impulse to commit suicide.

I sat in the car and turned on the radio. Mary Robinson was being interviewed three months after her inauguration as President of Ireland.

Her upbeat personality and optimism was in stark contrast to my own state of mind.

She spoke about her vision for the future of our country. She spoke dynamically and eloquently about the Irish Diaspora living in America, Great Britain and around the world.

She talked about how successful they were and how much pride they brought to the small island of Ireland. She talked about placing a lighted candle in window of Áras an Uachtarán as a symbol of remembrance to the Diaspora. I thought to myself "Hey, I am one of those people, I am new to this country, I ran with such pride in my green vest."

"Don't be stupid," I told myself. "Just go to the damned meeting."

I couldn't begin to tell you what transpired at the meeting that night. I was in a complete daze. By the time I got home that night I was in tears, mentally fatigued from the anxiety and stress caused by my "dream" job in BLE.

Eventually I sat down at the kitchen table with Yvonne and told her about the feelings that were overwhelming me and which resulted in me wanting to stay in bed all day and sleep.

She revealed that she knew all along that I was not right. She said that one of her friends had suffered from something similar and had finally gone for help.

"What you're describing sounds like the same thing," she said.

I made an appointment to see a doctor at the Blackrock Clinic who told me that I was exhibiting classic symptoms of a form of depression.

It wasn't just the job, although that was clearly the catalyst. He explained that there were understandable anxieties prompted by the end of my running career and the move back to Ireland that had been compounded by fighting the seemingly unwinnable battles I faced in my new job.

He said the transition from being a winning athlete and competitor to being an "ordinary" member of society was always going to be difficult to manage. The fact that I had left the winner's circle for a job bedevilled by political intrigue was truly a recipe for disaster and that he wasn't in the least bit surprised that I was suffering from depression.

On the plus side he said "You shouldn't feel ashamed about having come here – you'd be amazed if you knew how many successful businessmen and sportsmen have experienced what you're going through. You're not alone."

He prescribed an anti-depressant drug called Serax, and suggested that I take a break from the job.

"Take time off from work, relax, and forget about everything else, try your best not to think too much. Sometimes your thinking can exacerbate the problems."

I took two weeks off but didn't really feel that much better.

BLE President, Bobby Begley and a former President, Padraic Griffin, suspected there was something up – but I never divulged the truth.

They were worried that I might pack in the job and tried to convince me that it would all work out soon enough.

And while I found them both sympathetic and encouraging – they were soon to be proved wrong.

As summer approached, another issue blew up.

A number of the prominent international runners, including Marcus O'Sullivan, Frank O'Mara, and John Treacy, hadn't responded to a written request to turn over the 10% of their earnings into the BLE trust fund as they were supposed to have done.

The green blazers wanted to threaten them with suspension from the World Championship team which would travel to Seoul.

I told the committee that it was unlikely the boys would comply and that they'd be better off forgetting about it.

"These men are the face of Irish athletics, the ones we want to sell the sport in Ireland," I reminded them. "They're ones we want going into the schools and clubs on our behalf to promote athletics, if you'll just be patient and let me work with them, we'll sort this out," I told the board.

"No other federation in the world would demand a percentage of the few quid they're getting. And besides, these lads are my friends, I know what their needs are."

The response to this was withering. I was informed that my friendship was irrelevant and that I was to write to the athletes concerned and inform them of the BLE's view.

I was stunned. I told them that any such letter would probably be torn up and thrown in the bin, and that that's exactly what I'd have done had I been on the receiving end of any such missive.

"Lads," I told the committee as I walked out the door, "there's no way I'm writing that letter to anybody."

That meeting took place on the Friday before the June bank holiday weekend.

By the time I got home, I realised that this was going to be my way out of the job.

On Saturday, I rang up my solicitor and had him draft a one paragraph letter of resignation, saying simply that I was leaving because the Chief Executive of BLE had no executive powers.

When I posted it that night it was as if the weight of the world had been lifted from my shoulders.

From the newspaper headlines the following week, I learned that I'd lasted exactly one hundred and forty-four days on the job. The press were for the most part supportive, and I took the high road, declining to cite specific complaints and sticking to the "no executive powers" explanation.

I think the green blazers were delighted. They'd got what they wanted all along.

But I hadn't resigned for them. I'd done it for myself and my family.

Putting back the pieces

As I emerged from the BLE experience, I found myself casting about in search of a cathartic outlet for my energies. I didn't have to look far. I'd go back and do what I did best. RUN.

Running was my release and I knew the highs I got from doing it well would make me feel a lot better.

In golf, the Senior Tour was heading into its second decade of success, demonstrating that there was an audience for sporting heroes of yesteryear. George Foreman was midway through a comeback that would eventually see him regain the world heavyweight championship at the age of forty-five.

The world of athletics had seen a developing interest in so-called Masters events, pitting past-their-prime world-class athletes in nostalgic, head-to-head competition. The opportunity to watch the luminaries of their own era obviously appealed to the post-war generation. In some meets, Masters races had become the showpiece events.

At the time I tendered my BLE resignation, I was less than two years removed from competition, but between the stress of my embattled tenure with the federation and newly acquired proclivities for smoking cigars, drinking, and good food, I'd transformed from the whippet-like frame of a miler into a thirty-eight year-old light-heavyweight who could scarcely recognise myself in the mirror.

Having run seventy-seven sub-four minute miles in my lifetime, I quietly resolved to break the magical barrier just one more time. But as I embarked on an ambitious two-year plan to become the first over-forty runner to run the classic distance in under four minutes, there loomed obvious pitfalls.

For one thing, other milers of my generation were hurtling toward their own fortieth birthdays, and several of my contemporaries – Walker, Wessinghage, Dixon, Moorcroft, and possibly Steve Scott among them – were rumoured to be engaged in the same quest.

After Bannister smashed the four-minute barrier, his world record lasted less than seven weeks before it was broken by the Australian John Landy; four decades later Landy is but a footnote to history.

I realised that in order to cap off what would be the pinnacle of my career I not only had to accomplish what no man had before, but that I would have to get there first.

Forty years later, Roger Bannister was still a household name, but there would be little point in spending two years of hard training only to become the John Landy of over-forty milers.

Among my rivals, John Walker appeared to pose the most serious threat. The New Zealander had only recently retired from a competitive career that had seen him clock over a one hundred sub-fours by his thirty-eighth year, and through the running grapevine I knew that he was contemplating his own assault on becoming the first Master to go under four minutes. However, a more formidable rival was time itself. At this level, a forty-year-old runner is an injury waiting to happen.

When Samuel Johnson wrote that "He who competes against time has an adversary who does not suffer casualty," he probably wasn't thinking about athletics, but it couldn't have been more apt. The statement encapsulated the central problem faced by every athlete, but particularly the aging athlete.

Whether he's striving for a personal best, a school record, or, depending on his ability, a national or even world record, time is central to athletic performance. In our sport it's how we keep score.

I'd already been through all of those phases over the course of my athletic career, but when I decided to try to break four minutes as a forty-year-old I knew I'd be contending with an even more insidious effect of time: The ageing process itself.

The traditional view held that athletic performance inevitably diminished with the advent of mid-life. Whatever its causes, there is little debate on its effects: Flexibility decreases, strength declines, cardiovascular efficiency diminishes, and there is a significant decrease in lung capacity.

I was aware of all of this when I took up the challenge at thirty-eight. After the despair of the BLE experience, I needed an outlet for my frustration, and, simply put, I thought I should return to what I do best. It would not only provide me from an escape from the political minefield from which I had just emerged, but offered the opportunity to restore the focus and discipline I'd lacked since retiring from active competition. There were obvious risks involved. For one thing, the entire exercise might go for naught should one of the others get there first, and for another, what if I didn't break four minutes?

No one knew better than I how hard it was to run a four-minute mile at any age, but I recognised that once I embarked on the quest, anything less would be regarded as a failure by those who were, based on my Olympic results, already prepared to discount my other career achievements.

I consoled myself with the knowledge that even if I came up short I was going to be an uncommonly fit forty-year-old.

Fanahan McSweeney's cancer had metastasised again and he was back in a hospital bed. One of Ireland's greatest-ever quarter-milers, the Corkman had been suffering from multiple myeloma for years, but when I went to visit him my old friend offered only strength and encouragement.

"F*** the BLE begrudgers, boy. Get the sub-four and show the bastards what yer made of," he told me.

I had been down similar roads before, and this time I was determined not to repeat my own earlier mistakes.

Having watched others attempt to assume the workload they had been able to shoulder in their prime, only to wind up injured, I vowed to toe the fine line between adequate training and injury.

Although the quest was fuelled by passion, the challenge may have been more daunting than any I had faced before. As I plotted my course I likened the meticulous planning to assembling a jigsaw puzzle – looking for the corners, finding the crucial pieces and all the edges.

I knew that the more pieces I could successfully assemble, the greater the likelihood that the final picture would emerge.

I'd achieved a lot in my career, apart from an Olympic medal, but getting a sub-four at my age would allow me to do something that no other athlete had ever done.

And if I were successful in becoming the first to do it, no one else would ever be able to claim that distinction. It would give me the personal fulfilment I needed to retire from the sport with pride – and on my terms.

In my favour, was the knowledge that I'd have more than one chance at it, so the pressure was unlike that of, say, an Olympic Games, where it's one race, one race only, and in many cases, one-and-gone.

Realistically, I knew there might be failures before I got it right, and there was a safety net of sorts: If I didn't get the sub-four at forty, there would be a chance to try again at forty-one. Having an established timeframe and multiple opportunities eased the pressure and I vowed to myself that if and when I achieved my goal, I would retire gracefully right then and there forever more.

Marathon man

The quest had been encouraged by McSweeney from one cancer ward, and now the first step in its implementation would come from another. Fred Lebow, the president of the New York Road Runners Club and the impetus behind the New York City Marathon, had been diagnosed with a brain tumour and lay terminally ill at New York's Memorial Sloan Kettering Hospital.

A dreamer possessed of boundless energy, Lebow had taken an obscure race and turned it into one of the world's foremost marathons. An old friend, he'd urged me to run in the marathon on a number of occasions, knowing that the publicity attending the presence of an adopted hometown hero would provide a certain cachet.

I had always begged off. Running an autumn marathon had never fit with my schedule when I was preparing for the US indoor circuit, but now I had time on my hands and a two-year training schedule for the mile before me.

I knew that running the New York Marathon at last would be of some cheer to Lebow, a parting gift to my dying friend, but for the moment I kept the decision to myself.

Under normal circumstances, training for a marathon can be almost antithetical to a miler's preparation, but there is some overlap in training methods. During my competitive years, my standard regimen had included training runs of fifteen, eighteen, and even twenty-three miles, so I was confident that the requisite stamina was achievable.

Besides, I reasoned, I wasn't trying to win the New York City Marathon. I would just be using it to help pound myself into shape and regain the stamina foundations for the following year – a 26 mile, 385 yard "fun run." Yeah, right.

The months from June till November seemed to offer ample time to prepare, as I simultaneously attempted to recover from the trauma of the BLE experience.

For the first several weeks, I trained with slow, easy runs of five and six miles, but even that proved to be torture. After a year of almost complete inactivity, the old muscles and tendons were aching all over. It was difficult to stretch to touch my toes. There were days when I'd tell myself "This is f***** impossible!"

"Patience. Patience," I would remind myself that these were just the first steps in a bigger picture as I gradually worked up to ten and then fifteen miles.

By August, instead of dwelling on the torture to my body I began to take note of my surroundings – the rolling hills around the Munich lap in the Phoenix Park where I'd run as a lad began to reassert their beauty. I found myself taking pleasure as I ran past the reindeer, Áras an Uachtarán, the Ordinance Survey Office, the Glen.

"This," I'd tell myself, "is a good sign."

Along about this time, I also began to join the lads from my old running club, Metropolitan Harriers. On Tuesdays, Thursdays, and Sundays, I'd participate in "official club training runs." The others thought it was great to have the old man back.

Unbeknownst to them, I was also using them as an unofficial barometer to measure my own progress, and as I began to show more prominently on long runs, many of them began to suspect that something was afoot. The slagging commenced in earnest.

"The bollix is gettin' fit. He's getting' skinny in the face," John Whelan, one of the club characters from Ballyfermot, exclaimed after one evening's run.

"Yeah," answered Frank Nolan, who actually is the skinniest runner in the club. "The oul' spies have seen him doing secret training between club sessions."

It was then that I revealed to the boys my plans to run in a marathon, but at least a few of them were one step ahead of me.

"Bullshit!" came a disembodied voice from out of the shower. "You're probably going for the over-40s mile record, you son of a bitch!"

I didn't deny nor confirm it.

"Tell you what," I replied. "Let's see how the marathon goes and then I'll answer that."

I was labouring under no illusions about New York. I wasn't a marathoner, I had a profound respect for the distance, and I reckoned that under the circumstances anything under three hours would be a success.

My impending entry wasn't supposed to be public knowledge, but in early September I got a phone call from Eddie Coyle, a journalist for the *New York Daily News*. Looking, no doubt, for a bit of pre-race publicity, Fred Lebow had told him of my intention to run.

Eddie was supposed to be interviewing me, but in a way I wound up inter- viewing him. As we talked about the work I'd done over the summer, he talked about the regimens of top marathoners like Bill Rogers and Frank Shorter, and reminded me of the importance of getting in at least five twenty-plus mile runs in preparation for a marathon. I took his advice to heart and started to throw in a thirty-mile run at a very slow pace. After that, I allowed myself to think, twenty-six would be a mere trot.

As September rolled into October, I had begun to feel like a runner again. I felt in complete control of every stride, able to pick up the pace at will without courting oxygen debt. I optimistically and secretly revised my target time downward: 2:40 now seemed a realistic projection.

No one, myself included, expected me to contend in the New York Marathon. This was a private challenge, but the result was important because it would give me the psychological impetus I needed to press forward in pursuit of the magical four-minute barrier the following year.

Although I was an almost thirty-nine-year-old man running in my first Marathon, I was welcomed to New York like a returning hero and was invited to appear with the other guests of honour at the official press conference at Tavern-on-the-Green in Central Park three days before the race.

I was seated next to Scotland's Liz McColgan, who a just a few months earlier had won the 10,000 metres at the World Championships in Seoul. McColgan was the focal point of attention because she was the pre-race favourite in the Women's Division.

I was there because I was running for Fred and because "the former world champion, seven time winner of the Wanamaker Mile, ladies and gentleman, Eamonn Coghlan," as I was introduced to the assembled media, of the publicity it would bring.

But as I sat there listening to McColgan answer questions from the journalists, I experienced an epiphany of sorts. Liz, running her first New York Marathon, was aiming for a time of 2:28, and spoke of how she planned to run the race.

"How does this little woman think she can run that fast and beat me?" I found myself wondering.

There on the dais I mentally revised my projection for Sunday. I now resolved to break 2:30 – and I even had a pacemaker to show me the way. Liz McColgan would be my rabbit. I reckoned I'd have to run close to 5 minutes and 30 seconds for each of the 26 miles to achieve my new goal.

The trip out to the start felt like old times again. I was ready to go out and scrap. Of course, now I was an innocuous old-timer at the back of the bus, taking it all in – no nerves, no emotion, no problems.

The elite runners like John Treacy and Herman Silva and the mighty Kenyans kept to themselves, sipping their water as they eyeballed one another hoping to spot a hint of weakness, at the same time trying not to get caught looking.

I could now watch this pre-race tableau play out with some amusement. God knows I'd done the same thing enough times myself. This time, I reminded myself, I was here to have fun with 30,000 other runners and the two million party animals that would be lining the route to cheer us on.

All around me the tension was palpable. You could sense the adrenalin being kept under restraint until it was released by the starting gun – or in this case, cannon.

Once it fired, it was a struggle for me not to go after the early leaders. I knew that going out too fast would hurt me later, so I willed myself to keep the pace under complete control and not allow the adrenaline take over.

Instead I held back with the crowd and blended into the sea of humanity crossing the Verrazzano Narrows Bridge, which vibrated and swayed under the weight of 60,000 pounding feet. It was a bright, clear morning and I took in the picturesque view of the Manhattan skyline as it unfolded off to my left – the Twin Towers, the Empire State Building. The City that Never Sleeps. I tried to take it all in, if only to keep my mind off the long journey ahead. Central Park seemed so close, yet so far away.

The men and women had started separately, but I knew that the runners would merge in Brooklyn and that eventually I would find my rabbit.

As we came off the bridge at the two-mile mark a group of seemingly accomplished marathoners drew abreast, and at least a few of them recognised me.

"Whoa! Eamonn Coghlan!" exclaimed one. "What the hell are you doing in a marathon? You're a miler."

"Jesus," he said, "it's an honour to run alongside you, but what are you doing here?"

I told him I was on vacation, taking the Big Apple running tour of New York City.

Another of them asked how fast I hoped to run.

"About 2:45," I lied. "How about you?"

"We're looking for 2:19," he said.

"Well, you'd better not let me slow you down," I told him, and off they went.

"Good luck," I shouted after them, and added under my breath "I'll see you later alligators." I wished them well, but I knew in my heart they hadn't a prayer of going that fast.

If I was correct in my surmise, I expected to see them struggling along the course later that day. Around the eighteen-mile mark, I guessed.

When the male and female streams converged eight miles into the race, it wasn't difficult to find Liz McColgan. She was surrounded by her own pacemakers, as well as a police escort, TV crews and the press, huddled together on the back of a Sanitation Department truck.

For the next ten miles, I tracked Liz and never let her out of my sights. I just made sure that I'd stay well out of the sight of cameras because I knew they'd pick up on me.

Each mile mark, I'd glance over to the timing clocks to check and calculate that I was on target. It could have been so easy to pick up the pace, but control and patience were important.

What I'd gain in the first half would be totally lost over the second half and, I knew the real running in a marathon is over the last six miles.

As the course moved through the ethnic neighbourhoods of Brooklyn and Queens, I watched the crowds go from Hasidic Jews to Irish to Blacks and Hispanics.

The music of U2, Van Halen, and Led Zeppelin blasted forth from bands lining the course. New York comes alive on this day more than any other of the 365 in the year. People are on a high, handing out sweets, oranges, bananas and suspect water.

At the halfway mark I was right on pace, which I quickly calculated would convert to a sub-2:30 finishing time if I could sustain it. The steepest hill on the New York City Marathon course is the 59th Street Bridge, immortalised in song by Simon and Garfunkel. When I came off the ramp and into Manhattan, I encountered the uplifting spectacle of over a million spectators lining the course as the parade made its way up First Avenue.

The excitement of the crowd, the fact that the journey is two-thirds over, and the knowledge that the worst of the terrain was behind me contributed to a false sense of security.

That rush of energy had proven the undoing of many a New York competitor who succumbed to the adrenaline rush and I was well aware.

"Relax, relax," I reminded myself to hold back and conserve energy when I realised I'd lost sight of McColgan. I had no idea whether she was ahead of or behind me. At that point it mattered little, the rabbit had done her job.

But halfway up First Avenue, I did encounter another familiar face when I overtook the first of the intrepid group of runners who'd planned to run 2:19. The poor fellow was shattered, blisters having slowed him to a walk. I didn't have the heart to say anything as I passed him.

Shortly thereafter, I encountered the next runner from that ambitious band. This one was obviously suffering from diarrhoea. He was disconsolately seated at the side of the street, but looked up to shout a word of encouragement.

"Way to go, Coghlan!" he managed to cry out even in his misery.

I kept my head down and kept running, still quite comfortable.

At twenty-one miles I reached Harlem. By now the runners had separated to the extent that I was essentially running alone, apart from a few of the young "brothers" who'd join me and, showing off for their friends, run alongside me for perhaps a hundred yards high fiveing.

"Yo Bro, who are you, Carl Lewis?" I asked one of them. I used any psychological tactic I could muster just to keep my mind off the pain.

Shortly thereafter, I abruptly encountered the phenomenon that has proven the downfall of marathoners since Pheidippides.

I hit the Wall.

I could tell from the way the field was spread out that the front-runners weren't that far ahead of me, and at this point the crowd had thinned out a bit as well. It was a lonely place to be – especially when the cramps set in.

It came suddenly, like a bolt of lightening and without warning. It was unmerciful – like jamming on the brakes at 100mph. Every ounce of energy seemed to have sapped from my body.

This wasn't supposed to have happened. I'd followed the best advice, taken fluids at every station – first water, then Gatorade, then the glucose tablets, but somehow I'd hit the metaphorical marathon wall. I realised there was nothing metaphorical about it. It was all too real.

"S***," I muttered to myself, and the struggle began in earnest. This is what the marathon is all about – when the legs give over to force of will.

Give into it and you're finished. Fight it, and you'll learn what bravery is all about.

The cramps were unbearable over the next five miles. I'd heard and read about this, but I'd run thousands of miles throughout my career and never experienced anything remotely like it.

At times, it felt as if the muscles were being pulled right off the bone, or that someone was yanking the sinews out of my legs from toes to arse-bone, from behind the knees.

I tried to compensate by over-striding, hoping to keep my legs from seizing up completely.

As I turned from Fifth Avenue into Central Park, I still had three miles to go, but the spectators began to pick me up. New York crowds can be wonderful like that. They can read a runner's face and sense his pain, but not allow him to give up. I fed off this energy to push onward.

Amazingly, I noted as I checked my watch, I was still on a 5:30 pace, but the finish line couldn't come soon enough. It was the longest and hardest three miles of running I ever did in my life.

Approaching the finish line at Tavern-on-the-Green was a bittersweet experience – bitter because I was enveloped in a tortuous pain, but sweet with emotions. I could hear announcer Jim Sansevero, my great friend and former Villanova team mate, calling my name:

"Ladies and gentlemen, coming up to the finish line we now have Eamonn Coghlan and he's running an incredible time! Come on, let's put our hands together for the Chairman of the Boards and bring him on home!"

I posted a time of 2:25.14, good for forty-first place overall. I was delighted that this Big Apple Tour was over.

I was still catching my breath and wrapped in a tinfoil blanket when Liz McColgan arrived at the finish in 2:28, right on schedule. The crowd cheered wildly; she'd won the women's race alright and went on to be rewarded immensely.

I had my own reward, a mixture of relief and satisfaction: Relief that I had completed the first phase of my training for the sub-four so well, and satisfaction that I'd run so fast and that Fred Lebow, his health now in serious decline, had gotten to see his wish for me to run in his big event at last.

Once I recovered, the marshals shepherded me over to the elite athletes interview area. The medal I'd received for finishing dangled proudly from my neck.

I spotted John Treacy, slumped over a chair. John had been one of the pre-race favourites but right now he didn't look so good.

"Are you okay, John," I asked solicitously.

"F*****," he replied, managing a weak grin.

I asked him how it had gone.

"Awful," he replied. "I ran like a dog. How about you?"

When I told him my time was 2:25 and change he seemed genuinely surprised.

"Well, f*** me," he said. "How the hell did ye run that fast and I broke me balls training for this."

"I don't know myself," I admitted.

Eddie Coyle, my *New York Daily News* journalist friend, found us just about then.

"Eamonn, can I have a look at your medal?" he asked.

As I showed it to him he looked over at Treacy.

"I threw mine away," explained John.

Different strokes for different folks.

A new departure

Although my achievement went largely unnoticed by others, I departed New York with an immense sense of pride. Despite the agony of the experience, the time and effort had been worthwhile. I knew it had provided me with exactly what I'd sought out of it – the foundation upon which to build my training throughout 1992 and the realistic chance for a sub-four mile at the age of forty.

An important part of the puzzle was now in place. The key thing now would be to build toward that goal while simultaneously avoiding going overboard with the training.

Still buoyed by the New York experience, I found the notion of returning to live full-time to the States tempting, and sifted through the pros and cons on the flight back to Dublin. On one hand, I was out of a job, and even as a "retired" athlete still had a huge presence in America. In the States, I had been reminded, the attitude remained the same "What can we do for you Eamonn, will you come back and take over the Club?"

In Ireland, I feared, I would face still more of the begrudgery that had undermined my BLE experience.

On the other hand, I realised that Yvonne and the kids had just settled into their life in Ireland, and that they deserved a chance to get what they had longed for – the chance to grow up surrounded by all the Coghlans and Murphys, aunts, uncles and all the friends nearby.

But the dilemma wouldn't go away. I made contact with several estate agents with the view to selling up and moving back to the house we still had kept in Rye.

Several years earlier, I had been named to the Board of the Children's Medical and Research Foundation in New York and had helped to raise funds for Our Lady's Hospital for Sick Children in Crumlin.

Not long after my return from the marathon I was asked by Michael Hawkshaw, the Chief Executive to accept a staff position there. I told Michael that I was considering moving back to live in the USA.

"But, you can't do that. You've already lived there, it's Yvonne and the children's turn to live where they want to be, in Ireland," he said.

"It's tough living here, America is such a positive place to bring up the children and I can get work there no problem," I responded.

"Listen Eamonn, it's tough no matter where you live, I know you for years and I know what you went through. Don't let those bastards drive you out of here."

Michael was very persuasive and more importantly I felt he was the tower of strength I need by my side. Michael was a doer.

By the time our meeting ended, for better or for worse, I would remain in the land of my birth.

In agreeing to the job as Marketing and Communications Executive with the Foundation, I made it clear to Michael, that I had unfinished business on the track for the next year or two and that it would demand a little of my time. Michael understood, and offered his wholehearted co-operation. "And besides', he said, 'it will be good for us in the Foundation when you get that record."

Meanwhile, I could only monitor from afar as my rivals took their shots at the sub-four. Walker had scheduled an attempt on January 12th 1992, the day of his fortieth birthday in Mount Smart stadium in Auckland. But, shortly before the race came word that it was off. Walker had injured an Achilles tendon and decided to retire from the sport completely. I was sorry for John but relieved to here he'd retired and left another door open.

Rod Dixon had also given up on his quest, and there was no sign of Wessinghage. With those three out of the equation, Dave Moorcroft and I remained the only serious threats to break four minutes – and since I was a few months older than the Englishman and would turn forty in November, I would have the ensuing indoor season all to myself.

For the next six months, the plan would be a simple one. I would not try to attempt to do the training load of that of a twenty-something-year-old. I'd recover fully from the exertions of the marathon while training easily with long, slow jogs of up to ten miles. I'd factored in ample time for complete recovery and rest. Then during the summer I'd move up to light interval work, alternating fast strides with jogging on the grass to help rekindle leg speed. This could probably have been better accomplished on the track, but at this point I didn't even want to be seen on a track. It would only have raised suspicions and fuelled speculation.

The new job at the hospital fitted in perfectly with my plans. It enabled me to keep my mind on something other than running. The work was a welcome release, and provided me with a more solid perspective on life. I found it gratifying to be part of an organisation dealing with voluntary groups from all over Ireland, united in one common goal – helping sick children. Everyone was so positive and there was no one playing the "political game."

And it also allowed me to settle down and develop a routine. I was able to run to work some mornings, and home in the evening, or sometimes at lunchtime. Back at Villanova, Jumbo had always stressed the importance of maintaining a regular schedule. "Routine, routine, routine," he would say. "God damn it, live like a clock. Go to bed at the same time, get up at the same time, eat, drink and even shit at the same time every day." For the most part, my new career enabled me to adhere to that philosophy.

By the time of my birth in November 1952, the four-minute mile was still considered a feat beyond the scope of human endurance. Reputable physiologists staked their reputations on the publication of scientific papers which solemnly explained why no man could ever hope to surpass this seemingly inviolate barrier.

In an elaborate presentation called *The Ultimate of Human Effort*, published in 1935, Brutus Hamilton of the University of California at Berkeley had calculated the absolute limit of human performance over the distance to be precisely four minutes, 1.6 seconds. Man, Hamilton maintained, was physiologically incapable of running faster than that.

The myth was shattered in 1954 when Roger Bannister established a new world record by running a mile in 3:59.4. Bannister recalled, that upon learning of his feat, a Frenchman had breathlessly wondered "How did he know that he would not die?"

The answer, of course, is that Bannister, as a physician, knew better than most that both the distance and the time represented arbitrary numbers, and that the barrier was primarily a psychological one. Still, forty-six years later, *Sports Illustrated* would declare Bannister's feat the most significant athletic accomplishment of the 20th Century.

I had yet to turn two years of age when Bannister set the running world on its head, and forty more years would elapse before I would attempt to become the first person over forty years of age to break the once magical four minute mile. If successful, I'd have done it a total of seventy-eight times during my career.

Some of my American friends had speculated that hundreds of thousands, if not millions, of dollars might be made from running the first-ever sub-four Masters mile. Their reasoning was that the symmetry provided by becoming the first over forty-years-of-age to do it, four decades after Bannister's epic run would capture the imagination of the world.

If I was going to achieve the impossible and believe what all the experts said about the financial rewards, I thought I should put a marketing plan together.

But not too many were interested in a retired athlete and besides they didn't take the attempt seriously.

Their only interest was making money from the elite athletes, not an old man trying to make a comeback.

The masters indoor mile record stood at four minutes and thirteen seconds and previously, when former greats such as Jim Ryun and Lasse Viren ran in Masters' races they got more sympathy than welcome. Fans of the sport preferred to remember their glorious days in the sport and not the sight of beaten up geriatrics making a show of themselves!

So when I began to put feelers out to race promoters and shoe companies to explore the commercial side to the venture, it became apparent that the interest had been wildly exaggerated.

They did not believe for one second that it could be humanly possible to run under four minutes at forty-years-of-age. I had suspected that it was always going to be a tough sell anyway.

But, this was a private mission. It wasn't for money, it was for personal fulfilment. I wanted one more chance to go out of the sport on my terms, and not the way I did when I dropped out of the US Indoor championships in Madison Square Gardens a sorry sight.

I was more or less resigned to making this a one-man show. No agents, no promoters or middlemen involved.

In September of 1992, still two months shy of my fortieth birthday, I was invited to participate in a made-for-television Legends of the Mile road race which was being held on Princes Street in Edinburgh.

The field would be comprised of elite athletes 35 and older, and would include some of my old rivals Steve Scott, Sydney Maree, and Nick Rose. It seemed as good a place as any to chart my progress, and besides, there was a car on offer for the winner.

I knew I was in great shape, because on the Thursday before the Edinburgh Mile I'd run in my club's season-opening 10k handicap race, the Glen Trophy, in the Phoenix Park. To even my own surprise, I won in a course-record time of 30 minutes and 4 seconds over a very hilly course in atrocious conditions. That run confirmed that I was ready to race against the younger legends.

One hour before I got on the plane to Edinburgh, I had completed a charity swim in the river Liffey. I got a police escort to the airport and en-route towelled off and dressed in the back of the squad car.

I began to think that this is not the perfect pre-race preparation for my come back. When the Garda dropped me off he said "Good luck in the mile Eamonn, I'm sure you'll win."

"Thanks," I replied, "win – I forget how to race," I said under my breath.

Initially it was like old times in Edinburgh – checking in to race headquarters, hanging around the hotel, checking out the course and chatting over dinner about old times with the lads. We had all grown up and we were more concerned about raising our children than chasing medals. There were the pre-race interviews and the pre-race nerves, and as the race approached apprehension and self-doubt were beginning to surface.

"Do I really want to do this again," I asked myself.

The sensible answer would have been, "Hell, no!"

But I was here to run. I had to focus. I needed to find out where I was really at. I just wanted this to last until I achieved my underlying goal.

My confidence was restored when I won in 4:06, leaving Scott, Maree, & Co. well behind. I'd accomplished that without having done any real speed work, so I knew if I'd been able to go that fast under these circumstances the sub-four ought to be within reach. And, besides I went away with a brand new car for my troubles.

The Edinburgh win was the key that opened up some commercial doors. Aer Lingus expressed an interest in sponsoring my quest, but only to the extent of front vest signage and supporting appearances.

When I countered with a proposal that would include $65,000 in airfares in lieu of cash incentives, I was turned down flat.

Runner's World, Track and Field News and The Runner magazines, America's leading athletics' publications, agreed to do cover stories featuring my attempt at the record. The momentum was picking up.

Foot Locker sports stores, one of my long-time sponsors, came on board, albeit conditionally: The firm's financial commitment would be based on me becoming the first over-forty to run under four minutes. Anything short of this wouldn't count. Foot Locker took out an insurance policy to cover their investment and if I succeeded they'd be in for a bargain. Sonia O'Sullivan's agent Kim Mc Donald got Reebok to sponsor my gear only, but if I got under four minutes they'd throw in a few quid.

Another problem was presented by the decline in the US indoor circuit. In my heyday in the 1970s and '80s, I had been able to choose from among two or three indoor meets nearly every weekend from January through March – from New York to California, from Texas to Toronto, but one by one, they had fallen by the wayside. The Millrose Games and the US Track and Field Championships at Madison Square Garden and the Sunkist Invitational in Los Angeles remained the exception.

Based on their tradition and the quality of their fields, those meets had endured with a very high profile, but the tight, eleven-laps-to-the-mile track did not bode well for a fast time. I knew I might have to look around for smaller college meets on bigger eight lap tracks.

Masters plan

B y the time I turned forty that November and officially entered the ranks of the Masters, my ambition was well-known in the US. The CBS television network sent a crew to Dublin to film me on my home turf, strolling around Dublin, and to cover the Big Birthday Bash at my home. It was to be the feature story on *Sunday Morning with Charles Kuralt*, and would be televised to an audience of millions just before the Millrose Games.

Yvonne wasn't entirely pleased to have a television crew traipsing around the house during the festivities – especially when the strip-o-gram girl Chalkie White had hired made her appearance. She peeled off her nurse's uniform and then started to strip me.

Thankfully, CBS omitted the footage from the feature.

Having achieved the Big 40, I unwisely opted to tune up for the upcoming indoor season by entering the Manchester Road Race in Connecticut a few weeks later. I'd run in the Thanksgiving Day event several times in the past, and it provided an opportunity to thank my old friends there by making my Masters' debut. It was a tough, hilly and very fast four-mile course, and while I'd turned in some great performances in Manchester over the years, the course had not always been kind to me: On three occasions in the 1980s I'd wound up with shinbone stress fractures that caused me to miss the indoor season.

Forty years earlier, Bannister had noted that "The battle for the first sub-four minute mile was fought in the mind, not in the body," and while the aphorism was appropriate for an athlete in his prime, when a man turns forty the body assumes precedence.

I won the Masters' division in record time, but I came out of the race with an injury so severe that it threatened to wipe out the entire indoor season.

My hamstring tendon had torn from the ischium tuberosity: In layman's terms, the injury was to my arse bone – literally, a pain in the ass.

The attendant discomfort was so severe that it completely hampered my training, and the mere act of sitting down became an agonising experience. When I drove, I had to stop periodically and climb out to relieve the excruciating pain. I began to eat while standing up.

Consultation with several medical authorities produced a unanimous recommendation: Give it six months of rest and the application of ice packs to the injured area and hope that it would heal.

In my mind this was not an option. While there was no guarantee that the injury would be better after six months, two things were certain: One was that six months away from training would undo all the preparation I had endured to get to this point. The other was that Dave Moorcroft would by then himself have turned forty.

The races had been lined up and the deals had been done. I didn't want to let anyone down, and I wasn't going to squander a year-and-a-half of preparation. Besides, the boys from Metro running club and a contingent of friends from The Good Counsel Musical Society in Drimnagh had already booked flights to come over to watch me run in the Millrose Games. I didn't want to let them down.

Once my mind was made up, the only recourse seemed to be to train through the injury and do my best to ignore it. It wasn't going to improve, but it seemed unlikely that it would get any worse either. I didn't realise it at the time, but the pain was something I'd have to live with for the next year-and-a half.

The injury had rendered something so elementary as a five-mile training jog an instrument of torture, and the uncertainty weighed heavily on my mind over the Christmas holidays.

My work at the hospital proved a welcome distraction. I had been working on a promotional video, which proved to be a saviour of sorts, in that it diverted my mind from the injury while providing a valuable perspective: There were some very sick children who didn't give a damn about the pain in my arse. Some of them might never emerge from the hospital alive, while others might be burdened for the rest of their lives. I reminded myself of that as I did my best to squeeze easy training runs in between taping sessions.

Just after New Year's, I left Yvonne and the kids in Dublin and flew to Florida for a consultation with the noted physiotherapist Gerard Hartmann. A former Irish national triathlon champion, Hartmann had attended the University of Arkansas on a track scholarship, and while he'd never set the world on fire, he had subsequently achieved international renown for his restorative work with world-class athletes.

Following his initial examination, Ger told me that my body was "like a beat-up old Volkswagen with a Rolls-Royce engine." Only complete rest accompanied by long-term treatment would provide a likely cure for the ailment.

"F*** that Ger," I muttered, "I already heard that from the doctors in Dublin. I didn't come all the way here to hear it again. It's not an option. The Millrose Games are only a month away."

As patiently as he could, Ger explained that the doctors in Dublin had been right. Not only had I torn the tendon right off the bone, but there was an accumulation of scar tissue at the point of the injury, buried under a mass of muscle.

"And your flexibility is very bad," he added, "your alignment is completely out of balance. The poor flexibility is causing the tendons to pull even tighter, which causes the tear and thus the pain."

Then he offered a ray of hope.

"On the brighter side, you're fit," he said. "I might be able to help rejuvenate the old, worn-out muscle tissue with deep massage, flexibility exercises, and strength work. It will be a long, slow process, and at the end of the day all I can promise you is that it will take the brakes off and give your running a bit more freedom. But the pain may not go away."

"Fair enough," I said, "when do we start?"

For the next several weeks, I would be Ger's houseguest and patient at his Florida home. The former probably sounds more glamorous than it was, because while he'd only recently purchased a beautiful new house that looked like something right out of *Knott's Landing*, he had yet to buy a stick of furniture, making for some rather spartan living conditions. A formal dinner setting he'd acquired somewhere was the only concession to modern convenience. I had a small bed in my room, but otherwise there was no television, no radio, no couch.

"I haven't had time to buy furniture," he explained, "I've been so busy with my athletes I haven't even had time to fart."

In addition to his work with elite athletes, Ger worked full-time at a nearby health and fitness clinic. While he was off at work, I had the run of the place, and in the evening he would return for our nightly torture sessions.

There was much to be said to have escaped from an Irish winter. The hospitable Florida weather made it easier to bounce out of bed in the morning, and I quickly settled into a routine: I'd go for an easy, five-mile jog, followed by stretching exercises. Then, after a light breakfast, I'd sit for an hour on a block of ice moulded to the contours of my ass. Some afternoons, I'd go over to the University of Florida campus to work out with the college track team.

But mostly I'd sit around waiting for Ger to return. It was, frankly, boring. There were days I'd want to just pack up and go home, particularly since the routine didn't seem to be producing immediate results.

For over two hours a day, six nights a week, Ger chiselled his way through my skin to get to the muscles and tendons with his fingers, knuckles, and elbows. The objective was supposed to be to break up the scar tissue that had accumulated over three decades of wear and tear and tens of thousands of miles of running.

He would twist and turn every muscle in my body, and it was evident from his facial expressions that he was growing attuned to my body: It was if he could "see" inside me through his hands and pinpoint the source of the pain.

It was an excruciating process, unlike I'd ever experienced before. While he worked on me, I'd lie there roaring and screaming as I pleaded with him for mercy.

"It's the only way to get rid of the bastard," he'd grunt back. No matter how I begged he wouldn't stop until he felt the day's battle was won. Then he'd tell me to go ice my legs again.

In the first ten days there I managed to get in five track sessions at the University. It was dismaying to realise I couldn't even come close to running a sub-sixty quarter-mile, much less four of them in a row, but I reminded myself that I'd experienced these negative thoughts before and that they'd been expunged with the crack of a starter's pistol.

A week before the Millrose Games I decided to test myself by entering the mile in the Gator Invitational. It was a college indoor meet, and my entry set off some alarm bells thereabouts. Some of the college athletes I'd be running against saw it as an opportunity to test themselves against the world indoor record-holder.

Others, aware of how I'd been struggling, saw it as a chance to kick the ass of the "Chairman of the Boards."

Once the word got out, the newspapers began to phone up. I obliged, knowing that it would be helpful to the meet promoter, but I honestly had no idea what to expect.

All I remember about the race is that it was a struggle to keep up, and that I had a very heavy pair of legs on the final lap, where I had to make up eight seconds on my younger adversaries, but, amazingly, I broke the world Masters record of 4:13 by a full five seconds, running 4:08. It gave me a bit of confidence, but I knew that running eight seconds faster was going to take an almighty effort – even on the familiar boards at Madison Square Garden.

I was returning to the Millrose Games after an absence of three years. It had been six years since my last win in the Wanamaker Mile, but this time that historical race wasn't even the featured event of the evening.

The Chairman of the Boards was back in town, and all eyes were fixed on what was being billed as The Runners World Masters Mile.

Back to the Garden

For the first time in several years, the meet at Madison Square Garden was sold out and they were all here to witness the chairman break the four minute mile at forty. Over 19,000 jammed the rafters in anticipation, many of them waving green, white, and orange tricolours. A television documentary company had dispatched a crew in anticipation of the geriatric assault on the barrier.

Being back in New York awakened all the dormant memories. The sounds, the smells, the atmosphere of the Garden on the night of a big meet. I had enjoyed a long and loyal following here, and returning would be special indeed.

I looked at it as a way of saying farewell and Thank You to an audience I'd come to cherish over the years. At the same time, I realised that for many of them, any result that didn't begin with the number '3' was going to be a disappointment. A week earlier I'd set a Masters mile record and been deemed "a failure."

A sub-four was, after all, the standard I'd set for myself. I'd have loved nothing more than to achieve it in that setting, but I knew in the back of my mind that there would be other opportunities if I didn't.

Stepping out onto the floor of the Garden, I felt a bit like a gladiator about to take on the lions. The air of expectation was almost frightening. To ease the strain, I went down a ramp and went for my warm up run on the street outside, just like I did on so many previous occasions.

People were rushing to and from the subways. Police sirens wailed in the background. Yellow cabs jostled for position on the avenues. It was pure New York.

For years, I'd maintained a secret spot for stretching under an escalator beneath Penn Station, but on this night I found myself sharing the space with a bag lady, a homeless person who'd taken refuge from the elements there in a cardboard box. I was able to use the banter between us to relax and momentarily forget the pandemonium inside.

The television crew were following my every footstep, and the boys from Dublin were there in the stands. Yvonne was there too, along with Suzanne, Eamonn Jr. and our youngest two boys, Michael and John, who'd never seen their Da run before.

It's not often that you'll hear the Irish National Anthem sung at Madison Square Garden, but it was on this night – by Christine McCabe, whose father-in-law Charlie was the executive vice-president of Chemical Bank, the meet sponsor and President of the Children's Medical & Research Foundation. Michael Hawkshaw flew over from Dublin too. It was a very proud moment as Amhrán na bhFiann sent chills up my spine. The good news was that I beat my old Kenyan rival Wilson Waigwa to win, and set a new Masters World Record in the process. I received the Fred Schmertz award for being named Athlete of the Meet.

The bad news was that the time was 4:05.3. Although I'd run some of the best races of my life on this track, the old familiar surface had seemed almost foreign to my steps. When I'd tried to kick through that eleventh and final lap, the speed hadn't been there.

"Jesus," I reflected, "I used to be able to talk to this track – and it always responded."

Was it the track that hadn't responded, or was it my weary, forty-year-old legs? The questions were already plaguing my mind. I knew this had been the best opportunity, but it hadn't been the only one.

"Okay," I told myself, "you didn't do it at Millrose, so it's on to the next one."

This was, after all, still only part of the puzzle.

The celebrations at my New York local, the Old Stand on Third Avenue were somewhat muted that night. A blizzard pelted the city, covering the streets with snow as I joined Yvonne and the crowd over from Dublin for a pint and a sing-song before dragging myself self off to bed for a few hours of sleep before taking a flight to Washington DC. I had another race in Fairfax, Virginia two nights later.

At the Millrose Games, I had been the centrepiece of a Masters race. This time the field would be comprised of younger athletes, and while eager for a crack at the indoor world record-holder, the other runners evinced respect for me and for the magnitude of what I was attempting to accomplish.

A large crowd was on hand at the small-college arena, and on the eight-lap track at George Mason University, I won in 4:03.28, smashing the Masters record yet again.

Although I had left New York beset by nagging doubts, the Virginia performance encouraged me. To have run two races this fast in less than forty-eight hours was edifying – especially since I had done it while labouring under the continuing discomfort posed by the pain in my ass.

With three weeks to prepare for the next assault, at the US National Indoor Track and Field Championships, I returned to Florida and the healing hands of Gerard Hartmann. The University of Florida track had by now become a welcome refuge. I had come to enjoy the camaraderie of the younger runners on the college team, and found the training rejuvenating. Although the pain was unremitting, my 200 metre and 400 metre training times improved. So did my stamina: I was matching the young Turks when they went out for longer runs.

The back-to-back Masters records earlier in the months hadn't gone unnoticed.

This time there would be money on the table. Jimmy Rafferty and Ray Lumpp had negotiated a deal with Olan Cassell, the USATF Executive Director. Cassell had not only added the Masters mile to the program, but had taken out an insurance policy that would pay $75,000 were the elusive four-minute barrier to fall in the race at Madison Square Garden. I knew Cassell's motive for such an offer was to help sell out his dying meet and I was happy with the arrangement.

On the morning of the race, I was relaxing in my friend John Mauritz's house when a newsflash interrupted the television program I was watching. A car bomb had exploded in a garage beneath one of the World Trade Centre towers, plunging New York into a state of emergency.

Although the citizenry had been urged not to panic, bomb alerts were going off all over the city: The Empire State Building, the Port Authority Terminal and Madison Square Garden.

All proved to be unfounded hoaxes, but for half the day I wasn't sure whether there was even going to be a track meet at the Garden that night. Then, late that afternoon, it was announced that there would be no cancellations. The race was on again.

I did my best to regain my composure on my way to the Garden. Driving into the city, and walking the streets from the car park, I noted a strange air of caution among the populace. New Yorkers weren't accustomed to this sort of thing back in 1993. It was as if everyone was waiting for the next bomb to go off. (It would – eight years later.)

Despite the uncertainties posed by the day's events, the show was going on and the Garden was buzzing. Over 13,000 were in attendance, and I could sense the electricity.

In keeping with the pre-race regimen I'd employed for two decades, I first jogged around the wooden track, re-acquainting myself to its nuances, the soft spots, the familiar bends, before heading out to warm up on the street outside.

As I jogged down 33rd Street past Charlie O's, I was spotted by a number of fans, who shouted encouragement.

"Way to go, Ahmon," they shouted, "You can do it!"

After twenty years they could pick me out on the street, but they still couldn't pronounce my name. Nor, I realised, did any of them know, or probably care, how much my bum was hurting badly at that very moment. I could not keep my mind off the tearing pain.

When I lined up against my competitors on the starting line, I was truly hoping that this would be the last race of my life. I was fairly confident that I could beat the eight Masters in the race. The real race was against the clock, and if I could achieve my goal it would be an appropriate way to wrap up my athletic career and return to a normal, contented, and pain-free life.

Frank Conway, a Kerryman who'd run for Providence College had agreed to be the rabbit to ensure an even pace, and when the gun sounded he took off like a bat out of hell, producing a thunderous roar.

I could not keep up with him as he strode out ten, fifteen yards ahead. He stayed upfront until and eventually dropped out at three-quarters, leaving me to go it alone. The pace was a good one, and I was right in sub-four territory heading into the final lap, but once again the boards worked against me.

I came tantalisingly close. My 4:01.3 was a new Masters record, but even as I acknowledged the cheers I was muttering "Shit, shit, shit!" to myself.

I felt this had been my best chance, but my body had betrayed me again. The speed I'd always been able to summon on sheer will appeared to have deserted me. A mere 1% improvement would have sufficed, and that knowledge was enough to sustain my commitment. I knew that if I could rid of the pain I could still do it.

While I'd broken the Masters world record four times that winter, in media circles the comeback was largely perceived as a failure. I knew I was partly to blame for that. I'd put a number on the target, and at this level it was all or nothing.

I returned to Florida for a week of treatment before flying home to Ireland to resume my work at the hospital. The programme called for me just to coast through some easy training, perhaps pick an outdoor race or two for the summer, but for the most part to treat the injury and hope the pain would subside.

But as spring turned toward summer the injury persisted. I finally had to ease off, which proved to be even more exasperating when the rest produced no response.

I was aware that I might be running out of time on another front as well. David Moorcroft had passed his own fortieth birthday amid reports that he was well-conditioned and in pursuit of the sub-four. Through the running grapevine, I learned that Nike had agreed to underwrite his bid to crack the elusive barrier by offering sponsorship.

The pair of us had competed against one another many times over the years, from the first time we met in the 1976 Olympic final, and while I had come out on top most times, I was well aware of and respected his capabilities. In his prime, he had run a faster mile and 5,000 metres than me at 3:48 and 13:00.6 respectively, compared to my 3:49.78 and 13:19.11.

Dave was some tough runner and I knew nothing would give him more pleasure than to become, just like Bannister, another Englishman to go beyond the scope of human endurance. He never won an Olympic medal and this would be, similar to myself a great way to end the career.

We two were scheduled to go head-to-head in a B mile race, not a Masters event – at a Grand Prix meet in Stockholm that summer. Still hurting and under-trained, I seriously entertained thoughts of withdrawal. In the end I decided that if I was going to come up short on my quest, it wouldn't be because I had defaulted to Dave Moorcroft.

In the end, it was Moorcroft who withdrew because of injury, his body was breaking down also with the work load required to put four 440 yards laps together in under an average just below sixty seconds each.

I went through with the race, and struggled home in tenth place in 4:09. The only solace came in the fact that I was so buried in the back of the pack that most of the spectators didn't even realise who I was, much less why I was there, but it was a humbling experience I was eager not to repeat, and it served to reinforce my decision to pack it in for the summer.

Or so I thought.

John O'Shea had other ideas.

Own Goal

In 1985, O'Shea had pressed me into service on the world record four-mile relay team. Now he had come up with a brainstorm to incorporate an Eamonn Coghlan sub four-minute mile attempt into a highly public fund-raiser at Belfield.

It was an ingenious concept, one that couldn't miss. O'Shea thought so highly of his idea that he had already announced the event without bothering to consult with the guest of honour.

I'd learned long ago that you can't say no to John O'Shea. He just doesn't listen. But this attempt to hijack the sub-four promotion had forced me into a decidedly uncomfortable situation.

I knew I was hurt, I knew I couldn't do it, but he didn't want to hear about it. He'd already leaned on his media contacts to generate enormous television, radio, and press coverage, and when I rang him two days beforehand to explain that I just could not run, his response was decidedly unsympathetic. He would not believe me when I told him that I could not manage to run even sixty-three seconds for one 400 metre lap and that it was ridiculous to believe things would improve in two days.

"Coghlan," he said, "you can f*** off. You're running the mile and that's it. I have a pain in me own arse from listening to you complain about yours."

I was stunned when I arrived at Belfield to find a crowd of nearly 10,000 waiting. There was no admission charge, but GOAL was once again collecting donations near the finish line and did handsomely.

In a way it was like running back in New York, with thousands of expectant fans there to witness what they hoped would be history. But this was Dublin, my real hometown. These people had been there for me when I won in Helsinki, they'd been there when I'd lost in the Olympics. They were there to see me succeed one last time to give them, and me, closure on a golden era.

The invitational mile was sandwiched in between novelty races for sports stars from other disciplines like Stephen Roche, Steve Collins, and Michael Carruth, and it was in truth less a race than a conspiracy.

Although the field included Frank O'Mara, Marcus O'Sullivan, and Niall Bruton – all Irish world champions at the top of their games on the European Circuit – their purpose on this day was not to win, but to get me through three one-minute quarters in the hope that I could produce another on the last.

The pace was fair, but as I hit the three-quarter mark in just over three minutes I was battling not only the incessant pain, but an incredible gale-force wind. I managed to hold off the former, but not the latter.

O'Sullivan and O'Mara, both of whom had teamed with me in the 4 x 1 mile relay world record race eight years earlier, huddled alongside me, doing their best to create a human shield from the fierce gale, but my legs were heavy and I was plainly struggling. A cheeky young runner from the North came up alongside to challenge me as we entered the final bend, only to be rebuffed when O'Mara growled at him.

"Get the f*** back!" he ordered, "nobody wins this race but Coghlan."

By the time we hit the home straight, the "race" had changed from a time-trial to a nostalgic tribute. Although four minutes was clearly out of reach, the crowd was on its feet in a prolonged ovation. They knew, as did I, that this would almost certainly be my valedictory – my last significant run on a Dublin track.

The time was a disappointing 4:04. I felt as if I'd let the public down again, but consoled myself with the knowledge that the event had raised a tidy sum for GOAL, which this time had targeted the funds for war-torn Rwanda.

And it hadn't been an entirely pointless exercise. Any further racing that summer was definitely out, but I reminded myself, if I'd been able to run this fast in such inhospitable conditions while injured and relatively out of shape, the record might still be within grasp. Another piece of the puzzle had presented itself.

The next indoor season was seven months away. Now the question had become: could Moorcroft get there first?

The answer was: Close.

Moorcroft had entered the mile in a meet at the Mary Peters Track in Belfast that summer and knowing I could not compete, I stayed home in Dublin and nervously watched the race unfold on television.

After three laps the leaders were on a 3:53 pace, and the Englishman was right there with him. He began to lag over the final lap, and even though the gap between Moorcroft and the leader became significant, I knew the time was well within reach.

I was on the floor by now, torn my contradictory feelings. Part of me was screaming "Go, go, go!" and another was pleading and hoping "No, no, no!"

When the winner crossed the finish line I started my stopwatch and timed the difference to Moorcroft's finish. I smiled and screamed with relief, "Yes."

Moorcroft did break the world record for the Masters mile outdoors, but his time was 4:02.6. He had handed the puzzle back over to me.

The frustrations of the previous indoor season when I had come so tantalisingly close had been tempered by the knowledge that I had a fall-back position, but as I looked toward 1994, I recognised that this time there would be no second chances.

If I couldn't do it at the age of forty-one, I certainly wasn't going to do it at forty-two. Moreover, the once-flourishing American indoor circuit was in even more serious decline, and the opportunities had dwindled down to a precious few.

My best options once again seemed to be the Millrose Games and the US Indoor Championships a few weeks later. The latter event appeared to be most promising. The Championships had shifted from the Garden to Atlanta and would be run on a 200-meter track reputed to be fast. That meet would be nationally televised, guaranteeing widespread exposure.

With all of that in mind, I was determined to take a leave of absence from work at the hospital to become a full-time athlete, if only for a few months. In early December, I packed my bags and headed back to Florida and Gerard Hartmann to prepare for what would be my last hurrah.

Although I quickly settled into a familiar routine – five-mile jogs in the morning, speed work with the college runners on the Gainesville track, and torture sessions on Hartmann's table by evening – the injury persisted and the frustrations grew.

It was impossible to concentrate and relax. Instead of being able to focus positively while running, the pain dominated my thoughts. By Christmas, I was ready to give up the chase and return home to Yvonne and the kids and forget about the attempt. Sensing my discouragement, Ger sat me down for a heart-to-heart talk.

"Coghlan," he said, "there's no way you're going to quit on this thing. This is your suit, and you're the one who has to wear it. It's not Walker's, it's not Moorcroft's, and it's not Steve Scott's. It's yours, the indoor season is yours, and it's coming in a few weeks. By Jesus, you have to stick with it now!"

With that, he suggested that I should return to Dublin and enjoy the Christmas holidays.

Ger's little lecture had been a timely wake-up call, and the short respite over Christmas turned out to be a brilliant move. I returned with a renewed vigour. Unfortunately, I also returned with a new injury.

Over the holidays I'd gone out on a 10-mile training run with Kieran Phipps, my Metro club buddy, and somehow developed a torn calf muscle. It hurt so badly that I had to stop running and hitch a lift back to the clubhouse by bus.

In Florida I resumed my monastic existence, training twice a day, distance running, track works, weights, stretching and ice packs bound around my bum morning and night. Ger continued to work away on the injuries two hours a day, six days a week, but the pain persisted. Still, I was beginning to hit good times doing my repeat 200, 400 and 800 metres. I entered a small meeting at the University and ran 2 minutes 26 seconds to finish in 3rd position. I was pleased, it showed me that things were coming together. However, the race took its toll and the excruciating pain returned.

A few days before the Millrose Games, I decided that I had no choice and got a cortisone injection. The doctor said that because the tear was in such a deep awkward position right on the bone that it might have little or no effect. It didn't matter, I could not bear the suffering any longer. It was just like one continuous nagging toothache. The shot helped a bit, but only for a short time. By the morning of the meet in the Garden it was back nagging at me as much as ever before.

Yvonne and the kids once again flew over from Dublin to New York. I felt so good about my prospects despite the discomfort, that over lunch in Pasta Lovers on the day of the race I began writing down projected split times on a napkin, just the way I'd done when I was a kid: 59; 1:59; 2:59; 3:58.15.

I filed it away in my mind, and in my diary.

The buzz that had surrounded the Masters mile a year earlier was curiously absent. For one thing, the event hadn't been as heavily promoted, and for another, I suppose many people had given up on the idea and felt that at forty-one I'd already missed the boat. I won, but in a time of 4:04.55.

Any discouragement I'd felt was banished when I ran 4:03.23 at the Mobil meet in Washington two nights later. It felt easy, despite my having raced just forty-eight hours earlier, and I was running entirely on my own over the last half-mile. I knew if I could run back-to-back times like that there was still a chance I could run a sub-four in Atlanta at the Nationals.

I'd returned to Florida with a sense of purpose, but a few days later everything started to come apart. Ray Lumpp phoned up with the news that Ollan Cassell had decided against including a Masters mile in the US Championships.

There was a lot of hemming and hawing, but it came down to a couple of things. One was that Dwight Stones had turned forty and had announced his intention of becoming the first Master to jump over seven feet in the high jump.

"Ollan says he doesn't want to turn his meet into a Masters meet," Ray told me. "He said 'This meet is for elite athletes.' And he also said something else. He said 'Atlanta is a black town. They don't know Coghlan down there.'"

I was flabbergasted. I'd had a co-operative relationship with Cassell that went back twenty years. Twelve months earlier, he'd taken out a $75,000 insurance policy as my incentive in this same meet, and now he was pulling the rug out from under me in what was supposed to be my last, best shot. I had been one of his aces for so long and now he was throwing out one of his trump cards.

I was still convinced that I had a sub-four in my legs, but by now I was scrambling in search of an opportunity to prove it. The Los Angeles Invitational was coming up a week later, and Marcus O'Sullivan was entered in the mile there. I decided to call in an old marker from the promoter, Al Franken.

On two occasions – in 1979 and 1981 – I'd broken the world mile record in Franken's meets. In his roles as an agent and promoter, Franken had been a player in the world of track and field, seemingly forever.

The harsh reality of being an over-the-hill attraction hit home when Al sent back word that he didn't need me there at all.

"Eamonn is too old," was his answer, "besides, we have Gail Devers and Jackie Joyner-Kersee. They're my key players – and they'll put more asses in the seats than he would."

I had one response when I heard this: F*** him.

I was still seething, my ass immersed in a bucket of ice, when the phone rang. It was Victor Sailer.

In his day job Vic was a fire-fighter from Queens, but he moonlighted as one of the world's top photographers specialising in athletics, and he was a running junkie. He kept his ear to the ground and seemed to know everybody and everything that was going on in the world of track and field. He knew I'd been rejected by Al Franken, for instance, almost before I did.

I'd known Vic for many years, but he'd never phoned me before. This time he'd tracked me down in Florida. I confirmed that I got the cold shoulder from Franken, but told him I was still holding out hope that Cassell might change his mind about Atlanta.

"Forget Cassell," said Vic, "there's a big high school meet in Boston on February 20, and they're willing to put on a Masters mile as an added attraction. It's a good track, eight laps exactly to the mile, not 400 metres but 440 yards and it might just be the fastest in the country."

Initially he sounded so eager that I found myself trying to figure out what was in it for him, but as he pressed on his sincerity became evident.

"I've seen too many athletes over the years wait around hoping for a better deal and then miss the chance altogether," he reminded me. "You've got a window of opportunity of about two weeks where you'll be physically peaking – and you're in that phase right now."

He had piqued my interest, to say the least, but I found myself wondering if anyone would even notice. You know – if a tree falls in the forest with no one there to hear it, what sound does it make?

"Eamonn," said Vic, "go for it in Boston, and I guarantee you that when the word gets out, the hype will follow."

The longer he spoke, the more I realised he was right. I couldn't wait around for someone else to control my destiny. By the time I hung up the phone, my mind was made up. I would go to Boston and my final Masters examination would take place on the Albert J. Gordon Indoor Track at Harvard.

The summit of ambition

On the Tuesday before the Boston race, Marcus O'Sullivan arrived in Gainesville to spend a few days getting treatment from Hartmann before he headed off to Franken's meet in Los Angeles. We spent several days catching up on old times, and even engaged in a few runs together.

Although there was still some pain, I put together an impressive afternoon at the university: A 1:57 half mile, a pair of 56-second 440s, and then two 220s in precisely 26 seconds – each followed by a few minutes of jog-rest.

At the end of it, I warmed down with two miles jogging on the track's infield where I was joined by Marcus.

"Great workout, Eamonn," he said, "how fast were you going?"

When I revealed the times, Marcus replied "I wish I could manage that myself."

In the final days preceding the record assault, I spent hours on the telephone attending to the logistics of the race.

When I reached Jerry Canning at Foot Locker, it turned out Victor Sailer had already spoken to him, looking to have the company cover his expenses and give him a degree of exclusivity with the event photography.

"Well, I chuckled to myself. "Fair f***** to Vic!"

Canning confirmed that Foot Locker was in: "If we're sponsoring you and you get it, I want to organise TV coverage so we can get the word out," he told me. "And by the way Eamonn, we renewed our insurance policy because we believe you are not finished yet."

Putting together a field was another matter. I phoned Paul Mascali, a fellow Masters runner and my co-chairman of track and field at the NYAC. He promised that he would round up the usual suspects who'd love to get a chance to be in this race.

The next phone call was to Joey Goldstein, the indefatigable New York press agent. Joey would do his best to deliver press coverage, and also used his contacts to persuade Mobil to sponsor the race itself. Mobil agreed to put up $2,000 – just about enough to cover the weekend's expenses – if I and the other runners would wear its logo on the race numbers.

Bill Clark, the meet director, assured me that the electronic timing and technicalities would be in order to ensure certification of a record if there was to be one.

One significant problem remained: Finding a suitable pace-setter. Clark was pleased to have the event on his dance card; it represented a major coup for him, but his hands were tied in another respect. This was a no-frills race, not a commercial enterprise, and there were no funds available for the usual niceties.

Finally, the director said he would approach Foot Locker on his own and ask them to sponsor a rabbit.

The first encouraging sign appeared when I flew to Boston Friday afternoon, changing planes in Atlanta. I didn't even think of it until I got to my hotel room, but my ass-bone hadn't bothered me on either flight. It had been the first time in well over a year that I'd been able to travel in relative comfort.

Shortly after I arrived at the hotel, I got a phone call from Gerry Canning, confirming that Foot Locker had lined up a rabbit. Stanley Redwine was a former Arkansas University runner who'd fulfilled this function successfully on the European circuit. I knew he was a useful runner but still found myself somewhat troubled, because as far as I knew he'd never paced a mile race before. The longest I'd ever seen him go had been 800 meters.

"Are you sure Stanley can go three-quarters?" I asked Canning, who assured me that he could.

That question answered, sleep came easily that night.

I awoke to another North-eastern snowstorm and spent half the day watching television in my Back Bay hotel room while I awaited Johnny Mauritz's arrival. Johnny was driving up from Rye and had planned on going off to run with me that day.

When he hadn't shown by mid-afternoon I wandered out on my own. I ran along the river to the Harvard campus in Cambridge, and then crossed the bridge over the Charles River to the field house to check out the track.

Hoping to get a feel for the surface, I jogged for half-an-hour on the track and loved it. It was a finely tuned, continuous solid oval with steep graceful banks, but no soft spots or sinking boards.

I knew the track would help, but now had to decide which spikes I should wear the next day – the nice new ones I'd just received from Reebok, or my shabby old pair

After a few fast strides the decision was easy: I decided to use the beat-up old pair that fit me like a glove and had served me well.

On my way out of the empty arena I paused for one look around before I stepped back into the snow outside. It was a positively serene moment. I found myself wishing I could have a go then and there.

Johnny arrived just when I got back to the hotel. He explained that the snowstorm had caused traffic delays on I-95. He was disappointed that he hadn't been able to run with me, but when I suggested that he go for a run himself, he said "No. We'll just relax and have a few beers, shoot a game of pool and have an early night."

"I'm here to look after you, Coach," he explained.

John and I went downstairs to a sports bar in the hotel where we had our bite to eat and drank a couple of bottles of beer.

When we got back to the room it was 10.00 pm and there was no sign of Redwine and I began to fear that he'd been trapped by the blizzard and might not get there at all. He finally rang my room at midnight.

"Amon! Redwine here. Just got to town," he explained.

I confessed that I'd been really worried that he wasn't going to make it in the snow. We agreed to meet in the morning and go over the race strategy. I fell asleep, content in the knowledge that the plan seemed to be coming together after all.

Over breakfast I grilled Stanley to make sure he could get me through six laps to the three-quarters mark in 2 minutes and 59 seconds and take me through another lap as well.

"Sure, no problem," he said confidently.

Johnny and I headed off to mass and we invited Stanley to join us.

"Hell, no man. I'm too nervous," said Redwine, "I'm going back to bed to rest up and concentrate on the race.

We drove to a church in South Boston and quietly made our way inside. No one, I'm sure, knew who we were, which made it all the more remarkable when the priest started talking about athletics and running the four minute mile in his Gospel.

Johnny isn't a Catholic, but I was always threatening to convert him, and the subject of the homily obviously got Johnny's attention. He took it to be an omen. On our way out I dipped my fingers in the Holy Water, blessed myself and flicked drops into John's face, and told him "You are now a Catholic."

Stanley and I rode over to the track together, with John at the wheel. The arena was packed with over 3,000 kids and their parents. The State Championships were a big deal, the most significant meet most of these kids would ever see, so an air of electric tension permeated the place.

It wasn't Madison Square Garden, but there was plenty of excitement as the young athletes raced and their friends and team-mates cheered.

Victor Sailer had done his part. The camera crew was in place ready to record the event. Vic would take the "official" photograph, and Joey Goldstein had the reporters ready and waiting to send word around the world if I succeeded.

I decided to go for a warm-up run outside. It was both refreshing and relaxing. I reminded myself that this is what I'd been training for all this time, and did my best to banish the negative thoughts that inevitably start to creep in at crucial moments like this.

Then when I went through a series of eight strides over 100 metres, I noticed that the pain in my ass seemed to have subsided completely. I was no longer thinking of the baggage I'd carried around for nearly two years.

Was this some sort of miracle? I wondered. I closed my eyes, took a deep breath, and returned to the arena.

As race time approached, Johnny functioned as my minder, shooing away the young fans so as not to disrupt my focus, and helped to pin the race number onto my vest as I was introduced over the PA system.

As the noise level began to escalate, Johnny whispered into my ear "Good luck, coach. I know you're going to get it today. God is with us. I can feel it, because I'm converted, remember?"

On the starting line, I shook hands with each of the other runners. None of them had aspirations of winning on this day, but they wanted to be part of history.

"I'm nervous," Stanley Redwine said.

"Good, that means you're ready," I said, as I high fived him.

When gun went off, the crowd wasted no time in setting the roof to rocking. From high school kids too young to remember me in my heyday, to the coaches who had come to pay homage, I could feel the electricity in the air.

Redwine took off and took the pace through the first 440 yards in 59 seconds. He was doing just what he was supposed to do, but I found myself feeling suddenly sluggish and a gap of ten yards opened up between us and I could feel panic setting in.

We passed the half-mile in 1:59, right on target I began to hurt as I tried to close the gap. I began to doubt, and question myself. I eyed the inside rail of the track and briefly contemplated "accidentally" tripping over it to end my misery, but in a matter of seconds the gap on Redwine closed, and as it did, I was able to banish the negative thoughts.

"F*** 'em all," I told myself, "this is what I put my neck on the line for. This is what it's supposed to be like. Go for it."

Then, as we approached the three-quarters mark, the plan changed dramatically when Redwine eased off the track in front of me.

"No!" I heard myself pleading, "don't do this to me. You're supposed to go another lap! Don't leave me here all alone!"

The other runners were a good hundred yards behind and of no help.

It was then that the final piece of the puzzle loomed before me.

"This is it," I told myself as I gritted my teeth. "The last quarter-mile you'll ever have to run for the rest of your life, just two laps to go."

I'd been so startled when Redwine dropped out prematurely that I'd entirely missed hearing the three-quarter split, that I was virtually running on autopilot. I told myself to run the next-to-last lap as fast as I could and let the final one take care of itself. And as it turned out that seventh lap was my fastest of the day.

My legs felt like two pieces of overcooked spaghetti as we approached the line for the penultimate time. I was wilting at the knees. As the bell sounded I heard the announcer urging the crowd to cheer me on.

"He's on schedule for a world record!" he told them.

"Record, me arse!" I remember thinking, "I want the sub-four!"

As I passed by Johnny I saw him clenching his fist as he screamed "You got it, coach!"

I told myself "You've run thousands and thousands of 220s in your life. Let this one be your last."

With 150 yards to go my legs were buckling, they were all over the place, totally out of control, but the noise of the crowd told me I was on schedule. It was almost an out-of-body experience:

The din increased to such a crescendo that I was able to momentarily forget the struggle my legs were undergoing. It was as if they belonged to somebody else. My ears literally hurt from all the noise.

"Don't fight it, relax, relax," I reminded myself, as I gathered myself for the final drive up the finish straight.

Then suddenly, right in front of me, loomed the figure of an athlete about to be lapped.

"Jesus, not now!" I thought as visions of a collision two yards from the finish flashed in my mind. "Please get out of my way," I prayed. I needn't have worried. I crossed the finish line in 3:58.15.

It was the most profound running experience of my life – different to anything that had gone before. It really meant nothing to anyone else in the great scheme of things. But to me it was an emotional and physical triumph beyond my wildest expectations. Nothing compared to the feeling of ecstasy that enveloped me when I crossed that line.

After I crossed the finish line, Victor Sailer threw his arms around me. "You did it," he shouted.

"I know, I know," I replied, catching my breath.

"You did it! You smiled!"

Before the race, Sailer had reminded me that in every finish-line picture he'd taken of me over the years I had been grimacing with pain. "Would you ever smile?" he had pleaded before the gun went off. Strangely, I had actually thought about the conversation just as I hit the finish straight, and uncharacteristically managed to relax my head and neck muscles just in time for Vic to get the picture he wanted.

When I returned from my lap of honour, Ray Lumpp and Jimmy Rafferty were there waiting for me, along with their wives Annie and Margaret. So were Pat and

Margo Corr from the Old Stand. Other long-time friends began to materialise from the crowd. Unbeknownst of their presence until then, I asked what they were doing here.

Ray replied "We knew you were going to run the sub-four and we were not going to miss it."

Looking somewhat sheepish, Paul Mascali approached to offer his congratulations. Mascali had himself been nursing an injury, but he had desperately wanted to be part of the race.

"My nightmare," he gasped, "nearly came true."

I had no idea what he was talking about.

"I had a dream last night," said Paul. "You were going for the mile record, and then just as you were about to cross the finish line, I got in your way and blew the time on you.

"That was me you were about to lap there at the end," he confessed, "in fact, I broke the tape as they put it up for you."

"Paul, don't worry about it, I saw somebody there all right, but I didn't even know it was you. You may have broken the tape first, but I have the time."

It was the most euphoric feeling I ever had in my life. All the pain, all the sacrifices and more importantly all my self-beliefs were tested beyond human endurance.

Joey Goldstein almost got what he was looking for. A photograph with the Mobil Oil logo my vest on the front page of the newspapers. But, it was in Boston only, so he arranged a press conference in the New York Athletic Club the following morning.

The athletics fraternity he felt were somewhat robbed because my triumph at Harvard hadn't received the attention that such an event might otherwise have merited, but I understood.

Never a man to give up easily, Ray Lumpp had phoned Ollan Cassell the night before in an attempt to gauge interest in adding a Masters mile to the nationals in Atlanta the following Saturday. Ollan's initial response had been that "the bloom is off the rose" now that the four-minute barrier had been broken.

"Tell Ollan," I said to Ray, "that the bloom might be off the rose as far as he is concerned, but the rose always blooms again."

Ray had countered with a suggestion that Cassell did find interesting. My race at Harvard wasn't only an age-group record, it had been one of the fastest indoor miles run in the world that year, and qualified me to run in the Open Mile in Atlanta.

Ray told him he wouldn't even have to put on a Masters event to get me there. "Eamonn," said Ray, "people would pay to see *you* run one more time."

I told him that I'd promised myself that if I got the sub-four, I'd retire and leave the sport on a high note.

"Ray, people have seen me run indoors for twenty years," I added, "one more race won't make any difference. Besides, I want them to remember that last one."

The next day I got a phone call from Cassell, inviting me to compete in Atlanta.

"You can run in the Open Mile," he said, pointing out that the likes of Noureddine Morceli, Marcus O'Sullivan, and the Kenyans versus "The Old Guy" would make for a compelling storyline for the television.

"NBC is covering the meet and they want the Chairman of the Boards," he said, "come on, it would be great to have you."

I thanked him for the invitation and reminded him that I'd promised myself I would finish my career if I got the time.

"I'll tell you what," he said, "we'll give you the same deal we're giving Morceli."

"You will?" I almost choked. Allegedly the world record-holder from Algeria was getting $50,000 in appearance fees.

While it was a lot of money to leave on the table, I only thought about it for a few seconds as I drew a deep breath and collected my thoughts.

"Ollan," I said, "I've said it once and I'll say it again: I promised myself that if I ever got the time, I would retire. I've succeeded, and I am retiring. I am hanging up my spikes. You can keep the money. I'm taking my Master's degree from Harvard and I won't be in Atlanta."

With that I said goodbye and hung up the phone before I could change my mind.

The race was over, the puzzle complete.

For the first time in years I could sleep peacefully, totally fulfilled.

Ends

Acknowledgements

Writing this book was the hardest project I have ever undertaken. It was a marathon effort trying to get everything down on paper. It would not have been possible without the enormous help from many of my friends and family.

To the fore is the great George Kimball, my co-author, who devoted so much of his time and energy in helping to shape my life story at a time when he had is own marathon battle with illness to deal with.

To my mother, Kathleen, who made an invaluable contribution to the manuscript, recalling exactly how I was as a child growing up and our family history, while we quietly chatted alone over many cups of tea.

Thanks to my dear wife Yvonne, who endured the highs and lows and lived through the blood, sweat and tears of every sinew in my body and soul. Without her I'd never have achieved success on the track and without her guidance and encouragement I'd never have written this book.

To my brothers and sisters Bill, Brendan, Ann and Mary, your answers to my probing questions provided me with ammunition to write it as it was.

I would like to express my gratitude to the many who unselfishly shared their time, memories, and expertise, particularly Bobby Begley, Jerry Bouma, PJ Browne, Peter Byrne, Gerry Canning, Eamonn Dolan, Dr. J. Russell Ebbets, Sheila Farnan, Ray Flynn, Joey Goldstein, Frank Greally, Dave Herscher, Paul Howard, Brad Hunt, Phil (Tiny) Kane, Jerry Kiernan, Marge Marash Kimball, M.D., Gerard Hartmann, Franky Litsky, Malachy Logan, Ray Lumpp, Jimmy Magee, Paul Mascali, James O'Brien, Tom O'Riordan, Marcus O'Sullivan, Kieran Phipps, Stanley Redwine, Jim Sansevero, Ken Schappert, Howard Schmertz, Ellen Sweeney, Tommy Swift and John Treacy.

I am also grateful to Matt Semanision and Diana Nordquist, undergraduate interns from Fordham University, who did research and conducted interviews when George was indisposed, as well as to their journalism professor John Cirillo, who midwifed that arrangement.

I would additionally like to extend my gratitude to my guiding light, Stephen Ryan of Red Rock Press, who enthusiastically encouraged this project from its outset, and saw it through from beginning to end as its editor and publisher.

In attempting to re-create long-ago events it has obviously been necessary to rely on many secondary sources, and the body of work produced by Kenny Moore was particularly valuable.

Moore is that rare combination, an uncommonly gifted writer who happened to have himself been a world-class athlete. Kenny chronicled many of my more important races for *Sports Illustrated*, and moreover was able to bring another unique perspective to my career, having himself finished fourth in the 1972 Olympic Games.

A quarter century after Jumbo Elliott's death, Dr. Ted Berry's biography holds up well, and was an instrumental resource in recreating the background of the legendary Villanova coach.

And a special thanks as well to my fantastic children, Suzanne, Eamonn, Michael and John for the love and patience you gave me as I painstakingly devoted myself to the computer.

Finally, thanks to all my friends in the athletics community. You might not realise it, but your encouragement made a huge difference. Your inquisitiveness gave me the confidence to tell the story from my heart.

I hope you think I made a decent run at it.

— **Eamonn Coghlan, August 2008**

Bibliography

Books

Bannister, Sir Roger
THE FOUR-MINUTE MILE
Fiftieth Anniversary Edition
(The Lyons Press, Guilford, 2004)

Bascomb, Neal
THE PERFECT MILE
(Houghton Mifflin, Boston, 2004)

Butcher, Pat
THE PERFECT DISTANCE
(Weidenfeld & Nicolson, London, 2004)

Coe, Sebastian with David Miller
RUNNING FREE
(Sidgwick & Jackson, London, 1981)

Cleary, Kathleen
IF THIS IS HEAVEN, I AM GOING TOBE A
GOOD BOY
(iUniverse Inc., New York, 2005)

Denison, Jim
BANNISTER AND BEYOND
The Mystique of the Four-Minute Mile
(Breakaway Books, Halcottsville, 2003)

Ebbets, Russ
SUPERNOVA
(Off The Road Press, Seneca Falls, 1995)

**Elliott, James Francis and
Theodore J. Berry, M.D.**
JUMBO ELLIOTT
Maker of Milers, Maker of Men
(St. Martins' Press, New York, 1982)

Keane, Colm
A CUT ABOVE THE REST
Irish Sporting Heroes
(Town House, Dublin, 1999)

Kenny, Colum
MOMENTS THAT CHANGED US
(Gill & Macmillan, Dublin, 2005)

McGahern, John
ALL WILL BE WELL A Memoir
(Knopf, New York, 2006)

McSweeney, Fanahan
LIVING AND LOVING WITH CANCER
(Quill Print, Dublin, 1994)

Moorcroft, Dave with Cliff Temple
RUNNING COMMENTARY
(Stanley Paul, London, 1984)

Moore, Kenny
BEST EFFORTS
(Cedarwinds Publishing, Tallahassee,1998)

Magazine Articles

Bloom, Mark
COGHLAN OVER 40, UNDER 4 MINUTES
(Runners World, May, 1994)

Byrne, Peter
REST MAY BE A BOOST FOR EAMONN
COGHLAN
(Olympic Times, February 1984)

Byrne, Peter
AFRICAN THREAT TO COGHLAN
(Olympic Times, July 1984)

Callanan, Fionnbar
EAMONN COGHLAN SHOWS HIS WORTH
(Magill, September 1979)

Diamond, Peter
END OF AN ERA – START OF ANOTHER?
(Track & Field News; July 1975)

Doyle, Leonard
COGHLAN STILL NOT SURE
(Olympic Times, March 1984)

Hirsch, George
CHASE SCENE COGHLAN VS. THE COPS IN DUBLIN
(The Runner, June 1983)

Liquori, Marty
HE'S GETTING THE IRISH UP
(The Runner, June 1983)

Marshall, Joe
HANDS ACROSS THE CHASM
(Sports Illustrated, July 8, 1979)

McKenzie, Peter
THE MILE'S MAN
(Track & Field News, March 1979)

Moore, Kenny
GETTING IT ALL TOGETHER
(Sports Illustrated; Aug. 9, 1976)

Moore, Kenny
ALL THEIR MINDS WERE ON ONE TRACK
(Sports Illustrated, February 28, 1977)

Moore, Kenny
THIS WAS A TIME TO REMEMBER
(Sports Illustrated; Feb. 26, 1979)

Moore, Kenny
SHIFTING INTO HIGH FOR MOSCOW
(Sports Illustrated; June 25, 1979)

Moore, Kenny
A TALE OF TWO CITIES
(Sports Illustrated; February 25, 1980)

Moore, Kenny
PUTTING IT ALL ON THE LINE
(Sports Illustrated, August 22, 1983)

Nack, William
FAST TRACK TO… WHERE?
(Sports Illustrated, January 28, 1980)

Neff, Craig
HE HAD THE TIME OF HIS LIFE
(Sports Illustrated, March 7, 1983)

O'Brien, James
SEOUL 88
(Irish Runner, November 1988)

O'Neill, Paul
DUEL OF THE FOUR-MINUTE MEN
(Sports Illustrated; Aug. 16, 1994)

O'Riordan, Tom
UNIQUE ATHLETES UNDER UNIQUE PRESSURES
(Magill; August 1979)

Reid, Ron
A RECORD GOES BUST
(Sports Illustrated; May 26, 1975)

Smith, Gary
AN EXCLUSIVE CLUB
(Sports Illustrated; June 27, 1994)

Telander, Rick
NOBODY'S BIGGER THAN JUMBO
(Sports Illustrated, March 10, 1980)

COGHLAN BACK ON TRACK
(Track & Field News; February 1985)

Newspaper Archives

The Boston Herald
Delaware County Daily Times
Evening Herald (Dublin)
International Herald-Tribune (Paris)
The Irish Examiner
Irish Independent
The Irish Times
Irish Press
New York Daily News
New York Post
The New York Times
Philadelphia Evening Bulletin
Philadelphia Daily News
Philadelphia Inquirer
Pittsburgh Press
RTE Guide
The Sun (London)
San Diego Union-Leader
Sunday Independent
Sunday Mirror (London)
Sunday People (London)
Sunday Press
Toronto Star
The Villanovan

Index

RED ROCK PRESS FIRST FOR SPORT

redrockpress@eircom.net

Number 1 best-seller detailing the peripatetic life of Irish caddie Colin Byrne and the world of professional golf.

Recently published anthology of Irish Times sports columnist George Kimball's outstanding reportage over the last decade. A classic of the genre.

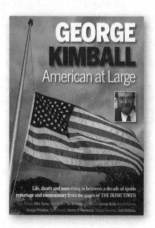

Winner

William Hill Sports Book of the Year Award.

Winner

Irish Book of the Year Awards, Energise Sport, best sports book.

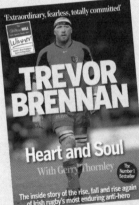

Trevor Brennan's award winning book, and his inspirational story as told to Gerry Thornley, caught the imagination of the Irish sporting public, becoming the biggest selling book over Christmas 2007 and the most talked about sports book of the year.

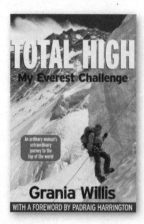

A remarkable, inspiring and beautifully crafted account of Grania Willis's determination to scale Mount Everest.

Catherina McKiernan's life story from humble rural background to internation-ally acclaimed runner as told to Ian O'Riordan